N.A.

Hope Dies Last

Hope Dies Last
Making a Difference in an Indifferent World

Studs Terkel

Granta Books

London

Remembering Clifford and Virginia Durr

Granta Publications, 2/3 Hanover Yard,
Noel Road, London N1 8BE

First published in Great Britain by Granta Books 2004
Published by arrangement with The New Press, New York

A CIP catalogue record for this book
is available from the British Library.

1 3 5 7 9 10 8 4 2

ISBN 1 86207 705 3

Printed and bound in Great Britain
by William Clowes Ltd, Beccles, Suffolk

In the Works and Days *Hesiod recounts that Zeus sent Pandora to Epimetheus who . . . was seduced by her beauty and made her his wife. Now, Epimetheus had a large earthenware pot, covered with a lid, which contained all the evils and one good: hope. Pandora had hardly reached Earth when, overcome with curiosity, she lifted the lid of the pot and released all the ills in the world. Only hope, which was at the bottom, was trapped in the pot when Pandora replaced the lid.*

Other versions of the legend say that the pot contained not all the world's ills but every blessing. By opening it carelessly, she let all the good things escape and return to the heavens instead of staying among mankind. That is why men are afflicted with every form of evil: only hope, a poor consolation, is left to them.

—The Dictionary of Classical
Mythology, *Pierre Grimal*

La esperanza muere última. *Hope dies last.*
—*Jessie de la Cruz*

I'm convinced Hope dies last
and it dies hard

Contents

Part III

Part IV

Acknowledgments

RIGHT OFF THE BAT, my thanks to the Big Four: André Schiffrin, my publisher for the past thirty-eight years; Tom Engelhardt, the nonpareil of editors; Sydney Lewis, more than a transcriber, an interpreter of indecipherable scrawlings and occasional critic; and Dan Terkel for keeping things moving.

My gratitude to Lonnie Bunch, president of the Chicago Historical Society, where I currently hang my hat, for granting me such latitude; to Usama Alshaibi, the sound engineer of the CHS, for his salvage job on my inept tapings; to Maria Lettiere, Sharon Lancaster, and Sylvia Landsman for help over and beyond the call of duty.

My thanks to Patricia Sullivan for her book *Days of Hope: Race and Democracy in the New Deal Era*.

As in all my previous works, a salute to the scouts and, especially, to those who have granted me hours of their precious time. I list them in alphabetical order: Fran Ansley, Andrew Bae, Joe Bast, Bruce Bendinger, Adria Bernardi, Father Brendan Curran, Mary Cygan, Father Chuck Dahm, Leon Despres, Ed Flickinger, Darren Fowler, Mary Gaffney, Merle Hansen, Quentin Ikozeo, Thomas Jeffrey, Tony Judge, Mark Larson, Jack Levine, Herschel Ligon, Marian McPartland, Jafar Moradi, Sandra Morales, Stella Nowicki, Hank Oettinger, McKinley Olson, Marie Perez, Crispino Peterino, Barbara Robbins, Steve Robinson, Tom Roeser, Walter Rosenblum, Ed Sadlowski, Florence Scala, Carol Steele, Gloria Steinem, Tish Valva, Tom Walsh, Robb Warden, Haskell Wexler, and Michael Wood.

Introduction

HOPE HAS NEVER TRICKLED DOWN. It has always sprung up. That's what Jessie de la Cruz meant when she said, "I feel there's gonna be a change, but we're the ones gonna do it, not the government. With us, there's a saying, '*La esperanza muere última.* Hope dies last.' You can't lose hope. If you lose hope, you lose everything."

She, a retired farm worker, was recounting the days before Cesar Chavez and his stoop-labor colleagues founded the United Farm Workers (UFW). It was a metaphor for much of the twentieth century.

As we enter the new millennium, hope appears to be an American attribute that has vanished for many, no matter what their class or condition in life. The official word has never been more arrogantly imposed. Passivity, in the face of such a bold, unabashed show of power from above, appears to be the order of the day. But it ain't necessarily so.

Letters to the editors of even our more conservative papers indicate something else, something that does not make the six o'clock news: a stirring show of discontent in the fields, a growing disbelief in the official word.

This is not a new story. It is a strain that has run through the century past, though not as in extremis as in this one.

During the Great Depression, after the crash came and *Variety*'s headline was "Wall Street Lays an Egg," hope was at low tide.* There was despair as well as breadlines.

Yet something was happening from below. True, the New Deal of President Franklin D. Roosevelt was endowed with enlightened

---

Variety was the trade paper of the entertainment world, renowned for its raffish headlines.

men and women who recognized the needs of the many. But that alone didn't turn the trick of transforming despair into hope.

There was always pressure from below: from beleaguered and embattled farmers coming out of the woods; from big-city neighborhood alliances, defying evicting bailiffs; from a threatened march on Washington by black trade unionists, leading to the passage of the Fair Employment Practices Act; and even from some forgotten man who swung from a chandelier during a Waldorf-Astoria dinner of baffled industrialists, shouting "Social security!" It was the very first time I had ever heard that phrase. Naturally, he was subjected to psychiatric care. Of course, that loner didn't cause social security to come to be, but he did help it along. At least I knew what it meant when, during the New Deal, it came to pass.

These troublemakers were, by definition, activists (*active:* 1. In action, moving. 2. Causing or initiating change. 3. Engaging, contributing, participating). They felt that what they did counted and that they themselves counted. Thus it was that out of the Depression, and during it, hope was springing forth.

Shortly after World War II came prosperity; there was "a chicken in every pot, and a car in every garage," and more, much more.* But along with it came the cold war, the witch-hunt. And silence.

Those who spoke out on behalf of those still dispossessed more than paid their dues. Hope for that more equitable society took an awful beating during these bleak times.

And yet, seemingly out of nowhere, came the '60s, led by students from all sorts of campuses. A great many of them knew nothing of the '30s, yet there they were. Along with African Americans, rediscovering a lost legacy, they helped end a maladventure in Southeast Asia as well as play a role in the advancement of civil rights. It was a time of tumultuousness and hope.

So we come to today, three years into the new millennium. As Sean O'Casey's Captain Boyle, gloriously drunk, mumbled to his buddy Joxer, "The wur-r-rld is in a terrible state of chassis." The chaos, and its accompanying terrors afoot, is in no small way attributed to the wantonness of our appointed chieftain and his armchair warriors.

---

*A phrase used by President Herbert Hoover during his 1932 campaign.

It would be manifestly unfair to blame the troubles wholly on one administration. It has been the dark dividend of all our adventures since the cold war. But now, with the world's hope, the United Nations, being constantly humiliated by our public servants, we are seeing enemies everywhere, even among our former allies. Thomas Paine's vision of the American is being profaned. What he wrote in 1791 is on the button in 2003: "Freedom had been hunted round the globe; reason was considered as rebellion; and the slavery of fear had made men afraid to think. But such is the irresistible nature of truth that all it asks, and all it wants, is the liberty of appearing. . . . In such a situation, man becomes what he ought. He sees his species, not with the inhuman idea of a natural enemy, but as a kindred."

Here is where the activists enter the picture, as they always have. Paine assumed a society not simply of citizens, but of *thinking* citizens. His slim books sold in the scores of thousands, equivalent to millions today.

In the following pages are portraits of the inheritors of the legacy of those past. They range in age from nonagenarians to young ones in their twenties. Activism need not be a profession in itself, as it is in many cases here. It can be in the writing of a letter to the editor or to your congressperson; it can be in taking part in a local action or a national one or, for that matter, a worldwide one; it can be in attending a rally or marching in a parade; it can be in any form, freely expressing your grievance or your hope.

Many had never participated in such matters before, at least not publicly. In expressing their grievances and hopes, they had become activists. Nicholas von Hoffman put it succinctly several years ago: "Often in putting right their private wrongs, groups of people have re-animated our public rights. You who thought of yourself as simply being a number suddenly spring to life. You got that most intoxicating feeling that you can make history; that you really count."

In these pages, Roberta Lynch, a Chicago labor organizer, observes: "It's about action. You feel that things can happen, the possibility, the hope. You feel ordinary people can do extraordinary things. Something comes along unexpectedly, something no one could have predicted." She is paraphrasing something Bob Travis, a strike leader, said in 1937, and Bob Kelly, a Harvard custodian, echoed in 2002: "People can surprise you."

Who would have thought that college students and blue-collar workers would have become a band of brothers at Seattle, and during the Harvard student sit-down strike on behalf of the university's custodians? Did these young troublemakers know they were in the tradition of the autoworkers who in 1937 sat down for forty-four days at the General Motors plant in Flint, Michigan? The difference lay in the students doing it for others, not themselves. This had never happened in the '60s, though that remarkable decade brought forth many unprecedented advances.

In all epochs, there were at first doubts and the fear of stepping forth and speaking out, but the attribute that spurred the warriors on was hope. And the *act*. Seldom was there a despair or a sense of hopelessness. Some of those on the sidelines, the spectators, feeling helpless and impotent, had by the very nature of the passionate act of others become imbued with hope themselves.

Today, from unexpected sources, comes a growing challenge to the official word. Not only among peace advocates, the silent as well as the outspoken, or among environmentalists, or among feminists, but also among small investors cheated by corporate Enronism, as well as those involved in other causes too numerous to recount. It may not be the stuff that makes a TV sound bite, but it's the stuff of neighborhood. It's the stuff set off by those who stepped forth and made the word *activist* a common noun in our vocabulary; a new vocation.

When I was first beginning this book, I had my doubts. Hope, as a theme, seemed too abstract. My earlier works dealt with specifics, visceral stuff: the Depression, war, the job, race, age, and death. It was a matter of personal experience, of people dealing with what happened or was happening to them—conditions that were imposed on them.

Activists have always battled the odds. But it's not a matter of Sisyphus rolling that stone up the hill. It's not Beckett's blind Pozzo staggering on. It's more like a legion of Davids, with all sorts of slingshots. It's not one slingshot that will do it. Nor will it happen at once. It's a long haul. It's step by step. As Mahalia Jackson sang out, "We're on our way"—not to Cannon Land, perhaps, but to the world as a better place than it has been before.

It's what Kathy Kelly and her Voices in the Wilderness project is all about. She is a direct descendant of Dorothy Day, who when asked why she was making so much trouble for the authorities answered simply, "I'm working toward a world in which it would be easier for people to behave decently."

Personal Notes

MAY 8, 1945, was the most hopeful day of my life as I had thus far lived it. It was V-E Day. Nazi Germany had unconditionally surrendered. That evening was especially exhilarating. My wife and I were guests of a Chicago artist and his wife. There was one other couple.

There were drinks before dinner, which promised to be a sumptuous one. I suggested we tune in CBS radio, as a program celebrating the event was about to be broadcast. Norman Corwin, radio's most honored bard, had written a one-hour program, *On a Note of Triumph*.

"It was also on a note of hope," Corwin recalled. "Consider how frequently we use that word. 'I hope all is well with you.' The idioms: 'Hope for the best.' 'Where there's life, there's hope.' We even have a hope chest. Think of the negatives, too: 'faint hope' and 'beyond hope.' The program ended with a prayer of hope." He shut his eyes as he recited from memory: " 'Let the singing fade, the celebrants go home. The bowl is drained and empty, and the toasts are drunk. The guns are still, the tanks garaged, the planes rest in the hangar. Only the night remains. Outside the dew of morning glistens like a hope.' "

As we listened transfixed during the whole hour, the dinner grew cold, but it didn't lose its flavor; it had the added nutrient: hope. Fascism was dead, and a new world was a-borning, its agency the United Nations.

Nancy Arnot Harjan, in Menlo Park, thirty miles south of San Francisco, shared that salubrious feeling. "I do remember V-E Day. Oh, such a joyous thing. It was in early May. It was my younger brother's birthday, and my older brother would most likely be coming home.

"San Francisco was chosen for the first session of the UN. I was ecstatic . . . somehow war would never happen again. They met in June of '45 at the War Memorial Opera House. They needed ushers, so I signed up to do that. I was still in my little Miss Burke School uniform. Little middy and skirt. I remember ushering as Jan Smuts of South Africa was taking the stand. I couldn't hear that very well. But I was thrilled to be there. I was part of it. And so deeply proud. And so hopeful. That was before Hiroshima."

We were, all of us, foggily aware of a new dimension being added to the adventurous nature of war: the atom bomb. The immediate reaction of most of us, myself included, was one of immeasurable relief. Our GI friends, Bill Mauldin's Willie and Joe, our sons and brothers still in Europe, were spared the invasion of the Japanese main island, where perhaps upward of a million of them might be killed.

On August 10, 1945—or was it the eleventh?—I was on the air, a commentator at WCFL, the Chicago Federation of Labor radio station. One of my few surviving contemporaries, who tuned in faithfully to all my meanderings, still remembered my letting go a public sigh: "Thank God it's over."

Though "the good war" was over, something else was getting under way, something less sanguine, less hopeful. The hovering presence of the most devastating means of sudden death en masse ever conceived by man, the bomb, possessed us all.

The cold war had begun. For professional patriots at home, it had become boom time in domestic as well as foreign affairs. The word *communist* had become the all-encompassing pejorative that was to include scores of thousands of liberal and left temperament.

Fear had replaced hope as the temper of the land. Today, we commemorate the tragic era as McCarthyism. And yet, even in those dark days, there were those who stood up for their beliefs. Clifford and Virginia Durr, to whom I dedicate this book, were among those.

*   *   *

An August evening, 1965. The Selma-Montgomery march had reached its destination: the mansion of George Wallace, governor of Alabama. A couple of hundred thousand *from all over the country* had appeared at this civil rights demonstration. It was open house at the Durrs'. It was always open house at 2 Felder Street for outcasts, scholars, libertarians, dreamers, troublemakers, waifs, and eccentrics: all those who insisted on being counted.

Clifford and Virginia Durr had lived in Montgomery, "cradle of the Confederacy," most of their lives, as had their parents and grandparents before them. Cliff had been Rosa Parks's lawyer when she was arrested for not surrendering her seat on the bus to a white man. Virginia was forever speaking out. They didn't court trouble, but neither did they run away from it; naturally, they were always in trouble.

Clifford Durr had a distinguished career as a lawyer in Washington. As a member of the Federal Communications Commission (FCC) during the administration of Franklin D. Roosevelt, he wrote the Blue Book, an affirmation of radio listeners' rights. When, during Harry Truman's administration, he was asked to sign a loyalty oath, he refused. "Not you, Cliff," the president explained, "merely your staff." Durr was adamant: "I will not submit any member of my staff to that indignity." And he resigned.

I first ran into Virginia Foster Durr, a sister-in-law of Supreme Court justice Hugo Black, back in the early forties. She and Dr. Mary McLeod Bethune, the African American educator, were touring the country on behalf of the Committee to Abolish the Poll Tax.

It was at Orchestra Hall, Chicago. On that Sunday afternoon, the place was packed to overflowing. Though Dr. Bethune was her usual eloquent self, it was the lanky fortyish southern white woman who set all hearts afire. I went backstage to congratulate her. As I extended my hand, she put forth hers. In it were about a hundred leaflets. "Thank you, dear. Now you hurry and pass them out. Dr. Bethune and I are speaking at the Abyssinian Baptist Church in two hours. Hurry, dear."

Naturally, she was called before the Eastland Internal Security Committee.* On the stand, she was most uncooperative, regarding the senator with undisguised disdain and his questions as irrelevant, impertinent, and vulgar. During most of his inquisition, she ignored the massa of Mississippi's Sunflower County, taking out her compact and powdering her nose. In explaining her behavior to the awed journalists, she said offhandedly, "I consider that man as common

---

*James Eastland was a senator from Mississippi in 1941 and between 1943 and 1978.

as pig tracks." A sigh: "Oh, I'm afraid I'm just an old-fashioned southern snob."

Eastland's target was the Southern Conference for Human Welfare (SCHW), consisting primarily of southern whites. During the mid-forties, the SCHW, in its registration drives, had tripled the number of black voters in the South. Mrs. Durr was a founding member.*

Another was Myles Horton, founder of the Highlander Folk School in Monteagle, Tennessee (now in Knoxville; it was driven out of its original home because of a state punitive statute, as a result of which their property was confiscated). The school was, of course, integrated, devoted to teaching labor and civil rights organizers the whys, wherefores, and hows of their missions. Among its visitors were Martin Luther King Jr. and Rosa Parks.

An afterthought: Mrs. Parks had worked as a seamstress for Mrs. Durr. Often they had conversations about conditions. It was Virginia who persuaded Mrs. Parks to attend Highlander. That Mrs. Parks subsequently became secretary to E. D. Nixon, head of the Montgomery NAACP, was no accident. Nor was it simply a spontaneous impulse that induced Rosa Parks to defy the Montgomery ordinance and thus make history. She now knew she counted.

I've always wondered what made Virginia and Clifford Durr tick. Mrs. Durr, as the daughter of a respected southern clergyman, had three avenues to travel. She could have so easily played the role of a southern belle, *Gone with the Wind*–style, gentle and sweet to her "colored help," joining a garden club or a respectable charitable society. If she had intelligence and conscience and did nothing, she could have gone crazy, as did her college friend Zelda Sayre Fitzgerald. She chose the third path: to go outside the magic circle and challenge the system head on, to become the rebel girl.† "The Depression changed it all. Up to this time, I had been a conformist, a southern snob. What I learned during the Depression changed all that. I saw a blinding light like Saul on the road to Damascus. [*Laughs*]

Days of Hope: Race and Democracy in the New Deal Era by Patricia Sullivan. University of North Carolina Press, 1996.
†*Outside the Magic Circle* is Virginia Durr's autobiography (reprinted by University of Alabama Press, 1990).

It was the first time I had seen the other side of the tracks. I saw the world as it really was."

Her husband, Clifford Durr, had a hard time of it, richly dossiered by the FBI and under surveillance for more than a decade. Though described by Wayne Coy, his colleague on the FCC, as "the shadow of a great rock in a weary land," he was blacklisted.

They came back home to Montgomery. Cliff's once-lucrative practice had become a shambles. Nonetheless, he was richly endowed with clients, mostly black and indigent.

On that evening in August 1965, the cause for which they had so long carried the banner had now almost two hundred thousand marching under it in their hometown. As we, at 2 Felder Street, were watching George Wallace on TV excoriating the demonstration, he was naming some of the guests in the room. Among them was Myles Horton. The governor indicated that Martin Luther King Jr. had attended Highlander, the "communist school." On more than one occasion, Wallace had paid similar acrid tribute to him, but this time, Myles smiled wistfully. He remembered earlier marches of this sort, with no more than a Gideon's army taking part. A good number of the usual suspects, gathered in the room, raised their glasses as he reflected: "We knew one another by name, by face. Old friends, old struggles. Today, there were so many thousands. I hardly knew anyone out there. They were from all over. It was great." Poignance and a quiet joy. And hope.

* * *

May I close on a personal note in the clownish mode? During the witch-hunt days of the late '40s and early '50s, I encountered some slight difficulties. Thanks to the Freedom of Information Act, I have seen my FBI dossier. It's not very thick, a mere hundred and some pages. Einstein's is eighteen hundred pages.*

A bit of background is in order. The political influences in my life were not the associations that made the attorney general's subversives list nor caught the gimlet eye of the director of the FBI, though my name was associated with a fair number of them. No, what most

*Fred Jerome, *The Einstein File.*

affected me during my formative years in high school and college during the boom before the Wall Street crash and the Great Depression that followed was the lobby of the men's hotel my mother ran after my father died. They were a motley, lively lot: skilled, semi-skilled, and unskilled workmen.

There were autodidacts who'd call upon Shakespeare, scripture, and Mark Twain, with added expletives. A number of them were old-time Wobblies, the idiomatic name for the Industrial Workers of the World (IWW). They were journeymen carpenters, boomer firemen, and seafarers, restless and transient in nature. Their dream was one big union. Their *bêtes noires* were equally voluble guests who believed that the boss, the man behind the mahogany desk, deserved to be there, deserved his privileges, because he'd *earned* them, and that the IWW was an acronym for "I won't work."

Oh, the debates, if you could call them that, were wondrous to hear (their perorations were seldom sotto voce). The Wobblies referred to their antagonists as scissorbills, "capitalists with holes in their pockets."

Most of the other guests didn't give a hoot one way or the other. Earning their daily bread wearied them enough, though, that I'm certain they looked forward to the entertaining nature of these lobby disputes, aside from a shot or two of sour mash and Sunday visits to the girls in the cribs a block away.

There were three bleak years at the University of Chicago Law School, where I was singularly silent, dreaming of Clarence Darrow and Wobblies and scissorbills, while hearing academic dissertations on real property, corporations, and partnership.

To escape the fate of becoming a lawyer, I became an actor in radio soap operas. I was always typecast as a Chicago gangster. Subsequently, I became a disc jockey with an eclectic repertoire: classical, jazz, and folk music. Among the artists I favored was a spiritual and gospel singer, Mahalia Jackson. She and I had become friends.

With the advent of a new medium, television, in 1949 or 1950, I joined that world. TV, heard from six in the evening till ten at night, was not the commercial and political force it is today, and the free-marketeers had not yet taken over. There were a few Chicago-originated programs that John Crosby, the preeminent TV critic, called "TV, Chicago style"; they were improvised in nature and live, of course.

One of them was *Studs's Place,* with which I was involved. There was no script, merely a plot. The dialogue was by the cast. I was considered a "hot property" by the New York agents. Parenthetically, my political leanings had become common knowledge in the trade. The influence of the Wells-Grand Hotel (that was the impressive name of my mother's place) had never left me. I found myself attending rallies, many sponsored by people of the left.

Some of the speakers were eloquent, some on the dreadfully dull and doctrinaire side. All were impassioned, reminding me of those Wells-Grand lobbyists. I walked picket lines. I signed petitions. I never met a picket line or a petition I didn't like. Eventually, I spoke at some rallies and became the emcee of a good number.

It was during this time that the cold war had taken off, as had Joe McCarthy. My past (and present) had caught up with me.

There were occasional visits from the FBI. They always came in pairs. Always polite. My wife was cool to them, suggesting that they had not been invited and thus were unwelcome. I, on the other hand, was always hospitable. Remember, I was an innkeeper's boy. Unlike the occurrence in the Book of Luke, there was always room at our inn. Even for couples without baggage. Even for the FBI.

The visits were brief and uneventful. For some reason, our uninvited guests seemed ill at ease, always seated at the edge of their chairs. Whether it was my wife's coolness or my overwhelming hospitality, I don't know. After a time, the visits ceased, but not my troubles.

While *Studs's Place* was still riding high, an emissary from NBC headquarters in New York appeared. We sat down in solemn conference, he, I, and the Chicago station's executives. "We're in big trouble," the visitor said. I was moved by his use of the royal pronoun. "I have a list of petitions that you have presumably signed." He ran off a good number, a dozen or so. "Is that true?"

"Oh, sure."

"Didn't you know that communists are behind all these?"

I remember my reply. It was in the form of a question. "Suppose communists come out against cancer. Do we have to come out *for* cancer?"

"That is *not* very funny." I was facing Queen Victoria. He continued, suddenly assuming the tone of a drill sergeant. "These days, you've got to stand up and be counted."

I stood up.

"That's not very funny, either. Sit down!"

I sat down.

"There is an easy way out," he suggested, a hopeful note in his voice. "All you have to say is that you were duped by the communists. You didn't mean it. You take it back. A lot of people have done that, and they're doing fine."

I demurred. NBC decided they could do without my services.

I was blacklisted for several years. I should point out that Chicagoans, by and large, knew little about this. It hardly made the local press. I'm certain that had I been in New York or Hollywood, I'd have suffered another fate. My kind of town, Chicago is.

During my persona non grata days in the trade, I'd pick up a few bucks lecturing at women's clubs on jazz, folk music, and such. After word got out that I'd been invited, each club would then receive, with railroad-watch regularity, a note from Ed Clamage warning them to desist. He was the Chicago Legionnaire who proclaimed himself a one-man Americanism committee. To their everlasting credit and my gratitude, not one club canceled.

One chairwoman, elderly and elegant, whose memory I shall always cherish, was offended by the note from "that vulgar bully." She insisted on doubling my fee from $100 to $200. Naturally, I sent Clamage a $10 check, explaining to him that it was his 10 percent agent's fee for making me a hundred dollars richer. He did not acknowledge the note. Nor the check.

One day in the mid-fifties, CBS hired Mahalia Jackson, now internationally celebrated, for a weekly network radio show. She insisted that I be the host. They reluctantly agreed. It had a live audience, about three hundred, in the Wrigley Building CBS studio.

During the third or fourth week of the series, another emissary from New York appeared. He was from CBS headquarters. It was during a dress rehearsal, an hour or so before the audience was let in.

He approached me onstage as I was going over the script (what there was of it; we mostly ad-libbed between her songs). He was quite polite.

"Would you mind signing this? It's pro forma."

It was a loyalty oath. I demurred. He insisted. Voices were raised.

Mahalia was passing by on her way toward Mildred Falls, her accompanist. She, of course, had known all about me. "Studs," she often said, "you have such a big mouth, you should have been a preacher."

Now she asked me, "Is that what I think it is, baby?"

"Yeah." I was worried about the audience impatiently waiting in the lobby. It was getting close to broadcast time.

"Are you gonna sign it?"

"Of course not."

"Okay, let's rehearse."

"Pardon me, Miss Jackson," said the emissary. "Mr. Terkel has to sign it." Orders from headquarters in New York, he explained.

Mahalia stared at him as though he were from Mars. "Studs just said no." But he simply didn't know when to quit. Finally, the now-weary singer said, "Look, you tell Mr. Whatshisname in New York, if they fire Studs to go find another Mahalia."

Our visitor disappeared and was never heard from again. Moral: Mahalia Jackson, in saying no, revealed more self-esteem, let alone what our country is all about, than William Paley, David Sarnoff, and all the sponsors and agencies rolled into one. In the beau geste of Mahalia Jackson, I saw the radiant vision once more of Clifford and Virginia Durr, affirming themselves, saying no to the official word. They may have always been in the minority, but it has been a prophetic one.

Prologue

BROTHERS

Father Robert Oldershaw and
Dr. John Oldershaw

Two tall, large-boned, bespectacled men enter the room. In their expansiveness, they appear to occupy the whole space: gentle giants. They could easily be passed off as Bible salesmen or can-do industrialists, except for the incongruity of the one's priestly collar. He is Father Robert Oldershaw, sixty-six, a Catholic priest. The other is his brother, Dr. John Oldershaw, seventy, a neurosurgeon.

I had intended to interview only one, the doctor. I was interested in his Vietnam War experiences. I had heard of his brother, the priest, but that was another matter. They immediately suggested that, since they had not seen each other for a long time, it be something of a reminiscent exchange, and that I play the role of prompter.

ROBERT: What led me to become a priest? [*Hearty laughter*] I don't know. When I was in fourth grade there was a sister in our school who gave us little holy cards with pictures. Boys got a picture of a little boy with Jesus in the background; girls got a picture with Mary in the background. Early memories. I went on through high school, and it kept nagging at me a bit—to do something. I wasn't quite sure what, but I knew I wanted to help people in some way. When I was in the seminary I almost got thrown out. The priest asked me why did I want to become a priest, and I said, "I think it's the grace of God." I almost got thrown out.

JOHN: After one year my brother thought he didn't want to stay up there.

ROBERT: It was not the first year, it was the second week.

JOHN: [*Laughs*] I talked him into staying with it.

ROBERT: I was terribly homesick. I didn't unpack for two weeks. I knew I didn't have a vocation. I was convinced I shouldn't be a priest. John wrote me and said that when he went on a retreat there was a priest who told him, "If you don't have a vocation, you can make a vocation if you're determined." I didn't think there was a future for me, but here I am.

My father was a convert; he used to sing in St. David's Episcopal Choir in Baltimore. He was excommunicated by the pastor when he hit the trail for Billy Sunday.* Then he came here to Evanston.

There's St. Mary's Catholic Church, there's St. Mark's Episcopal, just two blocks apart. My mother and father went to St. Mark's by mistake the first time. After the first ten minutes, he turns to her and says, "Gertrude, we're in the wrong place, I can understand too much." Everything in the Catholic Church was in Latin.

JOHN: When I was in high school, I wanted to get into the U.S. Naval Academy. I guess that was because my parents had people in the navy. The problem was, my vision wasn't good enough. As my second choice, I ended up getting into medical school at Loyola. From there I did finally go in the navy, as an intern at the Bethesda Naval Hospital. I became a flight surgeon.

I served in Vietnam for a bit more than a year. In Washington, D.C., they have the Vietnam wall [Vietnam Veterans Memorial]. That's not as important to me as the statue of the Hispanic, the Anglo, and the African American, young men that were maybe twenty years old.† These were the cream of the crop, the good boys, the boys I took care of overseas. They were the ones that volunteered. And I was operating on them. Some of them died. I was able to help a lot more, I believe. It was a privilege to be able to do that, the highlight of my military time.

Now, about the effects of war. I'm put in mind of its futility as described by Eric Bogle, a singer from Australia who wrote "And the Band Played Waltzing Matilda." It's about Gallipoli. If you really

*A popular evangelist early in the twentieth century. He was a former baseball player who was virulently anti-labor and pro–big business; quite colorful.

†*Three Servicemen* is a realistic statue by Frederick Hart near Maya Lin's abstract war memorial.

listen to that song, it tells you about the terrible damage that's done to people. In the Vietnam situation, there were so many young men whose lives were destroyed, crippled, and maimed, and many that died. Even now, we're talking about going to war with Iraq. Most of these people haven't lost a brother or a father, or gone to visit the veterans hospitals and seen the terrible physical and mental damage done by these things. Unfortunately, I think that mankind looks at war as some kind of a glorious endeavor. If you're working with the people damaged by it, it's not so glorious.

ROBERT: I have a real problem with the morality of war. Any kind of war. A week ago Archbishop Kassab, who is bishop of Basra, in southern Iraq, preached at our church. He told about the terrible hardship and the loss of life, the illnesses, all of the terrible experiences that they're having because of the sanctions our country has imposed on them. He told stories of some children who came to him before he left. They said, "Bishop, please ask the people not to bomb us." These are kids and they're malnourished. If you want hope, there's hope. Hope is that man named Archbishop Kassab. He's the guy who's taken everything. He's called the St. Nicholas of Iraq because of his care for the poor and for the kids and the elderly. I don't know how he does it with what he has.*

JOHN: Part of the training, part of the propaganda that's perpetuated in our military, their policy, and maybe it's even necessary in order to have them fight to kill, is that the enemy, people like Vietnamese or any of the other races or groups, like the Iraqis, are subhuman. They don't put any value on life. I remember hearing that about the Chinese. But once you get to know these people, you realize that they put just as much value on life and family as we here in the United States, if not more so. In many of these countries, their family cohesiveness is much better. We must realize that all these different countries, these people, their parents, their children, their brothers, their sisters, have value to one another, to each other. War disrupts that.

I've been told that in the Gulf War we lost only two hundred and some of our people, and most of those were by training accidents. But the bombing and the firebombing that was done, there were

---

*This conversation occurred several months before President Bush ordered the preemptive strikes.

estimates from ten thousand Iraqis up to a hundred thousand killed. When you get to know, which I've done, people who are Vietnamese who were on the other side, you get to know their values. They are important to their families, important to their loved ones, and they're no different than we are.

Father Oldershaw, your brother saw the humanity of people on the other side of war. I met you through Steve and Maurine Young, who lost their son because he was shot by a Mexican kid, Mario Ramos, who thought Andrew Young was a member of a rival gang, seated in a car, at a stoplight.* Mario had thrown a signal that Andrew ignored; he hadn't the slightest idea what it meant. You were the pastor in the parish of Mario and his family. John's experience was in the Vietnam War, yours was in a domestic war.

ROBERT: Right, it is, quote unquote, war. The boy Mario Ramos was an altar server in a parish that merged with ours. He used to serve mass. I remember him there. He was, like a lot of teenage kids, at the edges of the church, one foot outside the door. The day before this happened, he was there at the door. I saw Mario. He was a member of a gang, the Latin Kings. Next day, I hear that this shooting had taken place. I didn't know Steve and Maurine Young at the time. They were not part of our parish, but they were part of the community. Mario shot their son and killed him. It was a drive-by shooting. My first reaction was: lock him up, throw the keys away. I find out a week later that this is Mario Ramos, this is my Mario, this is the kid from my parish. So I went to his parents, first of all, and spent some time with them. Then I went to the prison to visit him. I just had this *why* question of him. He was feeling very sorry for himself at that point. At first, I really did not know what to do, but I knew I had to do something. So I just punted and I went to the community, to the church, to the people at Sunday services, and I said, "Our boy, one of our kids, shot and killed another boy in the neighborhood. Mario Ramos has killed Andrew Young." I said, "I want to ask you all to pray for Mario and his family, for Andrew Young and his family." So the people did. I preached on it the very Sunday after the shooting. Three or four weeks later, I made contact

*Steve and Maurine Young appear in *Will the Circle Be Unbroken?* (The New Press, 2001).

with the Youngs. I actually drove up with someone who offered to introduce me to Mrs. Young. It was frosty. It was a tense moment, but she also knew that I had asked the people of the parish to pray for them. At that moment I just said, "I'm here. Anything I can do to be helpful?" I gave them my telephone number. It was within a couple of days that I heard from Steve. We talked for quite a while on the phone. He asked, "Why would he do that? And where did he get the gun?" And then he came over a few days later and we talked way into the night. That was the beginning.

There were two letters that crossed in the mail a year after this happened. One was Mario's letter saying: *Please forgive me, I'm sorry.* And the other was Maurine's letter that said: *I don't know if you're able to ask forgiveness, so I'm going to take the first step. I forgive you.* That led to more correspondence. Eventually Maurine said, "I want to meet Mario." So I took her out to Joliet Penitentiary. She walks in, the very first thing she did, she takes his hands and says, "I want you to know that I am glad to be here. You came into my life through an act of violence, but I see you now as part of my family. So as part of the family, you have a responsibility to hold this family in prayer. To do what you can to help us recover. Because you've torn the family apart."

John, you were saying that in the military they teach people to fight to kill. Our court system, the prosecutors are taught to fight to kill to get a conviction, and if possible the death penalty. Because these people—just as you said—they're subhuman. Mario Ramos did a violent thing, but Mario Ramos is a child of God, and he has a human face. I've met other people who are inmates and you see the same thing: there's humanity there. Yet we demonize everyone.

How did you two get this way?

ROBERT: It must have been the Jesuit education. [*Laughs*]

JOHN: Bob says that jokingly, but I'm not sure he's wrong. The Jesuits teach you to think, to learn, to evaluate, to find out what is reality and how to deal with it. I've always looked upon the Jesuit ethic as being kind of special. I went into medicine because I wanted to do something useful. I wanted to be of some value. I wasn't interested in becoming rich and famous. My biggest satisfaction over the years has been taking care of people. I saw a fellow in the VA in New Mexico who had been injured with shrapnel back in 1943 on the Anzio beachhead near Rome. He'd had leg pain ever since. I operated on him about two years ago. His wife says it's miraculous: his pain is gone after fifty years. I can't take credit for that. The point is by being a part of that, I feel a great deal of satisfaction. The war situation is diametrically opposed to that. You see the destruction of young men's lives. It's usually the youngest and the best, the finest of our population. And it's probably—

ROBERT: The poorest.

JOHN: The same thing with the Vietnamese, the ones that I've had a lot of contact with and that I was most intimately involved with. I took care of Vietnamese when I was in Vietnam. I was chagrined to find when I inquired after their welfare that many of the people said our government killed them. This is after I'd spent a good deal of time, not trying to save them for interrogation but to save their lives.

ROBERT: When you were chief of neurosurgery at County Hospital, I asked you, "Why do you stay there when you could go somewhere else and make a lot more money in private practice?" You told me, "Someone's got to teach these young doctors compassion." I don't know if you remember that.

JOHN: I don't give up hope. Sometimes I'm just too damned stubborn. Through the course of years, I've always had this sense that things were going to get better. I've had an abiding faith. I do a lot of praying. I've spent some time in monasteries. I think that background has led me to keep trying.

ROBERT: I remember when I became pastor in Evanston fourteen years ago, I didn't realize that I was heading into a major depression, a clinical depression. I said to myself, *I shouldn't be pastor here, or be here at all.* Fortunately, I had a lifeguard who helped me—this guy, my brother. It was a very dark time in my life.

JOHN: One of the worst experiences I had was when my marriage was coming apart. There have been other times when I felt really down in the depths, a sense of hopelessness. I have to say that this fellow sitting to my left, he's saved my ass many times. Talk about hope. He embodies hope for me. He helps me even now, working out problems with my six adult children. I have great hopes for them. My brother, he's probably been the principal hope in my life.

ROBERT: That's payback for the time that he kept me in the seminary. If not for him, I wouldn't be here. We drifted apart for a while, but over the last several years, we've been close.

I'm an orthodox coward. John is the competitor. He was a great swimmer, and he'd get really ticked off if he didn't win the race. I didn't give a damn. I came in fifth in the Catholic League fifty-yard freestyle once. I got a yellow ribbon. I don't know where it is; I wish I still had it. That was a big achievement for me. I just could not push myself the way he pushed himself. I really need people to push me.

JOHN: I think for me I've changed from being a technician in medicine to understanding people. I never had much to do with feelings. As time has worn on, I've begun to listen to people. I'm not very good at it, but I'm doing better.

ROBERT: Now, isn't that hope? If you have a person who stands at your side . . .

What are your hopes now, or fears, or doubts?

ROBERT: "Hope is a thing with feathers" . . . Emily Dickinson. Hope is the people I see by day: parents really struggling to get their kids raised and through school, who take on two or three jobs to do that. Hope is people of my parish going through terminal illnesses but staying above it, not letting it dominate them. Hope is the people who minister to them. Hope is a group in the parish that came out of the recent scandal on sexual abuse by clergy, people who are really trying to make something positive out of this and who are really compassionate to those who have been hurt, both the victims and the victimizers. Hope is people working in the peace movement to keep us out of war in Iraq or working to provide affordable housing. Hope has a human face. Sure I'm worried, but as long as we have people who are speaking out loud and clear, and holding our leaders accountable, I'm hopeful. Hope dies last.

JOHN: My ideas of hope at this point revolve around the young men and women that I train: the example I can set for them, how I can show them what is important in taking care of patients, not just the mechanics, but the whole person. It sounds hackneyed, but that to me is what hope is about.

ROBERT: Hope is Maurine and Steve Young. Hope is Mario Ramos, who's turned his life around in prison. Hope is a woman named Arlene Boesak. She's a member of the parish who read a column I wrote in the bulletin asking people to write to Mario Ramos. She started writing to him, and then she started visiting him in Joliet. Hope is a guy named Paul Joseph, who would take public transportation every week from Evanston out to the Cook County jail to visit for half an hour with Mario. Five hours round-trip. That's what I mean. It's people like that. Who's ever going to know about Paul Joseph or Arlene Boesak?

Can I tell you about one more person in my parish? His name is David. He has cerebral palsy. He has two sisters. I married the parents and baptized those triplets sixteen years ago, and they were all premature. They've all been affected to different degrees with CP. David cannot walk. He can't stand. He had to go into surgery in February, very, very painful. I used to call him every night and we would pray together. He's an incredible kid who just absolutely will not give up. He said, "I would much rather play basketball than watch it. But if watch it is what I do, watch it is what I do." Sixteen years old. Unbelievable.

JOHN: To use a nautical term, a navy term, stay the course.

Part I

MR. SMITH GOES TO WASHINGTON

Representative
Dennis Kucinich

Congressman from Ohio. He is fifty-six. When I first met him in 1978, he was mayor of Cleveland. "The Boy Mayor," he was called; at thirty-two, he had the appearance of a teenage bellhop.

I ALWAYS HAVE LOOKED at each day with a sense of excitement, a sense of optimism, a sense of wonder and joy at the possibilities of that new day. I've had that since I was a child. I was growing up tough and growing up absurd. I was on the streets a lot. That's where I got my education. I made friends with all kinds of people, black and white. I'd stop in, talk to them, and run errands.

When I was in grade school, to pay for my tuition I would scrub floors and help with janitorial duties at the Catholic school. In high school, I worked as a caddy. I carried two bags. They called it workin' doubles, going forty-five holes a day, six days a week. I believe in the work ethic. There's a tremendous dignity in work. And it doesn't matter what it is. What some consider menial, I found to be just a chance to make a living. Work hard, get ahead, that was my American dream. *and it was Therapy*

This is a city run by the Mayflower aristocracy. It's as if the people didn't even exist here. Until recently. When I looked around, I saw many of the kids I grew up with trapped, not able to get as far as they would have liked. I started to wonder, *What the heck is this? No matter how hard they work, they can't get ahead.* Seeing all these people working their heads off, you find out the system is rigged.

You were pretty smart to figure this out so young 13

When I first started out, I didn't question the institutions. I never really put it together. I think it was the Vietnam War. I'd see that some people were profiting, when tens of thousands of Americans were dying. Friends of mine went over there and they died. Kids I rode the bus with to school. I started to think, *This is a dirty business. I'd better start to find out about it.*

Whenever I'd see something that was unfair, I said so. I was outspoken as a child. I'd raise my hand in class if I disagreed. I would always offer my opinion, even if no one was interested in listening. My mother taught me how to read when I was three years old. I read Emerson's essay on self-reliance when I was in the fifth grade. She read all the English poets, and from that I started my own exploration, at a very early age.

Now, like many young people in her generation, when World War Two occurred, she went to work in the factories right out of high school. Just as the war was ending, she married my dad.

Once I knew how to read, I was off on my own. My father used to call his friends in on Sundays. He'd entertain them with traditional boilermakers, shot and a beer, and also have me read the Sunday newspaper, so he could show me off. I was four years old at the time. Sometimes I'd read the sports page, sometimes I'd read the funnies. We had a big family; I was the oldest of seven. Every time we expanded, we had to move. We were always renters. My parents never really owned their own home. My dad's been a truck driver ever since he got out of the service as a marine. He's gung ho. His dream was to have all his boys in the marines. My brother Frank served four years, two and a half in Vietnam. My brother Gary served five years. My father never questioned authority. His authority was the guy who ran the trucking company.

My parents had a lot of ups and downs. From the time I was born till the time I was seventeen years old, we lived in about twenty-one different places. It was a lot of poverty, illness. Even though my dad was a good worker, he had injuries that caused him problems. He was hurt a few times on the job. There were medical bills. My mom gave birth to, I think, a total of nine children. Two didn't make it through childbirth.

We moved from house to house, trying to find a place that would take the number of children in this expanded family. There was a lot of upheaval, dislocation. There's a sense in which my own experience growing up doesn't really square with the optimism that I have. There was a time when within a period of about a year, we may have lived in six different places, including a car. We were five children, two adults, and a dog living in this car. It was a Packard. We didn't have a place to stay, so we stayed in the car, our whole family. We used to park the car on the edge of the steel mills. We'd use the bathrooms of the taverns in the neighborhood. We'd go and buy bologna sandwiches and white bread and some mustard.

In the evenings, I'd look out the window at this big sleeve of flame that was reaching towards the skies, coming out of the basic oxygen furnace of the steel mill. That pillar of flame gave me a sense of security and hope. It lit the night and it lit the darkness, and this child, with his nose pressed against the window of this car, was just agog at this incredible vision of light just brightening up the night. I had a sense that everything was OK. When I finally got tired of watching the flame over the steel mills, I would curl up on the floorboards of the backseat and go to sleep.

At that point, my country was my mother and father and brothers and sisters. That's what I knew about America. My religious education has always been an important part of my life: I had this understanding that even when all else appeared to be lost, I should hang on to my hopes.

In the late sixties, I didn't go right from high school to college. I worked for two and a half years. I rented an apartment above the steel mills, in the same neighborhood where *The Deer Hunter* was filmed. It was an awe-inspiring sight when you'd see the smokestacks against the starry night.

I was able to save up to attend Cleveland State University. I was there for three and a half years. After that, I had two jobs. I worked at St. Alexis Hospital as an orderly, then a surgical technician. I'd get up at six-thirty in the morning, I'd start at St. Alexis by seven-thirty, and at four-thirty I'd leave St. Alexis. By five o'clock, I'd start my evening job at the *Plain Dealer,* where I worked till two-thirty in the morning. I was a copy boy there. I learned about the city from being in that newsroom. This was before computers and before they sanitized, a real gritty-type journalism.

In '67, I made my first run for public office. I was still working as a copy boy. I was twenty. I was answering the phones at the city room one day, and somebody called from a bar, drunk, slurring every word. He was talking about running for city council. *Wait a minute,* I thought. *If somebody inebriated and half-conscious wants to run for public office, how does anyone actually run for public office?* So I asked my city editor, "How does somebody run for city council?" And he said, "Why? Are you interested?" I thought a moment and said, "I am."

The next day I went down to the board of elections and took out petitions. The *Plain Dealer* immediately wrote a story saying: *Protest with a guitar? Not this candidate. He's twenty.* And they had a picture of me, at twenty years old, trying to look like I was much older. It was pretty funny. It made the front page. I lost that election, but I ran a good race because I went door-to-door and talked to people. I didn't know anybody in politics. My dad had a friend interested in politics who said, "Dennis, you really want to be councilman?" I said, "Yes." He said, "And you want to win?" I said, "Of course." He said, "If you go and knock on every door in that ward, you'll win."

I started in early August, campaigned all the way through to November, knocked on every door, and came closer than anyone had ever come to defeating this particular guy. People just couldn't believe I was a candidate, but I'd talk about safety in the neighborhood, about air quality, about the condition of the streets, about whether the streetlights were working or not. I learned the importance of taking care of the real concerns that people had. People want someone who will be out there to articulate their hopes and to talk about their dreams. I saw that as my job. The next time around, I beat him and became a member of the city council.

By the time 1972 came around, I ended up being an antiwar candidate for Congress. I won the primary and lost a close race in the general election. I was twenty-five. I was still in city council. I got reelected in 1973. In 1974, I came back to run for Congress, this time as an independent, and finished third in a close three-way race. I got elected to Congress on my fifth try in 1996. I won against both political parties.

My involvement in government has always been kind of a calling. In 1975, I ran for a citywide elected office in Cleveland, as clerk of courts. I won that election. In 1977, I ran for mayor on a platform to save the electric system from takeover.

The campaign to save Muny Light started in earnest in 1976. I carried it into the mayoral election of '77, and my first act in office was to cancel the sale. In 1978, Cleveland became the only city to go into default in the nation's modern history, solely because the banks refused to renew the city's credit when I refused to sell the electric system to a private utility. Of course, I was blamed for it. All the media were involved in promoting the sale of the electric system, principally because they were getting advertising revenue from the private electric company. All the media and both political parties favored the sale, and the entire business community—banks, utilities, real estate interests—and a majority of the city council. All I had to do was sign my name on the dotted line. I was assured of fifty million dollars of extended credit for whatever projects I wanted in the city of Cleveland. But I really saw that as a defining moment for me as to whether or not the values of community participation meant anything at all. Was I going to stand on the side of a history of Cleveland being a city which had home rule, which had public control of electricity, or was I going to just do the convenient thing, and my political career would have been ensured?

I lost the next election. [*Slight chuckle*] The world media were there. This was an international story. Here's this kid, this young boy who became mayor and in short order brought this great city to ruin. It became a farce. Except it wasn't very funny. However, I want to point out as a footnote, I ran the city for those two years, cutting city spending by ten percent, and paid off the debt that was left to me by the former administration—without borrowing any money at all, because I was denied access to any borrowing. But the city went into default on December fifteenth. I then took the issue to the people of Cleveland and asked them to vote to maintain the municipal electric system.

The principal television station, where the private utility sponsored the news, took a poll six weeks from the election stating that ninety-five percent of the people wanted to sell the electric system. In February, we won two to one. We raised the money to go on television. I had the help of Ralph Nader, who came in to campaign with me. We ran a grassroots campaign, which took the issue right to the people. We had a tremendous turnout for this referendum and won.

People thought that winning the referendum was tantamount to reelection for me. I knew better. The incumbent lieutenant governor, George Voinovich, ran against me. We were outspent about eight to one. On the eve of the election, there was a horrible tragedy for George Voinovich's family and for our community. His youngest daughter was struck and killed by a motor vehicle. There are some things in life that eclipse politics. The election was essentially over. I folded up the campaign. By the time the election came in November, it was a formality, and George Voinovich won by about ten points.

I was shattered. That was a low moment. I had gone to Case Western Reserve when I was a councilman. I got a bachelor's and a master's degree simultaneously from Case. But I couldn't get a job in Cleveland. Opportunities were offered, and suddenly they evaporated like drops of rain on a hot summer sidewalk. It was tantamount to being blacklisted. So I traveled the country speaking. I did some writing. I scrambled for years to try to put something together. I had some rough times. I went out to the New Mexico desert on some sort of personal odyssey in the early 1980s. I tried to run again in 1982, for secretary of state of Ohio. I lost the primary election. I never thought of giving up, but I had no idea whether any of the efforts I made to get back would ever meet with success. I just felt this calling not to quit. It was shocking to me that you could actually do the right thing and still lose.

I had an ill-fated attempt to run for governor in 1986. I dropped out of that race. It was the only race in my life I couldn't finish. In 1988, I tried again for Congress, and I lost. In 1992, I tried again, and lost that race too. People suggested I should just give it up because, politically, no one was ever going to take me seriously again. Despite that, I had this sense, this feeling: keep on, persevere, don't quit. That's really what brought me back in 1994 to make one more try. Before I got there, here's what happened. In 1993, I got a phone call from a Cleveland *Plain Dealer* reporter. It turns out that Cleveland, in 1993, decided to embark on the largest expansion of its municipal electric system in its history, the largest expansion of any municipal electric system in the country at the time. When that was announced, there suddenly was a discussion: "Wait a minute, we wouldn't have an electric system if in 1978 the mayor had sold." It was almost like magic. Suddenly, there was a discussion about Dennis being right. Fourteen years I was out of office, and people start to talk about that decision back in 1978, that it was the *right* decision. [*Sighs*] So the *Plain Dealer* wrote the story, and I decided to give it one more try.

This time I ran for state senate. The Republicans had a very big year in 1994 in Ohio. Only one Democrat who ran for state office won, and that was me. I won on a slogan, symbolized by the signs I had: my name, Kucinich, behind a lightbulb with rays coming out. Underneath my name it said: *Because he was right.* And I won. I was returned to office with the help of the sudden awareness in the community of the importance of the decision that I made in 1978.

The city council came out with a resolution thanking me for saving the electric system and also recommending that they name the light system after me. In 1996, I ran for Congress again, fifth try. And the slogan in that campaign was "Light Up Congress." [*Laughs*] I was one of a few Democrats that year who defeated a Republican incumbent in a national election. I was elected with forty-nine percent of the vote, reelected in '98 with sixty-seven percent of the vote, and reelected in the year 2000 with seventy-five percent of the vote.

Next year will be the twenty-fifth anniversary of saving Muny Light. I had a sense of a connection to my constituency and a sense of purpose in my life. I was separated from that for a long time. That was very painful. But it was that calling that kept me moving, trying to re-create possibilities from nothing.

I have a faith in the nation. The optimism I have is optimism for a nation, despite all that has happened. I learned that the journey I had isn't so different from the journeys millions of people have in their lives every day, in terms of having some success and devastating losses. People go through that all the time. I've been able to include the experience of many within my experience, and that's given me a chance to understand people individually, but people in masses, too, and understand the nation.

Right now we're at a crucial moment where long-held aspirations for freedom and justice are under attack because of fear. Those freedoms enunciated in our Bill of Rights end up being political fodder in a terror-filled environment. So I have great concerns about what we need to do to stand for freedom of speech, for right of association, for the rights of defendants, for the rights of people to be free in their homes from illegal searches, concerns about a government which makes wholesale spying on its people a preferred way of control.

I don't believe we should give up any freedoms for a moment because we've been attacked by terrorists or anyone else. This is the time when we're challenged to insist even more strongly on the basic freedoms that we have, because it is through those freedoms that we're vindicated. If we lose those freedoms, we're not America anymore.

Representative Dan Burton

He is a Republican congressman from Indiana, serving his tenth term. He was first elected in 1982. He is of genial demeanor and a gracious host at the House lunchroom. At the time we spoke, he was worried about his wife's critical illness. She died shortly after this conversation.

I'M A PERSON WHO grew up in very meager surroundings. My father was a child abuser. He was six foot eight and weighed about two seventy, and he used to beat my mother and myself. When she finally got away from him, he broke in through the ceiling of the little place we were staying, over at my grandmother's, kidnapped her at the point of a gun. He ended up being captured, and he went to prison.

He beat my mother, and I'd hear her screaming in the middle of the night. I'd come down the stairs. I was five or six years old. He would tear her clothes off of her and beat her, and she'd throw a lamp through the window trying to get the police to come, and they never did. And then he would say to me, "Get back up those stairs or I'll give you some of this." And of course, it scares you to death.

When I had to go to the bathroom at night, he'd stand behind me in the bathroom and say, "You don't have to go to the bathroom. You just don't want to go to bed." And then, if I couldn't go because I was afraid, he would spank me or beat me for that, and then I'd go to bed and wet the bed, and he'd beat me for that. So it was a no-win. [*Pained chuckle*]

I think women have a penchant for believing a man when he says he's never going to do it again. She was married to him for about twelve years, and I think after the eighth or ninth year, she wanted to get away, but in those days, it was hard for a woman to find refuge. We went to the police department one night about one o'clock in the morning, and she had a black eye and her face was all swollen, and she had me and my brother and sister with her, and the policeman at the desk said, "Lady, you better get those kids home and get them to bed, or I'm going to arrest *you* for child abuse." It was tough back in those days.

I think part of my aggressive nature is because of my childhood. I could never stand to see a man abuse a woman or children. To this day, if I see that happening, I want to get involved and stop it. I don't know why I wasn't embittered. I guess maybe I was a little bit.

My mother finally got away from him when I was twelve years old, after he kidnapped her and tried to kill her. I was in the Marion County guardian's home with my brother and sister for a while and had a chance to see what other kids were going through, too. My mother finally remarried. After twelve years old, I was pretty much on my own. I came and went as I saw fit. I caddied at Hillcrest Country Club and I met a lot of businesspeople and saw a different side of life than what I was used to. I think things like that really helped me a lot.

My mother always read poetry to me and so did my grandmother, and they had me commit some of those poems to memory. The theme of all of them was: no matter how tough it is growing up, no matter what happens, you never, ever give up. So I guess I would describe myself as somebody who is optimistic, a person who would not give up or give in if I feel that we're in the right.

I remember a lot of those poems. One goes like this:

When things go wrong, as they sometimes will
When the road you're trudging seems all uphill
When care is pressing you down a bit
Rest if you must, but don't you quit
'Cause life is queer, with its twists and turns
As every one of us sometimes learns
And often the goal is nearer than it seems to faint and faltering
*   man*
Often the loser has given up
When he might have captured the victor's cup
And he learned too late, when the night came down
How close he was to the golden crown
Success is failure turned inside out
The silver tint on the clouds of doubt

So stick to the fight when you're hardest hit
It's when things go wrong that you mustn't quit.

I memorized that, gosh, fifty years ago.

When I was a boy growing up, I remember Jimmy Stewart playing in *The FBI Story*. I thought J. Edgar Hoover was probably next to sainthood. But when I became a congressman and chairman of an investigative committee here in Washington, they brought me some cases of innocent people who were put in prison by the FBI to protect Mafia informants and underworld figures. One man, Mr. Salvati, was put in jail after being convicted in the murder of a man named Deegan. The man who convicted him was Joe "the Animal" Barbosa, an underworld figure who killed twenty-seven or twenty-eight men and women. Mr. Barbosa, an underworld turncoat, was a loan shark who charged exorbitant interest rates. Mr. Salvati owed him $400 and decided not to pay him any more. He'd paid him way more than he should have. Barbosa fingered him as one of the people involved in this Deegan murder. Mr. Salvati was convicted and spent thirty-some years in jail. He had three or four children. They grew up without him. It was just tragic. I found memos that showed that they informed J. Edgar Hoover about what was going on. I am convinced that Mr. Hoover knew that innocent people were going to jail to protect underworld informants. I believe that any man who would put an innocent man in jail and ruin not only his life but his children's and his wife's lives to protect a killer who was an informant should not be honored. I believe his name should be taken off the FBI headquarters; I don't think it should be called the Hoover Building. I can't stand bullies. Hoover or my father.

In 1957, when I was about nineteen, I decided to go in the army. I had some college scholarship offers because I was a pretty good golfer. This girl I was going with convinced me I ought to pass up these college scholarships, because we had the draft, and then after the army, we'd get married, and I could go to night school. I was after Korea but before Vietnam, '57, '58, in a reserve program, six months active duty, and she married somebody else. [*Laughs*] Which is normal. So I decided to go to the Cincinnati Bible Seminary and study for the ministry.

I met my wife at a youth meeting over at one of the churches we visited. We moved back to Indianapolis, and I went to work as a special agent for an insurance company, traveling the state of Indiana. I went to night school. I was watching television one night. My wife had fixed me one of my favorite dinners: fried chicken, mashed potatoes, and gravy (which you can't eat anymore because there's so much cholesterol in it). I was lying on a couch, too lazy to get up and change the channel. Something political was on TV that I didn't think was right, and I said, "I'm going to get involved in politics." The thing that disturbed me was they had Norman Thomas on TV. He ran for president six times on the Socialist Party ticket. They asked him why he wasn't running a seventh time, and, I remember vividly, he said, "I don't think it's necessary because the American people will never accept socialism from the Socialist Party. But under the guise of liberal democratism, they will accept every concept." He predicted by 1970, this would be a socialist country. Well, he was wrong. But I felt like, *Hey, I don't want this to be a socialist country.* I had been mostly Democrat up until that time. I was a Reagan Democrat. I went down to the public library, started reading, and became convinced I ought to take a hard look at everything. I went to the Republican headquarters downtown and talked to the county chairman. I told him I wanted to be involved. The lowest position in the Republican Party was vice precinct committeeman, and he made me the assistant vice precinct committeeman. So I worked my way through the chairs. Many Democrats believe that the best way to solve people's problems is for the government to handle them instead of leaving it up to the free enterprise system. I think there needs to be an amalgamation of the two—government intervention to make sure the truly needy get help, but as much as possible, we ought to leave it up to individuals to run their own lives.

During the American Depression, the stock market crashed, business went down the tubes, we had people selling apples and doing everything they could to make a buck. Franklin Roosevelt promised a New Deal, and he came in and created various agencies to help get people back to work. Because the Depression was so severe, the government had to do something, and so I don't fault Roosevelt. I think they may have gone too far. I feel very strongly that the best government is the one that governs the least and leaves things up to the individual. I'm not so sure we couldn't see another Depression. They probably wouldn't call it that.

Because of all the corruption in the top levels of corporations, you're seeing a lot of confidence lost in the stock market. And I don't think you could call me a right-wing radical conservative. I've opposed the NAFTA [North American Free Trade Agreement] between Mexico, Canada, and the United States. The reason I did was because I thought if we're going to export jobs and business to Mexico and Canada, there ought to be reciprocity, there ought to be a balance. We see an awful lot of companies going offshore and taking with them a lot of good jobs. We have what they call free trade, but we don't have a balance of trade, and that needs to be introduced. I'm also opposed to GATT [General Agreement on Tariffs and Trade], and I've been opposed to the WTO [World Trade Organization]. I believe that when we have a trade agreement, it ought to be bilateral between one country and another; it ought to be balanced.

I think people in government should not have closed minds. People at all levels of government ought to look at things the way they are and not the way they want them to be. If you find out that there's corruption in any agency of government, whether it's the White House or one of the executive branch offices or in Congress, you should do something about it. For instance, when I was investigating Bill Clinton, my Democrat friends all said I was a radical right Republican, and they went after me with a meat cleaver. When Bush came in and we started to investigate the Salvati case, he sent an executive order up to Congress claiming executive privilege, saying that we could not have that information from the Justice Department and the FBI because it was not good for the national interest. We were entitled to that information. I was about to move to hold the president in contempt of Congress. Here we have George W. Bush, who I think is a wonderful man who's doing a great job. I think ninety-nine percent of the time he's right. But I think he got bad information, bad advice from Mr. Gonzales,* his chief counsel at the

---

*Alberto Gonzales has occasionally been mentioned by the Bush administration as a possible nominee to the U.S. Supreme Court.

White House. And so I took on the president of the United States, who now is a Republican. Many of my Democrat opponents, Barney Frank and a lot of others, all of a sudden said, "Hey, this guy isn't as bad as we thought he was because he's showing equal concern about what's going on under the Republicans."

Most people say if you treat one country one way, you should treat other countries the same. In the real world, you cannot do that. Foreign policy is not an exact science, but there are certain areas where I think we have a national interest. Where there's terrorism involved, I think we have no choice but to do whatever we can to root that out, in every form. If it's in our national interest to get involved, we do what has to be done, but if it's not, we should stay the heck out.

Let's go back to World War Two. You never like to kill innocent civilians. But Jimmy Stewart, who is one of my heroes, was a bomber pilot and became a general, and when they bombed Berlin and they bombed those factories, it was unavoidable that innocent civilians were killed. War is just bad and we should not go to war unless it's absolutely necessary. We need to hold people to a high standard, to make sure that the Geneva Convention rules are followed and that we're not bullies. But you're never going to get out of a war without these things happening. The problem we had with the Vietnam War, in my opinion, was that we saw a communist menace, and the menace was spreading. We saw it in Africa, we saw it in Central America, we saw it moving into South America with Che Guevara, and there was what was called the domino theory. I think our government, rightfully or wrongfully, under Kennedy and then Johnson—it was a bipartisan mess—felt like we had to do something. Once we decided to do something, we should have done what was necessary to win. A war of attrition against millions of people was an exercise in futility. I was a Goldwater supporter about whether or not we should have been there. That's a question that we'll debate for years. But since we were there, if we thought it was in our national interest, we should have done what was necessary to win.

I think of myself as a person who wants to do the right thing. I don't believe we should be the bullies. You have various organizations around the world that rule in a different way than we do, and you can't make the whole world over in our image. We can try to teach them our values and our system, but we shouldn't go around trying to be the world's policeman or bullying people.

The highest moment of hope in my childhood was when we finally got away from my father. When I was five, six years old, my mother used to stand between me and him when he'd start to beat me and take the blows. I was black and blue from my neck to my ankles. This is a terrible thing to say, but I developed a hatred towards bullies, any bully.

THE NEW DEAL:

THE OLD WAR

Clancy Sigal

A screenwriter living in Los Angeles. "I'm seventy-five and was married ten years ago. I have a seven-year-old son."

MY MOTHER WAS FULL of hope and pizzazz and bounce and energy. She was a radical, a single mother, a labor organizer. She had a really big burden on top of everything else, having a super-energetic kid to raise. I was her only child. She had red hair, dancing legs, a mouth like a river of fire. She was twenty-nine when I was born, which in those days was considered on the shelf, you've had it.

She had gone to work when she was about twelve years old. She organized her first shop when she was thirteen and went on from there. She wasn't a crazy lefty—she hated communists. She was a socialist, strong, militant, and really into justice for herself and for women; she was very much into women. She worked at what they called an overlot machine making knit goods, making sweaters. For people like her, the Depression lasted from the mid-1920s right up past Pearl Harbor. It was a sixteen-year depression.

This woman became a hero for me and a model. I was a kind of suicidal kid. If my mother's sense of hope, the movies, and pop songs hadn't saved me, God knows what would have happened to me. We all felt suicidal back then. I was born directly into the Depression in 1926, the year before Lindbergh flew the Atlantic. It's very easy to nostalgize, to put a veil of sentimentality over those years. In the middle of the despair and the abandonment of families, there was a curious kind of stability. The Depression was just sort of a natural condition for us; it was one endless summer. Nothing was expected of us. Our teachers didn't think we would achieve anything, so they didn't give us any homework. We spent all our time, from dawn until sunset, on the streets with the other kids. It was great, *total* freedom. And what kept us going as a community, what kept us going as individuals, was the thought that there was going to be something better.

More important than the relief and the WPA [Works Progress Administration] was the fact that we had a president, this aristocratic, cigarette-smoking guy, after whom my son Joseph Franklin is named, who had a kind of jauntiness in the face of terrible, terrible problems. My God, Roosevelt was incredible. When he was elected president you could feel almost the entire nation *willing* him to be in their corner, *willing* him to change things. Things couldn't get worse. There either had to be a fascist solution or something improvised that was going to be a whole lot better. And Roosevelt was the great improviser. He tinkered with this, he tinkered with that, totally freaking out reactionary millionaires. People gave him a lot of slack because they had a sense that he was tinkering with the system to help poorer people. We didn't know at the time that he was saving capitalism. He was somebody you could fight for because there was a sense that, hey, he was in our corner.

People in my neighborhood listened to two kinds of radio. They listened to Hitler's speeches from Europe and Roosevelt's fireside chats. Roosevelt's fireside speeches said, "Hang in there, things are going to be better, I'm doing something specific for *you*." People trusted him because he was the embodiment of the best in the system.

It's a double thing, hope and despair. Grimness and sunshine. The Depression was the greatest trauma that hit this nation in the twentieth century. Not even barring Pearl Harbor, nor 9/11. Its psychic repercussions are permanent. There is no question about it. The children, the grandchildren, the great-grandchildren in this country bear the scars of that Depression.

If you were a thirteen-year-old kid on the streets of Chicago, you experienced it in a very curious way. You were insulated by your youth. Remember, adults had nothing to do with kids when I was a kid. When we played sports, there were no grown-ups around. There was no such thing as quality time. There was no such thing as a mom in an SUV picking you up to take you to a private school. We were a kind of functioning democracy on the streets: rough-and-tumble, unfair, but it was a democracy. We kids raised each other in a kind of brutal form of love.

The man in the White House was telling us in one way or another, "Hey, it's OK, because what you're raising yourself up into may be a little bit better than what your parents have." So that was the closest thing to hope. Something was going to be better *or* we would die. Remember, we were training to be dead men. Either Hitler would come over and kill us all, or we would go into the military. There was no question about it. The Second World War was fought by people like the kids I grew up with in the neighborhood. I got into the tail end of the war. Only a few months separated me from friends of mine who died in combat.

What we learned in the Depression was stoicism, a kind of curious bravery. Ninety-nine percent of my friends married their girlfriends back in the old neighborhood, and a few people like me sort of flung themselves out into the outer space of what was going on in the world. On the radio, on V-E Day, we listened to Norman Corwin's *On a Note of Triumph*. All the networks shut down to listen to it.

I didn't believe it at the time because my second war was just starting—my third war, actually. The Depression was the first one. My second was the war itself. My third was I knew that something would be happening in America for lefties like me that would be something like a war. Almost immediately after the war came the cold war.

I was involved in labor activities, I was involved in left-wing activities. Any activity that was there to be involved with, I was involved with. It was the McCarthy days, and you were under the scrutiny of all of our security forces. People like me were either on the run or answering knocks on the door. In a funny sort of way, just as I turned the Depression into kind of a positive thing, I turned being hunted by the FBI into a positive thing. At a time when lefties were really isolated and fragmented, along comes the FBI. They knock on my door, I open it, they show me their service thirty-eights, and in effect they're saying, "You're the center of an international Marxist conspiracy to destroy this government," and I thought, *Wow, I'm really important.*

The FBI made me feel I was the center of the universe. I was in my early twenties, and just when I would begin to get depressed, boom, along comes the Red Squad, along comes the FBI, and makes me feel, *Hey, I'm important. These guys think I'm stealing atomic secrets.* God knows what they were thinking. But if I'm the center of their universe—and they took the trouble to build a big file on me—I have to be important, therefore my beliefs are important. J. Edgar Hoover validated my existence; he validated my beliefs for quite a long time. My beliefs were difficult to describe. Let's call them dissident left-wing socialism, premature anti-Stalinism, militant and activist, progressive, pro–civil liberties, pro–U.S. Constitution, down-at-the-grassroots work.

We thought for sure we were going to end up in jail or in concentration camps, so there was fear, absolute fear. Especially after the Rosenbergs were fried. There was terror among the liberals, especially progressive lefties. At the time, I was a taxi driver. I worked in a sawmill, I worked in a cement works, and I became a Hollywood agent after I got blacklisted. I worked for the studios for a couple of years. They blacklisted me and then I snuck back into the industry as an agent. I wanted to be Irwin Shaw, I wanted to be Hemingway, I wanted to be Proust. But I didn't have the talent. I knew I had to go somewhere and learn my trade. So I quit my job, and I went off to Paris. I spent six months in Paris and the next thirty years in London.

Then I returned to the United States. The suburbs had sprung up. I didn't know from suburbs. I came back to an America that was full of interstate highways, full of hippies, full of resistance to the Vietnam War, and it was a much more complicated America, and in that sense a much better America. I got involved with antiwar work. I was most comfortable with the draft resisters and military deserters. As I get older, I get more and more interested in people like conscientious objectors. It's very hard to write about conscientious objectors because they're not as romantic as *Black Hawk Down.* Shooting, killing, tanks, all of that, are visual, they're wonderful, they get our blood stirring. What's so stirring about some guy refusing to step over a line, or going to a camp in the woods? But I get excited by the idea of dissidents.

The day my son was born was my highest moment of hope. When he flew out of my wife's womb, sailed across the delivery room, squished into my hands, I looked at him, he looked up at me, and I thought, *Christ.* And you know, I could almost hear him say, "Hey, what the hell am I doing here?" I said, "Hey, welcome to the world, pal. And we go on together." In a slightly more anxious world than the one I grew up in.

Arnold Sundgaard

y-three. "*My mother and father were immigrants from* ⁞⸻ *y mother was part Laplander. My father, a machinist for the Northern Pacific, expected me to be one, but I wanted to write.*"

IN 1936, WHEN I FINISHED drama school at Yale, I was absolutely broke. I found myself in Chicago pretty hungry. I saw men fighting over the garbage down on lower Michigan Avenue, leftover stuff put out by the Harding Restaurant. I went to a saloon on North Clark Street where you could fill up a whole buffet plate for twenty-five cents. You also got a token on the Wheel of Fortune. Boy, was I hungry.

Luckily, I got on the WPA [Works Progress Administration]. Ninety-four bucks a month. What was so great, it was the government coming through giving you hope. In my case, as a writer. There were jobs for blue-collar workmen, but also for people in the arts. The Writers' Project, the Arts Project for painters and sculptors, the Music Project, and the Federal Theatre Project. I was with the Federal Theatre Project.

That was the one I latched on to, as a play reader. Boy, was it exciting. They believed an actor should work as an actor, a playwright as a playwright, and a dancer should dance. And get paid. Artists came from theater, vaudeville, burlesque, circuses, the movies. They played in small towns, too, where people had never seen live actors before.

Susan Glaspell, head of the Midwest Play Bureau, part of the Federal Theatre, hired me to read two plays a day and report on them.* Most were pretty bad, but the whole idea was to give writers hope.

The Chicago Federal Theatre was doing Eugene O'Neill's *The Straw,* about a young man with tuberculosis. Susan said to me, "Why don't you do one on a contemporary problem we don't know much

*She had won the Pulitzer Prize in 1931 for her play *Alison's House.*

about?" She was referring to syphilis. She suggested the Living Newspaper as a form. It was an invention of the Federal Theatre, a new way of speaking on the stage, a new form of journalism. We used everything: projection on screens, photographs, headlines, film clips, scrapbooks, charts, dance. And live actors of course. Always on important issues of the time.*

So I took on the job of doing a play on syphilis, a subject people shied away from. *Spirochete,* we called it, after the germ, and it was a medical history of the disease. At the time, the surgeon general was having a mass blood testing in Chicago. Everybody was shocked by the idea.

I went to all the research libraries in town, visited all the clinics. I remember visiting the county jail, where they had a clinic. One shot in the rear end one week, one shot in the arm the next. They tested all the actors, too. One old, old actor said, "Boy, oh boy, it's great to get that over. It says positive." He didn't know that positive was bad. Turned out he had to take treatment for it. To show the spread of syphilis in Europe, we projected a map with neon tubes running through it. Katherine Dunham's dance troupe was acting it out.† It was terribly exciting.

The tickets were twenty-five cents. It really grabbed the audience, really shook them up. They talked about it even after they left the theater. It made a lot of them aware, vocal, and active. At one of our performances, a committee from the state legislature came down from Springfield to see it. They had been debating the passage of the premarital blood test. My play *Spirochete,* I'm told, was instrumental in passing that bill.

That's what the WPA was all about, to give people hope. In some

---

*In New York, the Federal Theatre had staged several productions: *One Third of a Nation,* inspired by President Roosevelt's second inaugural address ("I see one-third of a nation, ill-fed, ill-clothed, ill-housed"); *Power,* dealing with the Tennessee Valley Authority; *Triple-A Plowed Under,* concerning the agricultural crisis at that time; and *Injunction Granted,* on the dangers of censorship.

†Katherine Dunham, as a member of the Federal Theatre Project, introduced Caribbean (especially Haitian) dance to the country.

cases, to get them involved, active. It didn't give them a hell of a lot of money, but it gave them the juice to go on. After all, private enterprise had failed them. The stock market had plummeted. A classmate of mine at Yale, his father jumped out a window, committed suicide at that time. God knows how many people did not have any help at all until the government stepped in.

Norman Lloyd

Norman Lloyd, an actor in the New York Federal Theatre, appeared in several Living Newspaper productions. "The audience often talked back to the actors. They thought the actors were making it up. It was very exciting. My salary was $23.78 a week. I got married on that. It didn't matter. I was really working at top speed in a glorious theater movement. It was creative stuff related to everyday life."

IN THOSE DAYS you were filled with hope. It's going to be better. We *can make* it better. Today, there is something else in the air. People are more cynical, feel more helpless. They don't believe something else will happen. Roosevelt and those around him were thinking of ordinary people, us, getting out of a jam, the Depression. I know Emily Dickinson's great line: "Hope is a thing with feathers." I think it's more like a hawk today. No, at eighty-eight, I'm not too hopeful. But I still think you can make it better tomorrow if you *struggle* for it.

* * *

During FDR's first two terms, Thomas Corcoran (Tommy the Cork) and Ben Cohen were special advisers to the President, "trouble shooters." They were known as the wonder boys. "I worked like hell for FDR when he ran for the third term. He called me in one day and said, Tommy, cut out this New Deal stuff. It's tough to win a war. He'd heard complaints from the people who could produce the tanks and other war stuff. As a payoff, they required an end to what they called the New Deal nonsense. To use his phrase, it was Goodbye, Dr. New Deal; hello, Dr. Win the War. I helped run the campaign against Willkie in '40 and then I quit. Ben and I felt since the New Deal was through, we'd better get out of the way."

37

Adolph Kiefer

During the 1936 Berlin Olympics, Adolf Hitler had no intention of meeting Jesse Owens, the black captain of the U.S. team. Instead, he sought out another American. At seventeen, the youngest team member, Kiefer had set all sorts of records as backstroke swimming champion. That year, he was to win a gold medal and set an Olympic record for the one-hundred-meter backstroke that held for twenty years.

"Actually, I met Hitler. He'd come to the swimming pool while we were training. He looked exactly like his pictures. He had a little mustache, a little crop of hair crawling underneath his hat. There was big fat Goering beside him. They had an interpreter. We talked back and forth, and the interpreter said that Hitler told him I was the pure Aryan type, blue-eyed, trim, and all that. Boy, if I knew then what I know now, I'd have thrown him into the water and drowned him."

We're seated in the modest offices of Adolph Kiefer and Associates, which sells every kind of aquatic equipment. "We sell swimming, we sell sports, we sell fitness, we sell safety." The store is huge, however, an entire building in Zion, Illinois.

At eighty-four, he has some trouble with the nerves of his legs and uses a walker, though in no way does it diminish his ebullience and enthusiasm. His wife, Joyce, occasionally interjects.

ADOLPH: What a hopeful moment that was. Jesse Owens and I were very close. I carried his bag and watched him work out in track and field, and he used to come over and watch me swim. Jesse won the hundred meters, the two hundred meters, the long jump, and the relay. He won four gold medals. He broke world's records in each of them. And I broke the world's record, too. I always sang while I was swimming. I forget the song, but it felt so good. Here I am, in the Olympics, full speed on my back, the water's fine, and I'm singing out loud and I finish way ahead of everybody else. It felt so free and easy. I can't forget that moment.

Then comes World War Two. I remember swimming that day,

Sunday morning, December seventh. We had the draft. My number hadn't come up yet, but I realized we were at war and I knew the best way I could help: as a swimming instructor for sailors in the navy.

More men in the navy at the beginning of the war were losing their lives because of drowning than bullets. I went to Norfolk, Virginia, the training school for swimming instructors. It left much to be desired. They didn't have adequate training. The chief petty officer who put us through our boot camp training said, "I can't swim." I said, "You mean to say that you're a chief, with all those hash marks, and you can't swim?" He said, "No. In the navy, we don't need to know how to swim." I went to see the captain who was in charge of all sports for the United States and told him of my concerns. He brought in the admiral and we discussed things to do to emphasize swimming safety and how to abandon ship. I helped institute the idea of compulsory swimming. I wrote a new program that required that the over two million boys and girls going into the navy must have twenty-one hours of instruction in swimming and survival. They must be able to swim two lengths of the pool and have a general ability to stay alive. I hope it saved somebody's life. Only three months ago, I ran into an old naval officer and he said, "I remember in training that we rolled over on our backs. By staying on my back, I saved my life when the ship was torpedoed."

My hope was to be a success in saving lives. So, after the war, I started doing research in developing safety equipment. That's how the company came into being.

JOYCE: I married Adolph three months before Pearl Harbor. Naturally, I was hoping he would survive the war. What I thought about the war at that time, I think differently now. Then, everybody thought we had a cause. I don't believe now that there are too many causes for going to war. It doesn't seem to me that anybody wins. We lose a lot of young men and spend a lot of money, and what do we get out of it? Nobody wants to gain another country because it's just a burden rather than an advantage. Sometimes people say politicians go to war just to enhance their own positions. I don't know if it's true. The people who have to go to war don't want to go. They're forced to. It's said you've got to be patriotic.

ADOLPH: I admire what Joyce said. I realize that our hopes and our prayers have to be synonymous with a better way of living. We have to find out what the key is for an understanding of all mankind. I think young Bush has tried that key and hopes that he presses the right button at the right time—not meaning war, but the right button for equality among all mankind. But we've been doing it for thousands of years and still haven't come up with real answers. Joyce is a very astute person; she reads a great deal more than I do. She likes big thick books, where I like the thin ones. [*Chuckles*]

JOYCE: I don't think they're pressing the right buttons. We're told that many countries do not like us. Why would that be? Because we put our nose in too many places. We think that we have the answer to everything. Even though we're all for democracy, it's hard to impose our ideas on another country. That's why they don't like us. At the same time, it annoys me that the Muslims treat their women the way they treat them. But I don't know what we can do about that except to educate the Muslim women, and a lot of them are pretty much updated on that.

ADOLPH: I have a simple answer—more exposure through sports. The Olympic Games started in 776 B.C. They were eliminated in A.D. 336 because of professionalism. They were started again in France in 1896. They brought back the meaning of mankind. We're getting ready for the next one, which is in Athens. There's a hundred and forty-one nations participating. The Olympic Games are given to a city, never a country. The olive wreath, the symbol of victory, is for the individual, not the country, not even the city. The honor is not in the victory, but in the opportunity to compete. Through friendly, amateur competition, we get to understand that all men are created equal, and women as well.

JOYCE: You sit in the stands and you're surrounded by people from all over the world. It gives you the feeling . . . I don't think making contact with a few athletes is gonna do it, but the fact that you have thousands of people in the stands, and you sit next to a guy from Yugoslavia or one from Spain or Nigeria . . .

ADOLPH: I really feel that through sports you learn the rule of give-and-take, winning and losing. Most people are afraid of losing. But if you get involved in sports at a young age, you learn how to lose. At the same time, sports gives you a sense of well-being, the feeling of hope.

JOYCE: Adolph and I have traveled to many, many countries. If we sit down in a restaurant, we always try to talk to somebody, and the people just seem like almost the same as we are. I bet even ninety percent of the Muslims are just like us. How do we get to know them better? Not by war. I heard on the news this morning that the American military presence is in a hundred and sixty-seven countries around the world. Why?

Admiral Gene LaRoque

A rear admiral, U.S. Navy (retired), he was the founder and di-
rector of the Center for Defense Information. "We keep an eye
on Pentagon spending. We're a group of retired military officers,
trying to hold down the growing influence of the military and
industry so that citizens can have a bigger say."

He had worked in the Pentagon for seven years and lectured
for seven years in the war colleges. "At one time, I was assistant
director for strategic plans, the best damn job you can get. I
would have done anything from then on: three stars, four stars.
I'm surprised they made me an admiral. I didn't want to be
one."

I SPENT MY LIFE planning, training, arming, practicing, and fighting in wars. I spent seven years in the Pentagon trying to find better
ways to kill people, destroy things. I was a strategic war planner. I
tried to find more ways to kill people all over the world. I spent
seven years in war colleges teaching people how to kill people, destroy things. I never once let myself think about hope. There was no
hope. I was looking for certitude. I lectured at the war colleges, as a
very young man, on enemy capabilities and limitations, and also a
little bit on their intentions. Never once do military people think
about hope. Hope in my view is a wasted emotion. People hope to
win the lottery when they buy a ticket. They hope to win it because
there's no chance. If we want a better world, we as human beings
ought to do what we can to bring about the change. Hoping is a
futile mental exercise.

There was no period in my life I can recall where I hoped for
anything. I was a boy during the Depression, in the little town of
Kankakee, Illinois. I didn't hope for more money or food or clothes;
I worked for it. I wanted to go to college. I didn't *hope* to go to
college; I said, "I'll *go* to college," and I worked forty hours a week
in the university to stay in college till I graduated. I didn't *hope* to go
into the military to fight the Germans; I went into the military.

I'm a military man since I was seventeen years of age. I went to

CMTC—Citizens' Military Training Camps—and learned to shoot a Springfield thirty-caliber rifle at a target of a man. At the University of Illinois, I was in the horse cavalry. I happened to be a marksman on a mounted horse, Fourteenth Cavalry, part of the ROTC. I trained for that. I tried the Army Air Corps. I didn't *hope* to be a pilot; I went to air training school at Parks Air Base down in St. Louis in the Army Air Corps. I didn't hope to be in the navy; I saw an opportunity and I went into the navy.

I didn't hope to be more efficient as a killer; I worked out ways to do it. I was a captain of five warships, and I trained my men mercilessly to become better marksmen, to be more alert, more attentive, to be better at detecting submarines, better at bombarding targets ashore, better at shooting aircraft, better at killing and destroying. I didn't hope anything.

At the end of World War Two, I thought it was okay to drop the atomic bomb, because then I could go home and back to my work. I had been working for the Highway Department in the State of Illinois. I found that pretty dull. When I went back, they said they'd pay me the same hundred and twenty-five dollars a month I was getting when I left. I said, "No, thanks. It's more exciting, more fun in the navy." My feeling then was not of hope, but that if the United States stayed strong and militarily capable, no one would attack us, and we then could live happily within the confines of our country.

But I misjudged. From 1945 until 1950, we weren't at war with anybody; we were even friends with the Soviet Union. Then came Korea, and President Truman decided to jump in without consulting the Congress or the United Nations, and we killed fifty-five thousand American kids in the Korean War.

Eisenhower came in, campaigning for office, and said, "Look, I'm going to bring an end to that war. Elect me, and I'll get us out." We elected him and he helped get us out. Eisenhower refused to let us get involved in Vietnam. He was a military man; he couldn't see any sense to it. Kennedy, noble in spirit, decided to help those poor South Vietnamese folks that we left out in the cold. Ten years later, after killing another fifty-six thousand American men and some women, that war ended.

Then we go along and the next thing we know, we're attacking different countries around the world, small countries. Many that

Americans don't even remember. Grenada, Libya, Panama. All of these without any remonstrance from the American public. We always find an excuse to do it. Before we went to war against Afghanistan, we had attacked five Muslim countries—Lebanon, Libya, Iraq, Afghanistan, and Sudan—in twenty years. Americans don't know, don't care how many we killed. Don't ask! Is it any wonder that some people in the world don't like us? Is it any wonder that after attacking Panama there'd be some Panamanians who don't like us, Grenadans who don't like us, Libyans?

If I did have any hope, I'd hope we'd improve, but I don't want to waste my emotions on hoping Americans are going to improve. We get one war and move along, and the president can easily declare another.

I'm very much concerned that the United States is becoming more militaristic with each passing year. We have become a nation increasingly intent on using our military forces to get our way, both in foreign countries and, surprisingly, here in the United States. I think that is something new in the American experience. The military-industrial complex that President Eisenhower warned us about is indeed alive and well, and increasingly influential.

When other countries are involved in war, they talk about when war comes. We Americans talk about when we *go* to war, because that's what we do: we go *somewhere else* to war. We are going to war with increasing frequency. The American public seems very happy about it because, I think, they are not aware of how frequently we go to war, and how powerfully our military influence is felt throughout the world.

I could explain the popularity of George Bush because, see, we were born in war in this country in the revolution against England. Then we declared war in 1812 against the British. In 1846, we declared war against Mexico. Then in 1860 to '65, we fought among ourselves. For the next thirty years, we fought the Indians, until 1898, when we declared war on Spain. Then we got in World War One, and World War Two, Korea, Vietnam, and then against Iraq. In the meantime, we have fought a lot of minor wars. Americans have become comfortable with war. It's a spectator sport for us on television. 9/11 was disasters, devastating, nasty, terrible things, acts that could only be explained as terrorist. But we dignify, we exaggerate the efforts of Osama bin Laden when we call it a war and do the things we're doing now to wage war against him.

When the Murrah Building was devastated in Oklahoma City, it was one of our own people. We didn't call it an invasion; we didn't declare war. But if you're the president and you're looking for a way to electrify the American public and ensure your ability to do whatever you darn please in national and international affairs, declare those 9/11 events as a war and you can probably ride that through to reelection. Americans are comfortable with war. They want the excitement and the pleasure of fighting a war, as long as we go somewhere else.

What we must do to counter the actions the terrorists took does not fit well with the huge expansion of military spending, with buying enormously new, powerful, destructive weapons systems and a missile defense system. These are wasted efforts, but it's something the right-wing administration folks want to do.

September eleventh was another excuse of the administration to declare another war. People said to me, "Didn't President Bush have to do something after 9/11?" And I said, "Yes, but he didn't have to go bomb and kill innocent men, women, and children in Afghanistan, trying to get Osama bin Laden." All we did in Afghanistan is to metastasize the problem of the terrorists. The craziest thing is to wage war against an ism, terrorism. You can't wage a war against an ism, it's too amorphous. You don't know where an ism is. We had a war plan against the Soviets because they had the weapons that could destroy us, and we could destroy them. We never had a war against communism. If we did, we'd have a war today against China. We like the Chinese today. But who can fight an ism?

Psychologically, mentally, I'm very bullish on the United States. I'm very optimistic. Today, there's reason for optimism. The glass is three-quarters full, not half empty. The blacks are doing better in this country. People in the United States are living longer than they were sixty years ago. I could go on with numerous reasons to be very optimistic. I think we ought to talk, travel, and trade, and cooperate with other nations of the world. My three *t*'s and a *c*. If we do that without trying to threaten them with military forces, we'll have people coming to our point of view. We have the best system of government. And we are the most powerful by any criteria. But if we force others to do something to join us, that's a mistake.

I have no despair whatsoever. I've been holding off telling you I have this terrible malady that is overtaking my whole system. There are no drugs, there are no medicines that will cure this. It's simply creeping contentment. I don't feel hopeless. I'm very optimistic. I think the world has a wonderful future. All I have to do is look back in the past sixty, seventy years of my lifetime and see when we had a terrible, stinking, difficult, disastrous period. The Depression, the wars, the killing. But it's not hope that's going to bring it about; it's going to be intelligent action.

Brigadier General Paul Tibbets

We're seated at a booth in a favorite neighborhood diner, good beer and great sandwiches: two old gaffers. Me, ninety, and Paul Tibbets, eighty-five years old, brigadier general (retired), in his hometown of Columbus, Ohio, where he has lived for many years.

I began, "I noticed as we sat in that restaurant, people passing by. They didn't know who you were. Once upon a time, you flew a plane called the Enola Gay *over the city of Hiroshima, in Japan, on a Sunday morning—August sixth, 1945—and a bomb fell. It was the atomic bomb, the first ever. That particular moment changed the whole world."*

THE PLANE WAS NAMED after my mother. She was Enola Gay Haggard before she married my dad, and my dad never supported me with the flying. He hated airplanes and motorcycles. When I told them I was going to leave college and go fly planes in the Army Air Corps, my dad said, "Well, I've sent you through school, bought you automobiles, given you money to run around with the girls, but from here on, you're on your own. If you want to kill yourself, go ahead, I don't give a damn." Then Mom just quietly said, "Paul, if you want to go fly airplanes, you're going to be all right." And that was that.

Now, my father said, "You're going to be a doctor," and I just nodded my head and that was it. About a year before, I was able to get into an airplane—I soloed—and I knew then that I had to go fly planes.

One day [in September 1944] I'm running a test on a B-twenty-nine. When I land, a man meets me. He says he just got a call from General Uzal Ent [commander of the Second Air Force] at Colorado Springs, who wants me in his office the next morning at nine o'clock. He says, "Bring your clothing—your B-four bag—because you're not coming back." Well, I didn't pay attention. It was just another assignment.

I got to Colorado Springs the next morning. A man named Lansdale met me, walked me to General Ent's office, and closed the door behind me. With him was a man wearing a blue suit, a U.S. Navy captain—that was William Parsons, who flew with me to Hiroshima—and Dr. Norman Ramsey, a Columbia University professor in nuclear physics.

Norman said, "OK, we've got what we call the Manhattan Project. What we're doing is trying to develop an atomic bomb. We've gotten to the point now where we can't go much further till we have airplanes to work with."

General Ent looked at me and said, "The other day, General Arnold [commander of the Army Air Corps] offered me three names." Both of the others were full colonels; I was a lieutenant colonel. When General Arnold asked which of them could do this atomic weapons deal, he replied without hesitation, "Paul Tibbets is the man to do it." I said, "Well, thank you, sir." It was up to me, he said, to put together an organization and train them to drop atomic weapons on both Europe and the Pacific—Tokyo.

My edict was as clear as could be. Drop simultaneously in Europe and the Pacific. Because of the secrecy problem, you couldn't drop it in one part of the world without dropping it in the other. And so he said, "I don't know what to tell you, but I know you happen to have B-twenty-nines to start with. I've got a squadron in training— they have the best record so far of anybody we've got. I want you to go visit them, look at them, talk to them, do whatever you want. If they don't suit you, we'll get you some more." He said, "There's nobody could tell you what you have to do because nobody knows." He said, "Paul, be careful how you treat this responsibility, because if you're successful, you'll probably be called a hero. And if you're unsuccessful, you might wind up in prison." I wanted to get back to Grand Island, Nebraska, where my wife and two kids were, where my laundry was done and all that stuff. But I thought, *Well, I'll go to Wendover* [an airfield in Utah] *first and see what they've got.* As I came in over the hills I saw it was a beautiful spot.

And now you chose your own crew.

Well, I had mentally done it before that. I knew right away I was going to get Tom Ferebee [the *Enola Gay*'s bombardier] and Theodore "Dutch" van Kirk [navigator] and Wyatt Duzenbury [flight engineer].

Guys you had flown with in Europe. And now you're training. And you're also talking to physicists like Robert Oppenheimer [senior scientist on the Manhattan Project].

I think I went to Los Alamos [Manhattan Project headquarters] three times, and each time I got to see Dr. Oppenheimer working in his own environment. Later, thinking about it—here's a young man, a brilliant person, and he's a chain smoker and he drinks cocktails, and he hates fat men, and General Leslie Groves, in charge of the Manhattan Project, he's a fat man, and he hates people who smoke and drink. The two of them are the original odd couple.

Dr. Ramsey said, "The only thing we can tell you about the bomb is it's going to explode with the force of twenty thousand tons of TNT." I'd never seen one pound of TNT blow up. I'd never heard of anybody who'd seen one hundred pounds of TNT blow up. All I felt was that this was gonna be one hell of a big bang. I think the two bombs that we used [at Hiroshima and Nagasaki] had more power than all the bombs the air force used during the war in Europe.

I was ready to say I wanted to go to war, but I wanted to ask Oppenheimer how to get away from the bomb after we dropped it. I told him that when we dropped bombs in Europe and North Africa, we'd flown straight ahead after dropping them, which is also the trajectory of the bomb. But what should we do this time? He said, "You can't fly straight ahead because you'd be right over the top when it blows up and nobody would ever know you were there." He said I had to turn tangent to the expanding shock wave. I said, "Well, I've had some trigonometry, some physics. What is tangency in this case?" He said it was a hundred and fifty-nine degrees in either direction. "Turn a hundred and fifty-nine degrees as fast as you can and you'll be able to put yourself the greatest distance from where the bomb will explode." I had dropped enough practice bombs to realize that the charges would blow around fifteen hundred feet in the air, so I would have forty to forty-two seconds to turn a hundred and fifty-nine degrees. I went back to Wendover as quick as I could and took the airplane up. I got myself to twenty-five thousand feet, and I practiced turning, steeper, steeper, steeper, and I got where I could pull it round in forty seconds. The tail was shaking dramatically and I was afraid of it breaking off, but I didn't quit. That was my goal. And I practiced and practiced until, without even thinking about it, I could do it in between forty and forty-two all the time. So, when that day came . . .

We were on Tinian [an island base in the Pacific] at the time we got the OK. They had sent this Norwegian to the weather station out on Guam, and I had a copy of his report. Based on his forecast, we said that the sixth day of August would be the best day. General Groves had a brigadier general who was connected back to Washington, D.C., by a special Teletype machine. He stayed close to that thing all the time, notifying people back there, all by code, that we were preparing these airplanes to go anytime after midnight on the sixth. And that's the way it worked out. We were ready to go at about four o'clock in the afternoon on the fifth, and we got word from the president that we were free to go: "Use 'em as you wish."

Well, we got going down the runway at right about 2:15 A.M. We made our flight up to what we call the initial point, a geographic position you could not mistake. Well, of course we had the best one in the world, with Hiroshima's rivers and bridges and that big shrine. There was no mistaking what it was.

We were told not to use the radio, but hell, I had to. I told them I would say, "One minute out," "Thirty seconds out," "Twenty seconds," "Ten," and then I'd count, "Nine, eight, seven, six, five, four seconds," which would give the airplane that followed us time to drop the instruments that would tell us what the bomb was going to do. And that's exactly the way it worked. It was absolutely perfect.

After we got the airplanes in formation I crawled back to tell the men. I said, "You know what we're doing today?" They said, "Well, yeah, we're going on a bombing mission, but it's a little bit special." My tail gunner, Bob Caron, was pretty alert. He said, "Colonel, we wouldn't be playing with atoms today, would we?" I said, "Bob, you've got it just exactly right." I went back up in the front end and told the navigator, bombardier, flight engineer, in turn. I said, "OK, this is an atom bomb we're dropping." They listened intently, but I didn't see any change in their faces or anything else. Those guys were no idiots.

So we're coming down. We get to that point where I say, "One second." By the time I'd got that second out of my mouth the airplane had lurched, because ten thousand pounds had come out of the front. I'm in this turn now, tight as I can get, that helps me hold my altitude and helps me hold my airspeed and everything else all the way round. When I level out, the nose is a little bit high and as I look up the whole sky is lit in the prettiest blues and pinks I've ever seen in my life. It was just great.

I tell people I tasted it. "Well," they say, "what do you mean?" When I was a child, if you had a cavity in your tooth the dentist put a mixture of cotton and lead into your teeth and pounded them in with a hammer. I learned that if I had a spoon of ice cream and touched one of those teeth I got this electrolysis and the taste of lead. I knew right away what it was.

The shock wave was coming up at us after we turned. And the tail gunner said, "Here it comes." About the time he said that, we got this kick in the ass. I had accelerometers installed in all airplanes to record the magnitude of the bomb. It hit us with two and a half G's. Next day, when we got figures from the scientists on what they had learned from all the things, they said, "When that bomb exploded, your airplane was ten and a half miles away from it."

Did you see that mushroom cloud?

You see all kinds of mushroom clouds, but they were made with different types of bombs. The Hiroshima bomb did not make a mushroom. It was what I call a stringer. It just came up. It was black as hell, and it had light and colors and white in it and gray color in it and the top was like a folded-up Christmas tree.

We had been briefed to stay off the radios: "Don't say a damn word, what we do is we make this turn, to get out of here as fast as we can." I want to get out over the Sea of Japan because I know they can't find me over there. With that done we're home free. Then Tom Ferebee has to fill out his bombardier's report and Dutch, the navigator, has to fill out a log. Tom is working on his log and says,

"Dutch, what time were we over the target?" And Dutch says, "Nine-fifteen plus fifteen seconds." Ferebee says: "What lousy navigating. Fifteen seconds off!"

Do you have any idea what happened down below?

Pandemonium! I think it's best stated by one of the historians who said, "In one microsecond, the city of Hiroshima didn't exist."

You came back, and you visited President Truman.

We're talking 1948 now. I'm back in the Pentagon and I get notice from the chief of staff, Carl Spaatz, the first chief of staff of the air force. When we got to General Spaatz's office, General Doolittle was there, and a colonel named Dave Shillen. Spaatz said, "Gentlemen, I just got word from the president. He wants us to go over to his office immediately." On the way over, Doolittle and Spaatz were doing some talking; I wasn't saying very much. When we got out of the car we were escorted right quick to the Oval Office. There was a black man there who always took care of Truman's needs, and he said, "General Spaatz, will you please be facing the desk?" Now, Spaatz is on the right, then Doolittle and Shillen. Of course, militarily speaking, that's the correct order, because Spaatz is senior. Then I was taken and put in the chair that was right beside the president's desk, beside his left hand. Anyway, when Truman walked in, everybody stood. He said, "Sit down, please." He had a big smile on his face, and he said, "General Spaatz, I want to congratulate you on being first chief of the air force," because it was no longer the Army Air Corps. Spaatz said, "Thank you, sir, it's a great honor, and I appreciate it." And he said to Doolittle: "That was a magnificent thing you pulled flying off of that carrier," and Doolittle said, "All in a day's work, Mr. President." And he looked at Dave Shillen and said, "Colonel Shillen, I want to congratulate you on having the foresight to recognize the potential in aerial refueling. We're gonna need it bad someday." And he said thank you very much.

Then he looked at me for ten seconds and he didn't say anything. And when he finally did, he said, "What do you think?" I said, "Mr.

President, I think I did what I was told." He slapped his hand on the table and said: "You're damn right you did, and I'm the guy who sent you. If anybody gives you a hard time about it, refer them to me."

Do you ever have any second thoughts about the bomb?

Second thoughts? No. Studs, look, I got into the Air Corps to defend the United States to the best of my ability. On the way to the target I was thinking, *I can't think of any mistakes I've made.* Maybe I did make a mistake: maybe I was too damned assured. At twenty-nine years of age, I was so shot in the ass with confidence, I didn't think there was anything I couldn't do. Of course, that applied to airplanes and people. So, no, I had no problem with it. I knew we did the right thing. I thought, *Yes, we're going to kill a lot of people, but by God we're going to save a lot of lives. We won't have to invade Japan.*

Why did they drop the second one, on Nagasaki?

Unknown to anybody else—I knew it, but nobody else knew—there was a third one. See, the first bomb went off, and they didn't hear anything out of the Japanese for two or three days. The second bomb was dropped, and again they were silent for another couple of days. Then I got a phone call from General Curtis LeMay [chief of staff of the Strategic Air Forces in the Pacific]. He said, "You got another one of those damn things?" I said, "Yessir." He said, "Where is it?" I said, "Over in Utah." He said, "Get it out here. You and your crew are going to fly it." I said, "Yessir." I sent word back and the crew loaded it on an airplane and when they got it to the California debarkation point, the war was over.

What did General LeMay have in mind with the third one?

Nobody knows.

One big question. Since September eleventh, what are your thoughts? People talk about nukes, the hydrogen bomb.

Let's put it this way. I don't know any more about these terrorists than you do; I know nothing. When they bombed the Trade Center I couldn't believe what was going on. We've fought many enemies at different times. But we knew who they were and where they were. These people, we don't know who they are or where they are. That's the point that bothers me. Because they're gonna strike again, I'll put money on it, and it's going to be damned dramatic. But they're gonna do it in their own sweet time. We've got to get into a position where we can kill the bastards. None of this business of taking them to court. The hell with that. I wouldn't waste five seconds on them.

What about the bomb? Einstein said the world has changed since the atom was split.

That's right. It has changed.

And Oppenheimer knew that.

Oppenheimer is dead. He did something for the world, and people don't understand. And it is a free world.

One last thing: when you hear people say, "Let's nuke 'em, let's nuke these people," what do you think?

Oh, I wouldn't hesitate if I had the choice. I'd wipe 'em out. You're gonna kill innocent people at the same time, but we've never fought a damn war anywhere in the world where they didn't kill innocent people. If the newspapers would just cut out the shit: "You've killed so many civilians." That's their tough luck for being there.

By the way, Enola Gay *was originally called number 82. How did your mother feel about having her name on it?*

Well, I can only tell you what my dad said. My mother never changed her expression very much about anything, whether it was serious or light, but when she'd get tickled, her stomach would jiggle. My dad said to me that when the telephone in Miami rang, my mother was quiet first. Then, when it was announced on the radio, he said, "You should have seen the old gal's belly jiggle on that one."

Herb Mitgang

He had for forty-seven years been a member of the staff of the
New York Times *in a number of capacities: feature writer, in-*
vestigative journalist, literary critic, member of the editorial
board. He has, in addition, written several political biographies
and plays. He retired in 1995. He recently suffered a stroke.

WE'VE FORGOTTEN WHAT WE FOUGHT FOR in World
War Two, when I was writing for *Stars and Stripes.** It was for the
freedom of all nations, large and small. Freedom from poverty—the
worst terrorism of all.

We World War Two veterans do not think we were the greatest
generation at all. Every generation has great people in it. Those who
went through the Depression, our fathers who sold apples, trying to
put us through college. When I think back on American history, the
greatest generation were the Founding Fathers, sometimes called the
Founding Brothers. They were revolutionaries. Another generation I
think was really great: the abolitionists who fought against slavery.
That took a lot of guts. The sixties was a great generation, too. They
were great truth seekers. Civil rights, antiwar, feminism. Now you
look on television, you see black faces, reporters. When I first joined
the *Times* there were no women covering stories. Now you have
women foreign correspondents. That happened because there were
people with guts who fought for them in the sixties.

I was just about old enough to vote for president for the first time
on a soldier's ballot from Italy when Franklin Roosevelt was running
for a fourth term, 1944. I think it's important to have somebody in
the White House whom you trust. I believed in the New Deal tradition of Franklin Roosevelt, and that there wouldn't be any more
wars. And so my hope was in the United Nations, and in the year

*A daily newspaper written and edited by World War Two GIs. Only en-
listed men were hired. It was often irreverent or critical of the top brass.
Bill Mauldin's two grunts, Willie and Joe, were a feature.

2000, I still feel the same way as I felt in 1945, after V-E Day, that the United Nations would bring an end to war.

I've had a stroke. I figure the best thing I can do is personal therapy, to keep writing and not give up. So I type with one hand, with my left hand, one finger of my left hand. Fortunately, I'm a lefty. I'm going to keep going. Good things happen. When I go to the park in my wheelchair for a little stroll, I cross streets. Now, because of the Americans with Disabilities Act, all the street corners have a place a wheelchair can go down, an incline, that's a great thing. See, things are improving. [*Laughs*]

VOICES OF THE '60s

Tom Hayden

He has served in the California State Senate and in the Los Angeles City Council. He is currently an author; among his subjects are his Irish heritage and street gangs of Los Angeles. He is sixty-two.

In 1962, he drafted the Port Huron Statement. "It was forty years ago this month. A very hopeful statement. It said that we were the students of this generation, that we had been raised in material comfort, but that we were unhappy with the world we were inheriting from our parents. It sketched out a view of human nature that required the system to respect each person's dignity politically, in the workplace, in the community. It said you had to build a social movement, for the first time in history based on students, that would realign the Democratic Party and change our institutions. We used the phrase, 'participatory democracy.' "

I CAME OUT OF MIDDLE AMERICA, out of Michigan. I grew up in a parochial Catholic family. They weren't very Irish; they had whited that out. Their goal for themselves and for myself: to make me the first one in the family to go to a university. That would complete the American journey for them. But it opened my mind. I'd never been exposed to so many currents of change and ideas. At the beginning of the sixties I was one of these guys who could have become a beatnik, could have hitchhiked to Los Angeles, could have hitchhiked to New York. I wanted to get out of the claustrophobia and the suffocation of this midwestern suburban upbringing.

My father was an accountant for Chrysler, my mother was a film librarian, I was an only child. We lived in Royal Oak, where the first shopping mall was built. It was called Northland.* My father had been a marine, stationed in San Diego, who didn't go into action in the Pacific. He was always a Republican, very self-made. Conservative guy, sense of humor. But his world was based on believing in the country, believing in what the president had to say. They were distant parents, not very warm or affectionate. They divorced when I was ten or eleven. I lived with my mother.

I started to live in my head, I started to live with ideas. My mother would say, "That Tommy, he's always got his nose in a book." I was a dreamer, disconnected from my upbringing. I wanted to be a foreign correspondent. Then I realized, because of the civil rights movement, that it was not just a matter of learning more about the world, but of trying to change the world. I came to Los Angeles to write about the Democratic convention in 1960. I was twenty. I saw Martin Luther King on the streets, and it changed me: it made me a part of something, an advocate. I hitchhiked to Berkeley, stayed in a commune. I saw the student movement up close. I became a troublemaker at the University of Michigan my senior year. They had never seen activism before.

I was writing editorials for the college paper, I was urging people to take action. Civil rights, peace demonstrations, taking back the university for the students, questioning authority. Everything that would seem quite commonplace today was very radical then. I was called in on the carpet by the administration. They told me I had a promising career. My first article in a national magazine was in *Mademoiselle*. That's how promising I was. They tried to put a leash on me, but I was stubborn. I resisted. I thought of myself as a crusading editor. My father's dream crumbled because he wanted me to be at least a foreign correspondent. He would have preferred that I be a lawyer or a doctor or something like that.

When I said, after graduation, "I'm going south, I'm going to live in Georgia and Mississippi, and I'm going to be an activist. Maybe I'll return to writing sometime," it really broke his heart. But he

---

*Royal Oak was the home of Father Coughlin, who was instrumental in the construction of Royal Oak's Shrine of the Little Flower and renowned for his Sunday evening broadcasts, which were polemics against FDR and the "international Jewish conspiracy."

couldn't say that. He was closed. He decided that something had gone wrong in the way he brought me up, that I had become subject to strange influences. My mother was always more supportive, but she didn't understand either. My father shut down. He didn't speak to me for sixteen years. My mother would speak to me, but in beseeching terms. "You're killing us. Can't you understand that you're killing us?" That was her message of maternal love.

I later learned that I was not alone in this experience. It happened in all kinds of families. The girl would go to Berkeley and the parents would go crazy thinking she was sleeping around. The son would have doubts about the Vietnam War, and the father would push him to join the army. The young man would come home wounded from the Vietnam War, or speechless, and the father would think that it was the son's fault. There was a generation gap, a silence that came over the heart that I think took people the rest of their lives to work out.

I actually reconciled with my father, but not until the beginning of the eighties. He remarried, had a daughter, a new child, and didn't tell her that she had a brother, myself. One day, his new wife, who was of Italian background, said, "Jack, you stubborn Irish son of a bitch, pick up the phone and call Tom. He's got a sister." This was when I had had a baby—in 1973—Troy. Jane Fonda is his mother. So my father was then a grandfather and he still wasn't speaking. I think the coming of Troy melted him a little bit.

There was a way that he could come around and keep his pride— to say that the government was lying to him. Once he understood that Nixon was a liar and that Johnson had been a liar, his hostility switched to the television. He became angry at the television set. [*Chuckles*]

At the beginning of the sixties was an extraordinary period of hope. From 1960 to the assassination of John Kennedy in '63. I don't expect to ever see it again in my lifetime. It seemed that the whole world was giving birth to new possibilities. Students everywhere in the world were rebelling. Japan, South Korea, Mexico. They became the so-called generation of '68. I don't know if it's because of my Irish heritage, but hope has always been a conflicting term for me. Because the people that impressed me the most in this world are people who stood up when their situation looked completely hopeless—like the Jews in the Warsaw ghetto. You really can't say those people had some hope of overcoming the Nazis. They stood up because it was the human thing to do. They stood up because there was some violation of their souls that was so deep they had to rebel. It was existential. That's the word I learned in college. I was very impressed by Albert Camus. You rebel because you're human, to prove that you exist. Not because you have a liberal, enlightenment form of hope that by taking action some result will follow. So I've always been conflicted about hope. Most of my friends feel strongly that hope is essential, so I accept the judgment of my friends.

From 1960 to '63, there was an absolute hopeful belief that if you stood up for the ideals of your country, the country would come back to its ideals. Everything would be healed. That moment was so hopeful, it was ludicrous. That was a high moment for the country, and I was pulled into it. But I had been educated in this more existential approach, or Irish approach, that expected doom, not a happy ending. So I was not completely surprised when Kennedy was killed. It certainly dashed the hopes of millions of people, but it confirmed more of my feeling about the world.

I think the assassinations of the sixties—of Bobby Kennedy, of Martin Luther King, of Malcolm X—all had an incalculable effect on a generation's psyche.

I see the sixties in stages. Stage one was the hopeful period. Stage two was an interlude. In 1964, there was this moment: Johnson was the new president. He could make a choice. He could escalate the war in Vietnam, then just a small skirmish, or he could take care of the home front and address the issues of racism and poverty. I don't know what John Kennedy would have done; no one really does. Part of the mythology is that if he had lived, he would have ended the war in Vietnam. The same thing was thought of Robert Kennedy, but what did happen is crucial to the history of the whole period. The liberal Democratic Party, represented by Johnson and vice president Hubert Humphrey, even Walter Reuther at that moment, chose Vietnam over civil rights. Or made no choice, living in the false belief that they could do both; Johnson called it "guns and butter," that you could have a war in Vietnam and a war against poverty. Because the ideals and the hopefulness of young people were so sky-high, so pure, this compromise was seen as a betrayal of Satanic proportions

that people would not get over for a very, very long time. The civil
rights activists brought the Mississippi Freedom Democrats to Atlantic City, to the convention, expecting to be seated by the Democrats in place of the segregationist party. Fannie Lou Hamer was the
symbol of this rising purity.* The American soul was going to be
redeemed. And who is in the way? Hubert Humphrey, Walter Reuther, all these people were saying, "Take a compromise." And compromise in those days was seen as exactly the opposite of what we
were driving for. The older generation could not manage the idealism
of the young. So you had this split. That was the interlude.

By going into Vietnam after saying he wouldn't, now Johnson's
got a hundred and fifty thousand troops there, and the latest reve-
lation of the tapes of Johnson portrays him as a man who thought
it was a mistake. He was yelling at his advisers, "What am I doing
here? What am I doing in Vietnam? This is madness." He's trying
to keep the coalition with the blacks together by offering them the
Civil Rights Act, the Voting Rights Act. But it's not working because the more militant young blacks are already in another place.
So the first stage is utopia and the second stage, the turning point
is '64, '65, when Johnson has a choice and chooses war. Then
from '65 till '70 comes the second half of the sixties, which is not
about hope or positive aspirations, it's about confrontation. Draft
resistance starts in '66. In '67, there's a huge march on the Pentagon. In '68, there's the riots at the Democratic convention [in Chi-
cago]. Nixon is elected. Draft resisters and antiwar protesters are
prosecuted, they're indicted. Nixon lived McCarthyism when he
was vice president; now he's president. So he uses the same formula: go out there and indict everybody as conspirators. I become
one of them. I was one of the Chicago Eight.† There must have
been fifty or sixty people indicted under federal anticonspiracy
laws, draft resisters, all kinds of people. That period became one of
confrontation and polarization in which generational lines became

*She was a sharecropper from Mississippi and was the eloquent voice of
the Freedom Democrats. She came to Atlantic City as part of its delegation.
†A group of eight activists tried for conspiracy in 1969–70. There was a
trial, farcical in nature due in no small part to the mischievous wit of Abbie
Hoffman, one of the defendants.

hardened. There was a lot of hate now. It almost came to a civil war because there were five hundred uprisings in black ghettos. I guess the lesson I draw from it is, as Jesse Jackson says, you have to keep hope alive continually. If you don't keep hope alive, then bad things will happen.

At the time, I thought my future would be in prison, or I would be dead. We were told by our lawyers in Chicago that we would probably be sentenced to ten years and get off in five. Actually, when we were found guilty on one charge and not guilty on another, we spent thirty days in jail waiting for federal courts to give us bail. If we had spent five years in jail, it would have been the time of the Attica prison riots. Attica came in the end of the sixties. And so, in my reflection, I would have been in prison in the midst of one of those riots. I'm not sure I would have ever gotten out alive. I'm a lucky man. No one really wants to speak of that period or remember it. I don't think anytime in American history, except the Civil War, has there been five hundred riots.

You can imagine how my parents felt. If my parents are the symbol of the older generation—they feel they've created a monster. Total shame. Their job, as they saw it, their mission in America, was to achieve respectability. In 1970, they thought that they had given birth to a son who had turned inexplicably into a communist menace, a devil. They felt everybody was looking at them, talking about them. You know how people gossip at the bakery or at the coffee shop. There's probably some truth to it. In a small town, gossip surrounded them and they magnified it, because I was the most important thing in their lives.

That period could have been even worse. Instead, it led to the end of the Vietnam War, the McGovern campaign, Watergate, the end of the Nixon presidency, the reform of the Democratic Party, the eighteen-year-old vote. So there was a second chance at the beginning of the seventies, where liberal hope started to reemerge, a new period after a storm, another interlude moment. Now the sixties generation was temporarily validated. People were willing to say that we were right. It was also a period of reconciliation with my parents.

People in the mainstream media are proclaiming that this proves the system works. This is the period that saw the beginning of the political careers of people like Bill Clinton. They had been inside the system all the way, but they shared the criticism of the war. They had worked for McGovern and now they were on their way.

Jerry Brown, who was really quite ahead of his time, was elected governor of California in 1974. He was about thirty-five years old. He ran for president two years later on a lark, and he scared the Democratic Party to death. I was sure that he or somebody like him would be president soon, and the country would be moving forward.

Again, I was deceived. Carter was president. When you look back, Carter was actually a good president and a better postpresident. But something happened. The conservatives rallied. They had a cause— to destroy the legacy of the sixties, and if possible, the legacy of the thirties. Social security, government programs, the Wagner Act, the civil rights laws, equal rights for women, environmental protection. To erase the thirties and the sixties. We had a false hope that the country was somehow good and that we would just keep pointing out inequities, and in the end, someone would be elected who would carry out this program.

So there was a round two of hopefulness. Every Democrat you know who's in office in Washington now came out of this period. Tom Daschle, the majority leader in the Senate, was a young staffer for Senator Jim Abourezk. Joe Biden, Chris Dodd, Ted Kennedy, they all were elected at this time. But the Republicans saw something, a real threat to the permanent interests of the business community. This was not about just getting out of Vietnam. That was bad enough, but Vietnam was thirteen thousand miles away. Now you had Nixon and Carter, both agreeing to the Clean Air Act, the Clean Water Act, the Environmental Protection Agency. There were four or five unheard-of reforms that became law that imposed a serious challenge to business as usual. They were associated with our friend Ralph Nader. We can call them consumer and environmental protection laws. I didn't realize it at the time, but this scared the hell out of the business community. So they formed, in the seventies, the Business Roundtable to consolidate business lobbying in Washington, to stop this march of reform. We proved no match for them. They found a candidate and they found a new formula. The candidate was Reagan and the new formula was to co-opt the symbol of the thirties, Roosevelt. Run Reagan as a new Roosevelt, while really sabotaging everything that Roosevelt stood for or accomplished.

If you think about the war on terrorism today, and al-Qaeda and bin Laden, this stuff all started in '79 in Iran. I don't think we took it too seriously, but it brought down Carter. The evening news would say: *Day twenty-six: the hostages. Day twenty-seven: the hostages. Day twenty-eight* . . . Imagine today if there was a news program that said: *Day two hundred and five: bin Laden is still at large* . . . It's an absurd way to define a crisis, but it worked. The Republican conservatives understood that. They were able to turn Iran into a Democratic weakness without calling for a new Vietnam War, which would have been a fatal mistake, and they were able to transform the civil rights issue into the crime and law-and-order issue. All of a sudden, they had a new message and they took power. As we speak today, they've demolished much of what was built out of the sixties and the New Deal. They had everything. They had money, they had candidates, they had focus groups, they had direct mail, they had grassroots organizations like the gun lobby, the right-to-life groups.

The low period continues because Clinton decided to outwit the Republicans by co-opting their program. He had inhaled the sixties a bit. Yeah, a bit. But he was trained to have it both ways. He wanted to represent the vindication of the sixties and to dump the Democratic Party baggage that had come out of the sixties. Clinton wanted to be more pro-business, more pro-police than the Republicans. It was a strange program that didn't satisfy either the supporters of the sixties or the sixties haters. The supporters of the sixties thought Clinton was betraying them, and the people who hated the sixties took any concession he gave them and asked for more, because they hated *him*. They hated *him*. They wanted to impeach him before there was a Monica Lewinsky. They hated Hillary because Hillary had been involved in her youth in the Watergate hearings that destroyed their champion, Richard Nixon. To them, the Clintons became symbolic of the sixties: smart people that kept winning but didn't deserve to be in office. I don't think we ever understood as well as Clinton did that these hate groups would do anything to win. Anything.

So you had an imbalance here. The conservatives had more money and the business community, and they also had a rage, a hate. On the other side, the liberals were fairly exhausted from the accomplishments of the past, and fairly comfortable. They were mayors, or city council members, or members of Congress. I remember talking with

Tony Cuello, majority leader of the House. It was January 1989. Dukakis had just been crushed under the barrage of Willie Horton ads. I went back to Washington, and I was crushed. I said to him, "I'm exhausted. This election was a disaster. Aren't you depressed? Why are you so hopeful?" He said, "Tom, you've got to understand, as you look around the House of Representatives, we're all winners here." Everyone had just been sworn in. He was the symbol of the new Democrats that would lead to Clinton.

For the Democrats, it got to be about the comforts of winning. I don't think that you would have heard the Republicans saying, "We're all winners here." They would have been happy that they had destroyed Dukakis, they wouldn't have had a care in the world about the character smears or the Willie Horton ad, but they would have been dissatisfied with the new president, Bush, because he was only a moderate Republican. They were already planning what became the Gingrich revolution.

Somehow, the energy shifted. In the sixties, the energy was on the left, in the eighties, the energy was on the right. What was it about? Was it about hope? No. It was about Republicans and the business community fearing the loss of their privileges more than the Democrats cared to overthrow those privileges. So you started to get Democrats who were comfortable with business contributors, you started to get Democrats who were giving tax breaks to business, Democrats who were courting business. And down it went. I was a California state assemblyman and a state senator for eighteen years. I ran in the seventies as an experiment, because I believed we were entering a new period of reform. Jerry Brown was the governor, Carter was the president. Unfortunately, by the time I got elected, we'd entered the Reagan era. Jerry Brown had been defeated. A conservative was governor of California, and a very conservative Republican was president of the United States. So I served almost all my time, sixteen of the eighteen years I was in office, under Republicans. Just when I shoved off in my little boat, the current changed. I was like a boat that was adrift, rowing against the current all during my time in office. It was terrible. Eighteen years, I served my time. [*Chuckles*] I was in a heavily Democratic district. I was able to do a lot but within a very tiny sphere. I think I became skilled at my business, at my craft. But it was hardly a time of great reform. In

Washington, the Gingrich Republicans took over the House. I had some confrontations with Gingrich. It was unbelievable. I could tell he still thought I was the devil. There wasn't much Clinton could do because he'd lost the House. He had a very crippled presidency. He had two problems that undermined him. Four of Clinton's eight years, Gingrich was the Speaker. The next four years, Monica Lewinsky was his nightmare. So Clinton was never able to push his agenda in a progressive direction. He was constantly playing defensive politics, and I was living in Sacramento under Pete Wilson, who had presidential ambitions himself. He was running anti-immigrant campaigns.

The war on terrorism has accelerated the push to the right, and we're farther than ever from where we ought to be. I don't quarrel with the idea that if the World Trade Center or the Pentagon is attacked, the United States has the right to go after those who did it. But what we have instead is an open-ended war on terrorism, a blank check, with no definition of enemies, no boundaries, no congressional oversight. We're at war in so many places at the moment: Afghanistan, Indonesia, the Philippines, the ex-Soviet state of Georgia . . . I can't remember all the places, and neither can the American people. Now we've had a secret memo divulged that says the Pentagon wants to develop more usable compact nuclear weapons. The conservatives are calling for the creation of an American empire. They're citing Tiberius as a role model. The curtain is coming down on parliamentary democracy. Congress has less and less power. Trade agreements are being realized without protections for labor, environment, human rights. Every day I tell myself it couldn't be worse, and then I wake up and I read the paper, and I hear the conservatives still aren't done. They think Bush isn't going *far* enough. Remember the statement by John Mitchell, the discredited attorney general, during the Nixon years? "We're going to push this country so far to the right that you won't even recognize it."

On the other hand, I haven't seen stronger, more idealistic protests than I did in Seattle since the sixties. Just before 9/11 there was a real movement beginning again that was on the level of the 1960s. I was in Seattle for all those days. I was gassed, I was in the middle of it, and I was overwhelmed by the emergence of this new idealistic generation. The backbone of the demonstrations was young people, but the coalition in Seattle was a dream one you couldn't have achieved in the sixties: young people and labor, environmentalists and labor. The issues were patriotic issues. We were standing for a democratic society in which our laws were respected: our labor laws, our environmental laws, our human rights laws. The multinational corporations and the WTO [World Trade Organization] were standing for a new international order in which American democracy would suffer. So that was the third moment of hope for me, Seattle. Because the progressives had done what you've always recommended: they had recaptured patriotism and the conservatives were losing their grip on it, because they were calling for more power for corporations and less democracy.

Then, boom, 9/11. Bin Laden and these guys handed the conservative right wing in America an opportunity they never would have achieved on their own. I just pray every day that there's not another attack on this country, because there's still time to rescue our ideals, to prevent further damage to democracy. September eleventh has eclipsed the memory of a stolen election and made it unimportant. Maybe John Kennedy's election was stolen in 1960, I don't know . . . but this election in Florida I *know* was stolen. So how did Bush become president? The conservatives have more rage. Rage and a strategy. They have message, they have money, they have corporate support, they have Supreme Court appointees. They have an apparatus in place, that's for sure, and are energized by a rage that doesn't exist on the Democratic side. You saw it in the faces of those guys who flew into Florida and literally broke into the county ballot-counting process and stopped it, *stopped* it. They physically stopped democracy. These are the people who are running the country. It seems to me that there is another opportunity coming, another period of hope beyond this current gloom, but only if progressives recover their rage. I mean rage in the Old Testament sense: a rage at injustice. I don't mean rage as in days of rage and wanton violence. I mean righteous rage. Righteous rage is what's missing. If you have righteous rage, then you can be a prophetic minority in the wilderness for a few years, but you'll never stop trying to get the country back.

There's a raging public out there that the Democratic Party is afraid of, that the Democratic Party doesn't understand. It's still out there, but it's been eclipsed by 9/11. And, ah . . . [*Long pause*] how do I feel? I feel that you can't take anything in life for granted. When there's an opportunity, you should seize it, and when you're victorious, you should not get comfortable. The struggle is just up and down, up and down. It's a little like that story of Sisyphus, I guess. Although we ought to have more joy about pushing the rock up the hill. It seems like the struggle is a burden. Whether you're hopeful or not, the struggle should be enjoyable, not a burden.

It's not surprising that the idealists are always young. Young people are like eagles, they can see a long way and they don't have any hindsight. They're always discovering something new, and they don't carry as much of the burden of the old. Then comes the second stage of life. I would call it your entry into a career, where you have to make money, you've got to settle down somewhat, and you become more like a coyote, more competitive with other people because this is going to determine where you are in the pecking order. So the idealism of the young is tempered by the competitiveness of the thirty-somethings and the forty-somethings. And then the third stage is you get as far as you're going to go in your career path, you become president of the United States, or a journalist, or a schoolteacher, or you get your seniority. And you realize that competition isn't going to get you farther. So you settle down more, you're the mayor of a city or the city council person or the editor of the newspaper. Here you try to bring together the best of the idealism you had when you were a kid and what you've learned about the world and the rat race. So at worst you're compromised, but at best, you're a smart idealist, you've learned something, you've matured. Then you get beyond that, into what in this society is usually called old age, but it's the only opportunity you'll have for wisdom. You're no longer really needed as mayor, because there's always some guy knocking at the door who wants to replace you, and the end is coming. So this is the last stage. You know what that is? To be an elder. The problem with the sixties, as I look back, was a problem of the elders. It was always defined as a problem of youth, a crisis of youth. But really, that was how the elders defined it. The real problem was that the elders weren't there. The elders missed the point entirely. I live now with one goal: to try to learn to be the kind of elder who was missing when I was a kid.

Staughton Lynd

Niles, Ohio, on the outskirts of Youngstown. He lives in semiretirement with his wife, Alice. He is seventy-one.

In the 1920s, his parents, Robert and Helen Lynd, wrote Middletown, *a study of Muncie, Indiana, that became a sociological classic and a metaphor for America. This was decades before Muncie joined the Rust Belt and the sunnier metaphors for America moved southwest.*

Ever since his young manhood, he has come to be regarded as controversial in many quarters, academic as well as political. His activities in the civil rights and peace movements, especially during the sixties, caused him considerable troubles.

His demeanor is gentle. He is soft spoken, and there is always the intimation of a sad smile. He is a Quaker, as were his parents, and could in his younger days have been a natural as the Quaker magazine cover boy.

WHEN I WAS SIXTEEN, I thought that the United States would undoubtedly be a socialist society, a humane one, by the time I was thirty. So I had hope. In fact, I had so much hope that a friend of mine wrote me a long letter in which he said that he was very worried about me because I had so much hope and I thought so well of human beings and I dreamed such big dreams, that he was afraid I would become disillusioned.

I didn't become disillusioned. Obviously, the United States did not become a socialist society either. Some very hopeful beginnings, as in Nicaragua or the Polish Solidarity movement, have not come to fruition. The Soviet Union took a turn, certainly with Stalin, and ironically, now. You can no longer speak of creating some kind of humane socialism. They have embraced out-and-out capitalism.

When my wife and I were in Eastern Europe three years ago, all our student guides were just beginning to realize that there would be no more free health care and no more free higher education. So if my old high school friend has occasion to write to me again, he'd say, "Now I'm more worried than ever, Staughton, because things haven't gone very well for what you were hoping."

If he knew of my personal experiences, he'd be even more worried. I got thrown out of the army in 1954, along with more than a hundred other people. It was at the height of the McCarthy period, and McCarthy had just discovered what he perceived to be a communist dentist at Fort Dix. The army was terrified that he'd come up with more such people. So anybody belonging to anything got a letter saying, "It is alleged that . . ." I still have this letter. One of the charges against me was: "It is alleged that your mother is a hyper-modern educator."

I was not killed, nor was I imprisoned for a long period, as I'm sure I would have been in a third-world society. But still, getting thrown out of the army, getting rejected for tenure at Yale . . . * That was in the later sixties.

There were three years, after the army threw me out, when I was at loose ends. My wife and I found our way to what would later be called a commune, an intentional community in the hills of northeast Georgia. Macedonia was its name. Almost every day for those three years, I got up early in the morning to feed the cows. I was on the morning milk detail because Alice and I were about ten years younger than most of the others. I was alleged to have more stamina. It got pretty cold in the hills of Georgia. I would pull my wool hat up over one ear to hear the cowbell, keep it down over the other so as not to freeze to death.

I'd kick the cows in their behinds, they'd start toward the barn, and I would follow. Along about then, the sun would start to come up. Everything I could see, all six hundred acres, was part of this different, cooperative life we were trying to build up together. Like any group of people trying to work out something new together, we had all kinds of problems. In the end, most of the others got religion, and Alice and I were left outside. But for those three years, I was

*He subsequently taught at Yale. His tenure was favored by all his department colleagues. The administration, nonetheless, denied him. He had, by that time, become "controversial," after his adventures in the southern civil rights Freedom School movement and a trip to Hanoi during the Vietnam War.

convinced on my pulses, as John Keats would have said, that people can live cooperatively. People can make decisions together. When problems arise, if they confront them head-on, they have a pretty good chance of working them out. If you ask me why I'm so hopeful, despite all the reversals in the world today, I chalk it up to my personal experience. Sooner or later, people will figure out a more cooperative way to do things. I've seen it happen. Those were the learning years, '54 to '57.

One day, a friend said to me, "What do you think about the sit-ins in the South?" I said, "The what?" I'm ashamed to say it. I had been immersed in graduate school and having two little children. I had not been in touch with the outside world.

That summer we went on a picnic in Central Park with an African American playmate of our older daughter. The playmate's mother said, "You should be teaching at a Negro college." I said, "A what?" I knew that there was something called the Tuskegee Institute, but that was about it.

Howard Zinn hired me to teach at Spelman College, a school for African American young women.* So we moved south. Alice said she wasn't sure she was up for a sit-in, but she was up for a live-in. We lived on the college campus.

One night at Spelman, half asleep and groggy, I was reading examination books. A particular one fully awakened me and excited me. I said to Howard, "Do you have a student named Alice Walker?" Alice [Walker] was going mildly crazy at Spelman. She was disciplined for having her light on in the middle of the night when she was reading French poetry.

Remember, it was an African American college that had been under siege for decades. Here were students going off campus and picketing and getting arrested downtown and then coming back to Spelman and getting stirred up by these young white radicals from the North. Howard Zinn was ultimately fired, and I quit. My wife, Alice, had been teaching in a day-care center. She got fired for joining a picket line in Atlanta. (My mother was teaching at Sarah Lawrence College. She helped Alice Walker get transferred there. She took creative writing, and the rest you know.) A year later, in the fall of

*Howard Zinn is an American historian.

1963, I was invited to be the coordinator for the Freedom Schools in the Mississippi Summer Project. It was the summer when the three young men were killed: Schwerner, Cheney, and Goodman. My experience with those Freedom Schools was the most hopeful you can imagine. Right along with my three years at Macedonia, it was the closest I've ever come to seeing a future that might work.

Next, we went to Chicago and I felt like a fish out of water. I got a part-time teaching appointment at Roosevelt University. The History Department recommended me for a full-time position, but the president of the university overruled it.

I had made a trip to Hanoi and had become quite controversial.* That visit was in its own way a very hopeful experience. We met a very small, very frail elderly man. Very soft spoken. He spoke through a translator. I'm not sure whether he was the foreign minister of North Vietnam or of the National Liberation Front of South Vietnam.

He said, "You don't understand, Professor. We're going to win this war." What he detected in me was the thought: *Oh, the poor Vietnamese, we're going to drop bombs and that will be the end of them.* He said, "That's not the situation at all. Your countrry has two choices: you can completely withdraw from my country, which of course, we would prefer. On the other hand, you may decide to send more soldiers to my country. But I want to assure you that whichever choice you make, we're going to win. Because, for every American soldier that lands, one more Vietnamese will come to the National Liberation Front." Here was a prediction from this small man that came in right on the money.

After his Roosevelt University experience, he decided to become a labor lawyer, and attended law school at the University of Chicago. By this time, he had become a notorious dissenter.

After I passed the bar exams in 1981, we moved to Youngstown, Ohio, an industrial city, where the unions and management were

*Lynd's two companions on the trip were Tom Hayden and Herbert Aptheker. Hanoi was the capital of the communist government in wartime North Vietnam.

engaged in tough battles. It was a culture shock to me to come from the movement of the sixties, the southern civil rights movement, the antiwar movement, to the labor movement. I've never gotten over it.

I was hired by the leading labor law firm in town. I recognized from the beginning that it might not work out, 'cause their clients were unions and I was determined to represent people who were being screwed both by the company and by the union.

Two years later, I was fired. I had written a little book called *Labor Law for the Rank and File*. You could put it in your shirt pocket or your hip pocket. Like a good earnest Quaker, I thought I should first show it to my boss. So we invited him to dinner, gave him a copy, and I was fired at eleven o'clock the next morning. [*Laughs*] The book starts by saying, "We all know Dr. Spock's baby book. Dr. Spock says, if your infant has such-and-such symptoms, don't panic. Try this, try that. Only if the temperature goes above such-and-such, call the doctor. Don't call the doctor right away, don't waste your money. It's the same way with lawyers. Try to figure it out yourself, just like you would if there was something wrong with the ignition in your car. Don't spend a hundred bucks on a lawyer, spend a few bucks on these two books I'm gonna tell you about." [*Laughs*] I think that's what he didn't like.

Now, in retirement, I'm very much involved in prison reform. In Youngstown, all the steel mills closed, and after about ten years the city fathers decided they had an idea. They couldn't get any other big corporations to move to town, but maybe they could get some prison business. So they got the first supermax prison in Ohio, and the first private prison in Ohio. My wife and I have been pretty busy ever since. At the moment, I'm involved in three major cases. One of them has to do with a 1993 prison riot in southern Ohio, at a prison called Lucasville, which lasted eleven days and would have had a lot more publicity except that the Branch Davidian thing in Waco was going on at the same time. Nine prisoners and one hostage officer were killed. Five prisoners were sentenced to death. For five years, my wife and I have been associated with the appeals of one of those prisoners. I'm trying to represent them as a group. Three are black and two are white. At the time of the riot, the two whites were members of the Aryan Brotherhood. But I'm telling you that those guys have really stuck together in a way that is very admirable.

It's a conventional thing in academe these days to say, "Well, why did they ever think the white working class would amount to anything? They're just a bunch of racist slobs." In the early sixties, between white and black students, we caught a glimpse of interracial solidarity. To find it among these working-class guys, these outcasts, is, to me, incredibly moving.

The hope, first of all, is in a labor movement that will not be narrowly nationalist. In other words, capital has gone international, and so working people have to find a way to do the same. I think the real reason the steelworkers were in Seattle [for the antiglobalization demonstrations] was to keep imported steel out of the United States, and the real reason the Teamsters Union was there was to keep Mexican truck drivers from crossing the Rio Grande. Nevertheless, I think that working people are moving in that direction. We've made considerable efforts in Youngstown so that workers can go to a labor school in Mexico. I have hope in that. I think that the use of e-mail makes it much easier for people across borders to coordinate their efforts. It has to be a bottom-up sort of thing.

Workers feel more than one thing at the same time. Workers are not at an Ivy League sherry party where you can be completely wrong and nasty, but you have to be consistent. That's not workers. Workers react to things. There are those notions about being middle class, but there are also certain communities, and Youngstown is one of them, where people feel somebody is pushing shit on us.

It was a special situation in Youngstown, where people came home from the mill, walked up the hill, and lived in houses where the neighbor in every direction also worked in the mill. It was like a mining community. In that kind of community, it's obviously a lot easier for workers to feel themselves a community separate from the rest of the world. Those communities are dying out because of the use of the car.

I'm not minimizing the role of the working class. I now feel that students and workers are like two hands. In many situations it's gonna be the students who act first. They don't have kids at home, they're not paying a mortgage, they're not tied down to a thousand responsibilities the way workers are. There are many situations where students act first. I still believe in finding common cause with all kinds of people and creating what in spirit is the same kind of community that we were privileged to live in in the Georgia mountains. It's not that one gets up in the morning and stirs up a little porridge of hope for breakfast. That's not how it feels. You get up and the sun is shining and there are tasks in the back of your head for the day, and the phone rings and it's a friend who wants to discuss some common project. And . . . [*Long pause*] that's how the day begins.

Arlo Guthrie

A folksinger and songwriter. His most celebrated work during the sixties was "Alice's Restaurant." He is the son of Woody Guthrie, known through the thirties and forties as "America's balladeer."

I WAS ONE OF A FAMILY of troubadours and hopers and dreamers. I've got ancestors who were doing that, I've got kids who are doing that, I've got grandkids that are starting to do that. I seem to be caught in the middle of a multitude of generations who have been interested in making music and at the same time making it worthwhile to listen to. My dad was Woody Guthrie. A lot of people know who he is. It seems that his ancestors were all fiddle players. They came from a long line of Scots, who were in this country since the very early seventeen hundreds. They all made their own fiddles. My dad wasn't a very good fiddle player, but he had one and he sawed on it occasionally.

We used to look at Woody Guthrie as the Dust Bowl balladeer, because that was the very first of his works that got out to the public. He started traveling around with Will Geer, Cisco Houston, Pete Seeger, and others. He became known as a protester, the guy who would show up at your union hall and sing something that would earn a little money for the outfit or make people feel pretty good. That lasted for a while. Then he became a sort of social commentator. As the decades drift by, we've seen different parts of him. Now in the new millennium, we're seeing parts of him that have never been seen before—love songs, baseball songs, songs about space . . . He wrote songs for little kids, songs for fighting, and songs for death. He wrote in an era when songs were more than just entertainment, they were a part of *life*. In everyday life, music played a part. Nowadays, music is something that most people go hear other people do. It's not something they do themselves. He was opposed to this kind of mechanized, lambs-to-the-slaughter mentality, where you just go to hear other people live. He was convinced—Pete Seeger, too—

that people should be making their own music. That's what it's all about.

The best part of my dad's work has been distilled into some of the ideas that he wrote in prose that say that the value of being human is you cannot be imitated by anybody else. No matter where you come from, how big or tall, how fat or thin, how educated or uneducated, how much money you have, who your parents were, what your tradition is, you have a unique value. He wanted people to take pride in who they were. If you look at the world today, all of the conflicts that are going on involve people whose lives, they feel, are valueless. There are people around the world today whose traditions, whose values, whose ideas are being threatened by what they perceive as being a conscious effort on the part of corporations, governments, other vested interests. So they're struggling, they're defending, they're terrorizing, whatever it is. The same two people in a conflict have the same fear that their way of life is being threatened. These are values that I think my dad put his finger on. So I see my life as trying to hang on to the values that were picked up by him in his time. They are just as valuable, if not more so, now.

I'd say there's a certain familiar herd of people who have traveled with me on my life's journey. I remember the first controversial concert I attended was a Pete Seeger concert. I was a kid in grammar school, about nine or ten. We got to the show and there were these people outside the hall with signs and pickets saying that he wasn't worth going to see, that we should stop seeing these commies. I went up to one of the pickets with my classmates, I said, "Is this true? Is he really one of those?" And the man said, "Yeah." I said, "Give me those pamphlets! I'll help pass them out." Of course, we threw them away. When we didn't have any more pamphlets, we went inside. That was my first political action in support of the rights of people to say what they want and be who they are without other people second-guessing their patriotism.

I have lived through a number of different things. Sometimes I've been disappointed in history and sometimes I've been proud to be a part of it. I'm fifty-five now, about one month older than my dad got to be. Most of the time it occurs to me that history is made up of events that are not healthy for human beings. Every once in a while there's a historic event that makes you proud to be a human being. But all of the other things that mark human history are wars, disasters, famines, floods, earthquakes, diseases. At every show, I say to the audience, "Somewhere there's somebody ducking for cover. Somewhere somebody's shooting at somebody that's hiding in a hole, hoping that somewhere in the world somebody's singing, somebody's playing, and life is worth living."

After this 9/11 thing, I didn't feel like playing, I didn't feel like singing. But I realized that there were people around the world who were counting on others to keep that hope alive. It's good to be reminded that there are people who would love to be at these events we so casually attend, where life is celebrated. Every time the troops go overseas, they come back with ideas, they come back with values. They come back with liquor or drugs. Good things, bad things, all kinds of stuff. But nobody goes away and comes back untouched. We've had millions and millions of men and women involved in wars overseas. When you put together all the money that's been spent on all of these wars, just in the last fifty years, and you compare that to the money that people have spent getting along with each other, it's no wonder the world is the way it is. We put our money where our mouth is. I saw my friends go overseas and come back different times. I see it today. Nobody gets untrained when they come back. We have used up most of our humanity in inhuman ways. That's the great disaster. So we end up weak instead of strong.

My job is to continue the work of my dad: making people feel good about who they really are. Somehow or other, we have to put that back in our consciousness. It's not to go back to walking around in coonskin caps or loincloths, although that would be nice. The truth is that we have to bring our history with us and not abandon it as we move forward.

You have millions and millions of schoolkids who think there's nothing to do, there's nothing worth watching on TV. All the effort by the community to support drama programs and school programs is out the window now. So what are they learning? They end up getting stoned for a break. Just a rest. Then we take that away, too. We say, "No, no, you can't do that, that's bad for you," without realizing it's *life* that's bad for them. It's living in this world that we've created that's bad for them. We've poisoned the water, we've killed the air, we've automated everybody so there's no value to them anymore. As soon as one guy leaves, you can plug in another one. This is *insane*. No wonder people are flipping out. No wonder there's countries overseas that are saying, "Leave us alone. We'd rather ride our camels around without ya."

I think these problems are solvable and that maybe we'll get to 'em, but not without leaders. I don't see where the leaders are. Where are the Roosevelts? We kill the statesmen on their way up. Not only are we digging ourselves into a deeper hole, but the people who know how to talk us out of it, we've pretty well bumped them off, too. What I've noticed throughout all of this, it's like a river. It doesn't go straight. History goes from side to side. One time it goes off to one side, bounces off the wall, and comes back. I think we're in one of those extreme moments when the entire river seems to be off on one side. It looks like it's created an entirely new direction, but I don't think it has. I think it'll start going back the other way.

Just look at nature. That's how people really are. Nobody just has an idea and sticks with it forever unless he's a stick of wood. How do you know if your idea is real or not, if your values are real or not, without testing them? How do you know that your relationships are real until they come under stress? The truth is until you bounce them up off the wall of reality, you don't really know.

Instead of having a community understanding as in the Great Depression, my dad's time, when everybody was broke, everybody's now depressed and taking Prozac. [*Laughs*] We did have that sense of community in the sixties. There was a real coming together of all these divergent communities: of women, men, kids, adults, grandparents, blacks, whites, red people, yellow people. All of those people got together in the sixties to end the war, to end pollution, to talk about education, to deal with nuclear energy, and yes, to fight for civil rights. Since then, all those people seem to have drifted off into their own worlds. At our shows you will hardly ever find any black people, red people, or yellow people. Everybody's got their own audience now.

Pete [Seeger] talked to me the other day. We're doing a show in Newark, and I called him up: "Pete, would you come and do it with me?" He said, "I'll do it with you if you'll make some tickets available cheaply for some of the people in the community." Pete has no idea that the reason they're not coming is not a matter of expense. They're not coming because they're not interested in the kind of music that Pete and I make anymore. This is a different world. Everybody has gone off to live in their own culture.

When radio first started, you would hear a very diverse format, a whole variety of stuff. Now, all the radio stations play one kind of music. The great benefit of the broad variety was that even as a kid, if I wasn't listening to country music, at least I knew what the country music hit was. I knew what the classical music hit was. I knew who the famous opera singers were. Even though that wasn't my thing. I had a knowledge of a broad spectrum of community stuff that's gone now. All of these different communities have their own music, they have their own clothes. I'm not saying it's a bad thing. What I love about it is that people have to be bicultural now. You have to live in your own world, but you also have to know the language of communicating with everybody on equal terms in global society. This is the model that I think will save us in the long run, because the only way that the guys in the Middle East or the guys in Asia are going to feel comfortable is when they realize that they can be themselves. They can live in their own world, and at the same time they can contribute, they can interact on a global scale with everybody else. At the same time, as we're becoming smaller, we're becoming bigger. This is what appeals to me. There's no authority behind this movement, there's no invested interests. It's just the way it's going. I'm noting, while we're all becoming separate, we're also learning how to be together. Because we do have to meet above all the differences.

We were the first generation to come to the brink of a global disaster the likes of which no other civilization ever felt. The Aztecs, the Incas, the Romans, the Vikings, the Chinese—if you put them all together, none of them would have had the destructive power that we had to deal with in the sixties when we came to the Cuban missile crisis. We were all told to hide under the desks when the bombs went off. I think we kids were so impressed by the fear that we sensed that we all decided spontaneously to do things differently. We realized that the traditions that had brought us to this brink could no longer play the only role in our history. That led to the sixties. There was not a majority of people that moved, but it was a critical mass. A critical minority formed the revolution that moved us into the sixties. This was the beginning of a new world where we suddenly realized all of this talk about equality couldn't be just talk anymore. We actually had to live it or forget it. And we decided to put it to the test. So we started living together in all kinds of strange ways. We accepted people who were really different and far out. You could wear what you wanted; you could grow your hair two feet long. We broke all the barriers. Some were worth breaking, some not. But if we hadn't done it, we would have continued down this trail of total annihilation, which was unacceptable.

I remember the day it ended. We were protesting the building of the Seabrook nuclear power plant in New Hampshire. We had been at a bunch of these things for the last decade—civil rights, ban the bomb, stop the war, clean the water, whatever—and we had always marched down these streets and boulevards singing the usual songs, "We Shall Overcome," "I Ain't Gonna Study War No More" songs. All of a sudden, I saw a placard that somebody was holding. It said: *Lesbian Plumbers from Albany, New York, against nuclear power.* Although it was very funny and wonderful in some ways, I also realized that this was the end. Now people were using these events to justify who they were and not simply to end the nuclear threat in the area. And I think I was right.

I remember the last time the Names Project quilt, the AIDS quilt, was unfolded in Washington, D.C. I was there, I spoke, I'm walking down the street, and they were playing canned music. I thought to myself: *Isn't it interesting? None of these people could possibly have been at the civil rights demonstrations or anywhere else where live music played such an important role. If they had been, they would have* known *the power of playing our own music. And they've totally missed the opportunity. We're playing canned stuff over the speaker systems as if we were all supposed to sing along with a record.* I thought, *What a shame.* I felt my world had ended in some ways; that that time of the sixties was definitely over. The great tragedy of these times that we're living in is that we have given up the voice of the average guy and we now listen to the people who profit from canned stuff.

The older I get, the more I realize that most of the people I know are already dead. My dad, my mom, my grandparents, my great-grandparents, even some siblings are gone now. And most of my friends. My other great hope is that this isn't it. I hear from them more and more, I'm closer and closer to all of these ancestors, even the ones I've never met. Because I realize that most of my history, what I'm made up of biologically, genetically, goes back for millions and millions of years. So I'm very curious about these guys. And in a personal way, I'm hanging out with my dad, not Woody Guthrie the great balladeer.

It's not a question of afterlife. I'm talking about something you can touch while you're still alive, if you have the discipline to do it. I hope that I'm learning them. And if not, that's OK, too. It's still worth attempting. I hope it's worth all the effort that I put into my life being me, but if not, that's OK, too. I'm not less of a person for living my life, even though it may not pan out to be exactly how I have it in mind. I heard the Dalai Lama speak one time, and somebody asked him, "Why do you meditate all the time?" He says, "Well, there might be an afterlife and there might not be. So when I meditate, I put myself in that afterlife right now so that if I ever have to die, I won't even notice it." He says, "If there is no afterlife, OK, what the hell? It wasn't such a bad discipline anyway." [*Laughs*]

Part II

CONCERNING ENRONISM

-ism. 1. An action, practice or process . . .
3. A characteristic behavior or quality . . .
5. A doctrine, theory, system or principle.

— *The American Heritage Dictionary of*
the English Language

John Kenneth Galbraith

Economist, memoirist, former ambassador to India. Who's Who
in America refers to him as a retired economist. It may be mis-
leading: his trenchant commentary on "private affluence and
public squalor" (a phrase coined in his most celebrated work,
The Affluent Society *[1958]) has never been more relevant.*

THE FIRST THING I remember from my early youth was the
sinking of the *Titanic*. I was then approximately four years old. I was
born in 1908, and have been trying to live with that date for the last
several years. The *Titanic* is almost a metaphor, isn't it? The tip of
the iceberg. A metaphor for the big corporations, including Enron
and WorldCom, and Tyco, that were thought to be invulnerable. And
then, within a space of a few weeks—in the case of Enron, a year—
they all suddenly hit the rocks. The real problem of what's happening
right now is the unlicensed transfer of power to less-than-responsible
enterprise.

The word *capitalism* is somewhat obsolete because power has
passed in the modern corporation from the owners, now nicely called
the investors, to management. The complications associated with
running a corporate enterprise, like General Motors or General Elec-

tric, or Enron for that matter, are beyond the information, the ability, the authority of the so-called investors. They just can't usefully participate. And power, therefore, has passed almost entirely to management. That only works if you have two things: a competent management, and one that is honest. In these last days, we've seen exposed the depth of the error in those assumptions. After all, they can give themselves very nice salaries, and nobody reacts, out of ignorance or an assumption that this is the national reward of the rich. They can raid the economy for enormous sums of money, as in the case of these who have just gone down, at a cost not only to the stockholders, but to their own workers. Someday, this will be known as the year of the 401(k).

History doesn't in any precise way repeat itself, but the 1920s were a decade of increasing optimism leading to insanity. If you got possession in the early twenties of the right kind of Florida real estate, by which I mean any acreage in Florida, then you got rich in the New York stock market. And you attributed the wealth you raked in to your own insights, never to circumstance. When the crash came, it not only destroyed that illusion, but of course dispatched a lot of people into a lower-middle-class living. Out of Washington came a flow of optimistic comments about the future of the economy and the future of the market. That Rockefeller was optimistic and investing money to prove it brought forth one of the great comments: "Who else had any money?"

I wrote *The Great Crash,* which still outsells any other book of mine. That is because when everybody got carried away in these last years by general optimism, I got free advertising. So in some ways I've been a considerable participant in the recent boom, thanks to people who have been told to study 1929. One of the great errors of our time is the assumption that economists or some other magic group have the key to prediction, can predict when we're going to have a recession, that their training and acuity make their predictions valid. The truth is nobody knows.

Up until a year ago, the basic economic assumption was that we were in the hands of corporations of great distinction and able leadership, and nothing in my lifetime or yours has happened more completely than the loss of confidence in corporate leadership. The great force in the modern economy is corporate management. It's faceless and powerful. Nobody had heard a great deal about Enron, or a great deal about WorldCom, or a great deal about Tyco. It was an enormously influential community that was largely unknown. And no ordinary stockholder in those corporations had any particular authority. There are some problems that can be solved. Let's go back to the Great Depression. There were lines of action putting money in people's pockets, whether in the farm field or the WPA [Works Progress Administration], which would then be spent and revive the economy. There was a cure. The situation we're talking about now is one for which there is at the present time no readily available remedy. No question about it, we're going to have to accustom ourselves to more regulation, but we're going to have to accustom ourselves to the fact that the difference between avarice and self-service and intelligence and public responsibility is not something that yields to the passage of law. This is human behavior beyond the reach of the law.

As we put power in the hands of corporation management, where it is bound to stay, this is going to be one of the great problems of the future. Intelligent, competent corporate management that is law-abiding and effective is something you cannot get by legislation. We do not have available any clear alternative.

Those of us who were associated with the New Deal were slightly insane on the wonderful vision we had of the United States, and of its economy. And that was something that I remember with both pleasure and a detailed array of doubts as to how anybody could be so optimistic.

We had the central problem of preventing inflation during World War Two, which had been the great hazard of World War One, when prices doubled in the matter of a year. That responsibility devolved on me. I was in charge of price control. I started with a staff of seven and ended with several thousand. There was a strong but rather simple course of action. You simply told people they couldn't raise prices. I enjoyed that to the extent that anybody could enjoy that pressure of responsibility.

At the age of ninety-four, I don't think of myself as the national source of great remedies anymore. I am limiting myself to the enjoyments that are associated with defining the problem and defeating the palpable nonsense that this is a problem easily solved by enjoining better behavior, which is the president's design, or by regulation. My pleasure is in opening up the problem, not providing the solution. I would point out that at my age, there are no untrammeled hopes for the future.

There's a possibility, though, that the American people will discover it isn't necessary for their happiness and well-being to have a continual high and increasing economic production of goods and services, that we might graduate into an atmosphere of contentment with a lower supply of goods and services.

We cannot have the present kind of economy without a great series of bureaucratic establishments, and the result is that we depend very much on honesty and competence. We have learned in these last months that honesty cannot be counted on. As things now stand, we allow enormous incompetence and enormous compensation to those who have power. I see that as a great unsolved problem of our time. And since it is all quite legal, I call it the likelihood of innocent fraud.

I entered the world of politics at a time when there were Fifth Amendment communists, and I've reached the age of ninety-four, when there are Fifth Amendment capitalists.

Wallace Rasmussen

In 1967, when he was appointed senior vice president of Beat-rice Foods, the company was worth $4.3 billion dollars. In 1975, when he retired as president and chief executive officer, it was worth $7.8 billion. He won the Horatio Alger Award in 1978.

Big-boned and heavyset, with calloused hands, he had the ap-pearance of the archetypal workingman in Sunday clothes. "I'm just a country boy. Born in Nebraska and came up right through the Great Depression . . . I'm convinced it will repeat itself in time when it's time, and probably it'll be good for the country. It will be hard on people who never experienced doing without, but it's amazing what you can get along without." By means of an electrified armchair, a necessity for him, I am lifted into his office, one flight up. I am deeply appreciative, being two years his elder. He has aged remarkably little since I first interviewed him in 1980, his bolo tie lending him a rakish air.

I GRADUATED FROM HIGH SCHOOL when I was sixteen. It was during the Great Depression and drought. In order for my father and mother not to have to feed another kid, I left home. I went to California. I got different kinds of jobs. In those days, you'd take anything. I peddled handbills for ten cents a hundred. I got a job in the Mojave Desert on a hay ranch, ten dollars a month, room and board. I didn't get paid for the last month, so I went home and finished shucking corn. I sold one load, a hundred bushels, for ten cents a bushel. Never got paid. That taught me: in God we trust, and everybody else, you better audit.

My uncle got me a job where he worked, at the Beatrice Foods Company in Lincoln. It was ice, butter, milk, ice cream, and cold storage. Their sales at that time were something like three hundred and fifty million dollars a year. I started out doing a bit of everything from cleaning out sewers to pulling ice. I could do anything with my hands, fix anything. I still can. A gift, I guess. But I wasn't educated. So I went to night school to learn welding. I told the chief engineer I'd pay for it myself. He gave me the go-ahead. I was nineteen. That was in 1932. Butter was selling for seven cents a pound. When you put it in cold storage for a length of time, it becomes off-flavor. So they got a Roger's Deodorizer. They said, "Wallace, put it in." I never saw it before in my life, but I got it working.

They sent me down to the butter plant at Vincennes, Indiana. The deodorizer had been sitting there for six months 'cause nobody could hook it up. I did it in a jiffy. I was just a kid.

Somebody said to me not long ago, "You must have been ambitious." "No," I said, "I only wanted to be a little better off than I am today." Because if you're too ambitious, it'll chew you up, and I've seen it destroy people. So I went up step by step. I had to step over a lot of people, but not run over 'em. I would always do my job.

Forbes was listing the toughest CEOs in the country, and I was in that article. They had me saying, "Do unto others before they do unto you." [*Laughs*] I don't know whether I should have been happy with that, but I was OK. You have to show strength. Any sign of weakness and people are going to take advantage of you.

Even though I've retired, I still serve on boards of various companies. I've always made trouble. I was on the board of a company here, and I found out they cooked books. They were not working for the company, but for themselves. I had them fired. That got me into trouble, but it also got me where I am today. I can face anybody.

What's happened at Enron and WorldCom—cooking books—is criminal. A great country lasts about four hundred years. We're in the declining-morality period. That is what ruined Rome. . . .

Greed. I think a lot of it comes from people in our educational system who are teaching things in business colleges that are not for the benefit of the world but for the benefit of themselves. I listened to some of the hearings, and those guys were all egomaniacs. Is it going to turn around? Not in my lifetime. Not in my children's lifetime. The corporate life, it's going down the drain. Greed. When I was on the boards of companies, I insisted that they give *all* employees stock, not just the CEOs, the top people, because it's the workers are the ones who put me where I was.

I understand unions. I worked with them and I got along well with them. The only time I didn't was with Jimmy Hoffa. Making a profit no matter how, that's what the free market is today. Making a profit, without humanity and morals. It's not just a few rotten apples in the barrel. It goes all the way from here to Washington, D.C.

They have one goal in life: "How much money can I get out of this for myself?" I was chairman of several auditing committees, and I always said: "In God we trust, everything else we audit." When I didn't believe what the auditors were giving me, I would say to them, "Bring me the work papers. I want to review the work papers." "What do you want to do that for?" "I want to find out what you're not telling us." Because it's the work papers and the words of the workers, who report everything; I did that at every company I was at. They said, "Do you know how many boxes that is?" I said, "Yes! I want to see them." Boy, I straightened a lot of things out by looking at the work papers. Who is taking their girlfriends to posh places? Who's entertaining people they shouldn't be entertaining and putting it all on company bills? Who's bought a boat, who's bought a car and charged it to the company?

Since 1980, I have spent a lot of my life helping young people. Ten years ago, I was discouraged. Today, I'm encouraged by how bright those young people are. Look at that girl right there. [*He indicates a woman at an adjoining desk.*] An Aztec Indian from Mexico. She's a brilliant writer, and I'm going to help her through college. As far as I'm concerned, I'll survive, and you will, too, because we know how. With a young person, I see the frustrations that they go through with conditions as they are, people making a lot of money over here and people not making any there.

BREAD AND ROSES

Victor Reuther

He and his brother, Walter, were founding members of the United Automobile Workers (UAW-CIO). Subsequently, Walter served as president of the UAW until he died in a plane crash.

In his Washington, D.C., apartment, there are multitudinous plaques, certificates, and objets d'art, mementos of long-ago labor battles, triumphs, and ordeals.

I WILL BE NINETY YEARS OLD when the bells ring on January 1, 2001. One of the earliest memories I have was growing up in Wheeling, West Virginia. It was a highly industrialized town, better known than Pittsburgh in those days. When I was a child, my father was elected president of the Central Labor Council. That was all AF of L [American Federation of Labor] in those days. An immigrant child from Germany, he brought with him some European concepts of industrial unionism. He became a champion of building industrial unionism, not just craft unionism. He also was a fond admirer of Eugene Victor Debs, from whom I got my name, Victor.* When I was six, he took me to the penitentiary where Debs was being temporarily held for protesting World War One. Debs, like my father, was committed to social democracy: we were not only in a political union, but a social union as well, committed to broad social issues like civil rights, decent housing for working people, and minimum wages that would help them live

*Eugene V. Debs was a revered labor leader early in the twentieth century. He was the Socialist Party candidate for president five times. While serving time in a federal prison for speaking out against World War One, he polled a million votes.

their lives more decently. Those are wonderful childhood memories that have stayed with me all these years.

Many of the immigrants brought that concept with them. Even though Wheeling, West Virginia, was still racially divided, still affected by Civil War concepts, the immigrant community brought with them some social concepts that helped us build a better life. There were lots of coal miners and later those who worked in the tobacco industry and steel. They had a social agenda. They had, of course, their own language societies, the immigrants. Those societies included singing groups, lectures, theater, discussion groups. But some of the children of the immigrant families absorbed the racist attitudes that were prevalent in the South in those days.

When my father, as the head of the Central Labor Council, invited a black delegation to his home, the kids in the neighborhood called me a nigger kid. A nigger-lover. I came home one day in tears. My father and mother explained to me that that was a prejudice I had to overcome, and not to respond to those catcalls from less-informed children in the neighborhood. So, as a child, I saw that I should welcome all with the same feeling of solidarity as I would welcome a member of my family.

I was very small when World War One hit the immigrant community. Some of the divisions in that world war were felt even in Wheeling. Here again, my father was a champion of peace. He did his best to help the community weather that terrible storm, which had divided so many of us.

After high school, my family sent me to the university in Morgantown, West Virginia. I was the first child in the family to go to college. But I couldn't stand it in Morgantown because they compelled me to take military training. So I quit school. My brother Walter was already in Detroit, in the auto industry. I joined him there. I attended Wayne State University. I lived with Walter and three other skilled workers from the Ford Motor Company, all toolmakers like Walter. I prepared their meals and kept house for them until I could get my own job in the auto industry and learn the skilled trades. It was before the crash of '29. The auto industry was young and booming, and there were jobs available in the industry for both skilled and unskilled. I saw it as a potential center for powerful industrial trade unionism.

The Ford Motor Company was contemplating advancing Walter to a management position in their new aeronautical division. Walter was excited about that offer, but his own social conscience began to surface and he realized that what was lacking in the auto industry was a powerful voice for the workers. We needed a trade union. When Walter began to promote unionism—he had fifteen older men working under him in the tool room of the River Rouge plant—he was fired by Ford.

The Ford Motor Company had signed an agreement with Russia and had brought three hundred young Russian workers over to the Ford plant for training. And Walter met many of those young workers. When we confronted Hitlerism in Germany, we accepted Roosevelt's appeal to help build an ally in Eastern Europe. We applied for jobs and were granted them.

We went to Russia in 1934, as skilled toolmakers in the great automobile plant in Gorgy. Walter was, of course, rehired by Ford. We came back in 1936, in the spring. After two years of work there we knew that we did not believe in communism, we believed in democracy, but we also knew that we didn't want Adolf Hitler to take power and run the world. And so we came back determined to support the military efforts in the United States.

When Walter and I returned, our first objective was the organization of a democratic union in the auto industry. Walter said to me, even though I was a skilled toolmaker by then, "We've got to organize the production workers, the unskilled, too." Many of them were women, immigrants who spoke little English, hired to take the place of the hundreds of thousands of men who were inducted into the armed forces. Walter suggested I take a job in a parts plant that supplied the Ford Motor Company with wheels and brake drums. Two plants with a total of five thousand workers. I hired in for thirty-three and a half cents an hour, running a punch press in department forty-nine, where there were five hundred women and a handful of men.

I was running a punch press next to a Polish immigrant woman. I could use my Russian in speaking with her for those few minutes when we could talk to each other. I also had married the child of Polish immigrants, my dear Sophie Gudaleyavitch. She called herself Sophie Good. She became the first woman hired by the International

Union as a staff member. She would meet with immigrant women in the evenings, at their homes, or in their Polish or Ukrainian or Hungarian gatherings.

I was working there on the punch press, and when the Polish woman next to me suddenly fainted, I was worried she would crush her hands in the press. I stopped my press, went over, turned off her press, picked her up, and stretched her out on the floor with old newspapers nearby as a pillow for her head. The superintendent of the factory came running down, cursing me, shouting, "Dammit, get back to work. We'll take care of her." Everyone in that department of five hundred saw what happened.

I told Walter about it that night, and he said, "I want to meet with her." Walter listened to her story and said, "Do you think you could faint again, but on schedule?" Yes, she said, she would be happy to, but when should she faint? Walter said, "Not tomorrow, but Tuesday, just before the change of shifts."

I talked to the few we had already signed up in the union, and said, "Be sure to be here tomorrow. Come a little early." So the second-shift people came in early. She went into a faint again, and I went over and shut down her machine and put her on the floor again, until the health people picked her up. I began, then, making a speech. We had the workers turn their machines off in the whole department. They crowded around me. The superintendent came down again, cursing me. I said, "There's only one person who can get us back to work." He said, "Who in the hell is that?" And I gave him the card with Walter's name, address, and phone number on it. He called Walter, and Walter said, "What can I do? I'm here in my office, and they're sitting down in the plant." "We'll send a car." When they brought Walter in, I was still on a soapbox, carrying out my organizing speech. I introduced Walter and he got up and took over right where I left off. The superintendent grabbed Walter's trouser leg, pulled on him, and said, "You're supposed to get them back to work." Walter said, "I will, but I gotta organize them first." And that began our sit-down strike, which ended in two days with a three-fold increase for every Kelsey Wheel worker. The women who were getting only twenty-two and a half cents an hour went to seventy-five cents in one sweep.

This was just days before the great sit-down in Flint. I was in to man the sound trucks through the great forty-four-day sit-down strike. Bob Travis was there. And Genora Johnson Dollinger.

GENORA JOHNSON DOLLINGER

"We sat down in the winter of December 1936 and didn't come out till the end of January 1937. I was twenty-three." As she recounted the events she was eighty, and in the last days of her illness; with the telling, her voice assumed the timbre of a passionate young woman.*

"The United Auto Workers Union was in the process of organizing, fighting to be recognized. The first big corporation they took on was General Motors. The two GM plants where the sit-in occurred were known as Fisher Body One and Fisher Body Two. For the first time in labor history, we organized a Women's Auxiliary. We did everything. Mainly, it was to get women to understand why their husbands were taking the big chance.

"The battle began when General Motors ordered some goons and the Flint police to throw the workers out of Fisher Tool. They were afraid that it would spread to the fifteen other GM plants across the country. So they started tear-gassing. The police were using buck shots and tear gas and everything against us. The men were throwing back whatever they could get their hands on: nuts and bolts and hinges.

"When the fight was at its height, Victor Reuther, who had been on the sound truck, encouraging the people to keep on going, came over and said to us, 'The batteries are running down. We may lose this battle.' I said, 'How about me getting on that truck?' Women were never on the sound car. The men thought they had to win everything. He said, 'We've got nothing to lose.' So I got on and tried a new tactic—an appeal to the women.

"Somehow, the sound car was reaching them. On the top of the truck, through the loudspeaker, I directed my remarks to the women on both sides of the barricades. I begged the women to break through those lines of cops and come down here and join with us.

"One woman started forward and a cop grabbed her coat. She pulled out of it and marched down to join us. After that, other women came. The women poured through and that ended the battle. I was smack dab in the middle.

*From Studs Terkel, *Coming of Age* (New York: The New Press, 1995), 97–101.

"We won. Our union was recognized. GM decided to sit down with us. John L. Lewis came in and they conducted negotiations in Detroit. The guys in the plant couldn't believe it. They were struck with astonishment.

"That period was the high point of my life. It was the time of the Depression, when working people had a feeling for each other. We helped each other out in times of trouble. It was a time that most people never get a chance to live through. We started to organize against hunger, poverty, sickness, everything that's hard. We were just at that point where so many of us decided we'd rather die first before we'd go back to being union scabs."

It was an exhilarating feeling because here we were, a handful of workers, taking on General Motors, the largest and most powerful corporation in the U.S., with tremendous resources against us. They not only controlled the city police in Flint, but they had great influence over the state police and others. When that strike was over and the UAW was finally recognized, there was a celebration, dancing in the streets.* It was in large measure due to Murphy's being the governor of the state of Michigan. Frank Murphy was a very religious Catholic and very sympathetic to the human problems involved in the sit-down.† He didn't want the forces of the state used to repress. When he sent the state troops in, we fraternized with them, and

---

*"We finally got the word: THIS THING IS SETTLED. The guys in the plant didn't believe it. We had to send in three people, one after the other. When they did get it, they marched out of the plant with the flag flyin' and all that stuff.

"You'd see some guys comin' out of there with whiskers as long as Santa Claus. They made a rule they wasn't gonna shave until the strike was over. Oh, it was just like—you've gone through the Armistice delirium, haven't you? Everybody was runnin' around shakin' everybody by the hand, saying, 'Jesus, you look strange, got a beard on, you know.' Wives kissin' their husbands. There was a lot of drunks on the street that night.

"When Mr. Kudson put his name to a piece of paper and says that General Motors recognize UAW-CIO—until that moment we were nonpeople that didn't even exist. That was the big one." Bob Stinson in Studs Terkel, *Hard Times: An Oral History of the Great Depression* (New York: Pantheon, 1970), 101.

†Frank Murphy subsequently became a member of the U.S. Supreme Court.

received them warmly because we knew that Murphy's voice would be heard in their ranks.

Afterwards, there were a couple of years of bitter internal struggle to reach the Ford workers, because the Ford Motor Company had hired a vicious so-called labor relations man, a thug, Harry Bennett, who had goons who threatened us. There were attempts on Walter's life and on my life. Those intervening years between the successful sit-down in Flint with General Motors and the incredible struggle at Ford were frightening years. My dear Sophie, for instance, as the mother of our young children, when she would take the garbage out, she would carry a loaded revolver underneath her skirt. We had security men sleeping on mattresses in the living room.

One of the reasons we were successful was because of our record in support of civil rights. And the leaders of the great civil rights movement, black speakers, came to our assistance in the Ford organizing drive.

The war came. We had to concentrate not only on organizing, but on supporting the national war effort. The Ford Motor Company finally gave way and got rid of Harry Bennett, but the gangsters that Bennett brought into the region continued to do their dirty work. Walter was shot in 1948. I was shot in '49, losing my right eye. But the victory—the recognition of the UAW—overcame all barriers. [*Long pause*] And then came the cold war and the McCarthyism. It frightened some of our most active people into silence. But the truth of the matter is, we had been so successful in raising the stature and the strength and the income of ordinary working people that many of them decided, "Well, we'll hang on to what we've won and we won't jeopardize it by becoming too active again." So we had difficulty keeping alive the membership role in shaping its own future. A kind of new leadership came to power in big unions, less focused on internal democracy than in building a partnership with a corporate structure, and feathering their own individual nests. It helped enrich the income of high officials in the labor movement, and junior officials in the corporate structure. And that was unfortunate, and we paid the price for that.

Carole Travis

I said, "Your father, a dead ringer for Robert Redford, as I recall, led one of the most momentous strikes in American labor history: the forty-four-day sit-down strike in Flint, Michigan. Now it is sixty-seven years later."

"Is that so?" Carole laughed. "I was born in 1942, five years later."

She is an official in the Service Employees International Union. "The largest union in the United States now, with 1.4 million members.

"In the 1960s, I was in my twenties and wild in the streets. I was in the student antiwar movement. Some of us believed the way to change society was to join the working class. [Slight chuckle] So I went to the working class from college. I worked on assembly lines at Motorola, at Zenith, in picture frame factories. In fact, I led a sit-down strike at a picture frame factory, along with a Puerto Rican woman.

"Then I worked on the assembly line at a General Motors plant for nineteen years. I became the president of the UAW local, served for twelve years. During those years, I went to night school and became a lawyer."

I WAS THE ONLY CHILD. My mother and father separated when I was quite young, although I saw him a lot throughout my life. I remember my mother told me that we lived in a railroad flat on Chicago's West Side. She put a child's swing in between the living room and the dining room so that during the endless meetings, I could be entertained by swinging. The phone rang so much that at nine months old, the first words I would say were, "Hello, hello." I would go play with a toy phone, because my father was on the phone so much. [*Laughs*]

I didn't hear about the 1937 sit-down strike until quite late in my life because my father was a Red, a communist. As a result of that, few historians know who he was. Reds went underground because of the McCarthy era. There was not a lot of talk about what did my father do. In fact, I used to get in trouble for saying out loud, "My father is a communist." People would say, "Oh, oh, don't say that!" I couldn't understand why not. During the *Daily Worker* picnics we children played games. The FBI would have these cameras out. The kind of cameras in the old days where the guys would crank these big reels and they'd be taking pictures of the cars to get the license plates. All the children would dance in front of the license plates, so the FBI would have pictures of the children doing these crazy dances and marches instead of the license plates. So that's one game. The game I invented had to do with the Rosenberg trial. I was eleven or something. We children of communists played a game where we would talk on the phone and pretend we were transferring atomic secrets. We would say things like, "My father told me to tell you to tell your father that the fudgesicle is dripping on my left knee." [*Laughs*] We would talk for hours because we knew the FBI would have to transcribe this, discuss it. We knew we were being tapped, so we thought it was a funny thing that we did that. I knew my father was a labor leader. I knew he was not around. For most of my life he had trouble getting work because he was blacklisted. He had been trained as a machinist. It was when I got to college, I understood who my father was. I went to him and I said, "What is all of this? What did you do?" I did not grow up in a house like Walter Reuther's, where everybody said, "Oh, Walter Reuther, leader of the labor movement." I grew up in a house where my father wasn't there.

He signed Walter Reuther's first union card in Indiana. You can ask Victor about that. When I was born, he was working for the farm equipment workers, and then for the Illinois CIO [Congress of Industrial Organizations]. He was the vice president. He used to ride the train with old man Daley down to Springfield and play cards with him on the train.* He worked for the United Mine Workers in the fields of southern Illinois, for John L. Lewis. We figured it out one time that he organized forty-seven UAW locals. That's quite a few. He was born in 1907 and he died in '79. Seventy-two. He had

*The elder Mayor Richard J. Daley of Chicago, father of the current mayor.

strokes. Heywood Hale Broun told me a story about his father and mine.* They were at a strike in Cleveland that was having trouble. He and my father found some old tires and cut them in half. Then they found some young trees. They used the tires and trees to make gigantic slingshots to send bricks through the plant's windows a block away. He was in another strike, and they were losing. It was a Thursday and the committee was saying, "Should we go back to work?" And they decided, "Well, let's use all weekend long to pass out leaflets and ask people to come support the strike lines on Monday morning. If not enough people come, then we'll see if we can go back into the plant on Monday afternoon and end the strike." They worked all weekend and ten thousand people showed up. When he told me this story, it was after his first stroke, he was kind of shaky, and he burst into tears. He said, "You never know what's going to happen. Sometimes people will surprise you and come out, and you never know when it's going to be." He was so moved.

Let me tell you more about that day when ten thousand people came out. They had huge crowds, and then the mayor brought the police out. So my father is walking down the street, talking to people on the picket line, and suddenly the man next to him falls, shot in the stomach. Clearly, somebody was trying to kill my father. The whole place freezes. The police, the strikers, this man down, bleeding on the street, it's a moment when it's not clear what's going to happen. Strikers picked up this man and rushed him to a hospital. Then the mayor came into the street waving his handkerchief as a truce sign. My father met him in the middle of the street. He said the mayor was shaking so badly, he couldn't speak well. "Wha—well—well—wha—what—what are we going to do? We don't want a massacre. Wha—wha—what are we going to do?" My father said to him, "What we're going to do is you're going to order all of your police right now to stand still. You and I are going to walk down the line and we're going to smell every person's weapon to see if we can find out who fired the shot. I want you to order that right now." So the mayor turned around and said, "I order all of you to stand

*Heywood Broun, father of Heywood Hale Broun, was the celebrated columnist who founded the American Newspaper Guild.

still. All the police stand absolutely still." My father went down the whole line, smelling the weapons, and couldn't find the gun. Of course, the guy got away. And then he said to the mayor, "Now you're going to dismiss the police. You can leave two policemen on horseback for traffic reasons. Everybody else is to be dismissed." And so the mayor did that. And then they went on with the strike. Isn't that a great story?

My father was a tactician. My father organized the factory that was the origin of the Haymarket affair.* People had tried to organize the McCormick plant since Haymarket and had been unsuccessful. My father organized it. And there was a moment in time when they thought they were going to break that strike by busing in scabs every day, and then there was a police wedge that would push back the strikers, and they'd blow a whistle, and the scabs would run like hell through the police corridor to get into the plant. My father went and got guys from other places, who nobody knew, to be scabs. They were fake scabs. Their orders were, when they blow the whistle, deck the guy next to you. Deck 'em. They had twenty or thirty guys on the scab buses and they knew each other 'cause of a little thing they were wearing on their lapels. All they had to do was find somebody who didn't have a thing on their lapel, and when the cops blew the whistle deck the real scabs. The cops couldn't tell who's who, what's happening. And that killed the ability to have the scabs. Isn't that great?

When my father was dying, he was having delusions that revolved around stool pigeons. He thought that there were stool pigeons and recording devices in the closets and under the tables. Having been pursued and harassed at a critical point in his life, at the end it haunted him, it haunted him.

Once, he was blind for a few days because he was beaten up so

---

*In 1886, there was a strike at the International Harvester plant in Chicago. It was for an eight-hour day. A bomb was thrown, long after the meeting was over. No one knows who threw it. The speakers, who had long since left, were convicted of conspiracy. Four were hanged after a farce of a trial. A few years later, the survivors were issued a full pardon by the new governor, John Peter Altgeld. It went down in history as the Haymarket affair.

badly. One time, a guy came to him in Flint and told my father that he had been hired to kill him. He was so moved by my dad's speech that he decided to leave town, but he wanted him to know he had been hired to kill him.

There was one time my dad was driving between Flint and Kalamazoo when some thugs ran him off the road. They wrestled with him, got his car keys, threw them into a cornfield, and when he went into the cornfield to try and find them, they started shooting at him as a game. A woman who came by and saw what was going on started screaming at these men. And they left. So this strange woman, whom he never knew, saved his life.

My union, the SEIU, is janitors, low-wage workers, a lot of immigrant workers, nursing home workers—people at the bottom who, twenty years ago, unions were not interested in organizing because they seemed too weak a social base to do anything. Now SEIU is one of the most militant unions in the United States, and growing. It's a big shift. In the labor movement there are sectors that are growing. There's been a big movement around the Charleston Five, a group of dockworkers in the port of Charleston who were beaten up because a Danish ship tried to use scab dockworkers to unload. The hotel and restaurant workers are also growing.

I suspect that we're going into a recession or a depression and the things that we're trying to accomplish as unions will be harder. Up until now there's been some wealth, some more money in taxes, enough in the economy to grant union demands. If the economy fails, the unions will have to start paying attention, not just to wages, but to social issues. Let's say you represent prison guards. Do you want lots of prisons built so that you can get lots more members? I don't know, maybe not. That would be the dilemma you could get into, whereas, really, you want more schools. What worries me is how strong the other side is, how controlled the media is, how they can move from one part of the world to another. They can move the jobs and everything else. And the delicate state of the earth, I worry about all that, too. When I was young, I knew everything, and I knew where to go and how to get there. Ah-h-h, now . . . there's lots of big questions that can't be ignored. I don't know where they're being discussed and debated. I don't see it.

I have hope. But I am not full of hope. I have worries, deep worries. When I was young, as an antiauthoritarian, I thought that history was made by the masses. I can't think of any union leaders who everybody in the United States knows like they knew John L. Lewis. Where they all wanted to hear him. Or like Eugene Debs. We live in a society that's very much based on how you look. Are you good-looking, are you fancy? It's all visual.

I think we're at a historical moment, and it's not clear how things are going to go. The means of communication are so controlled, emphasizing trivia. There's the big march of history, and there's people and the planet and the future at stake. We should keep our eye on the big issues.

My father's dream was for a wonderful world. My father had a great sense of humor. He always remembered Bill Haywood's quote, "Nothing's too good for the working class." [*Laughs*] People will surprise, my father said.

I ran for president of the UAW, Local Seven-nineteen, in 1986. I had met Victor Reuther a few months before in Flint, at a reunion of the Flint sit-down strike people. Victor and I and his wife, Sophie, had become good friends. The day before the election for my first run as president of the Local, a leaflet came out on the plant floor. It was a very interesting, sophisticated leaflet. The first paragraph of the leaflet focused on my father, which was bizarre, because nobody knew who my father was. It said he was a sellout union leader. It quoted Victor Reuther calling him a sellout union leader. So there was a false quote in this opening paragraph.

I called Victor Reuther on the phone and I read him the leaflet. He said, "Oh, my God, what do you want me to do?" I said, "Well, I want you to get on a plane this afternoon so that to-morrow morning at five A.M., you can be at the union door with me, so that when we open up to start voting you'll be standing there with me repudiating that leaflet." So his wife's birthday was the next day. Sophie was going to be seventy that day. April ninth, I think it was. He said, "Sophie, Sophie, Carole wants me to get on a plane...." She said, "Of course." At five o'clock the next morning, he was standing at the union hall with me. Two hours after I talked to him on the phone, there were leaflets all over the plant saying: *Victor Reuther will be here tomorrow to stand with Carole Travis at the polls. Come meet Victor, come vote Travis.* [*Laughs*] And that was it. He just stood there. Some people came and had long conversations with him, some people just shook his hand. It was terrific.

Ken Paff

He is tall, gaunt, professorial-looking. He founded the TDU (Teamsters for a Democratic Union), challenging the union bosses long before the current reform movement.

I'M FIFTY-SIX, from a small town near Pittsburgh, a Rust Belt town, Bear Falls, Pennsylvania. I'm the youngest of seven children. When I think of the fifties, I think of my mother. She was born in 1906. She worked up the nerve for about thirty years to leave my father, and did it in 1956. I moved to Santa Ana, California, that year with my mother. She had never worked in her life, being a housewife and having seven children; it was a big deal in those days to strike out on your own. To me it was an adventure. I was a kid. We hadn't been anywhere. Hell, Pittsburgh was far to us, and that was twenty miles. We took the train in if we went to the Pirates game. California was a whole new world.

My mother's idea was just to get away from the past, and her youngest kid was going to get ahead. A 1950s kind of hope. She had told me since I was little I was going to college. The older kids didn't have that opportunity, and my mother only had a grade-school education. In 1964, I went to Berkeley. I got a diploma signed by Ronald Reagan. That ought to be valuable. I could sell it on eBay. In those days they had no tuition. You could go to any public university in California for nothing.

What a new world to go to Berkeley. I had been to a Catholic grammar school, and now I'm at Berkeley. This cosmopolitan student movement breaks out. Mario Savio was there. That was a good time to be coming up, the sixties. We believed that ordinary people could change things. The civil rights movement became like a religion to me. We'd have marches in Oakland and people would just come out of their house and join the march for fair employment. I feel lucky that I grew up and came of age in that kind of period.

My first involvement with labor was as an outside supporter for the United Farm Workers of America, Cesar Chavez's union. I leafleted supermarkets. In 1970, in the Salinas Valley, there were thirty thousand farmworkers on strike. Ironically, that strike was actually against the Teamsters. The growers had enlisted the Teamsters to sign a sweetheart deal, quote, representing thirty thousand farmworkers. The California Supreme Court later ruled that the Teamsters had never consulted one single farmworker. That week in Salinas kept me going for ten years. Events like that have changed my life. The experiences, the victories, the people that get involved, and you just feel proud when you're standing near them. I felt that was the course of the rest of my life. It was set then.

Labor's a great place to be. I was one of the founders of TDU, Teamsters for a Democratic Union. We call it a movement. It was founded in 1976. I was a truck driver in Cleveland in the seventies. A member of Local Four-oh-seven. At that time the union was run by a very mean-spirited old guard associated with organized crime. Jackie Presser, who later became the president of the Teamsters, was from Cleveland and was a domineering presence. Obviously, that was a difficult environment for us. We had constant threats.* There had been dissidence in the Teamsters, even in this difficult atmosphere. In Chicago, in Los Angeles, in Cleveland, in other places in the trucking industry, truck drivers had started to rebel against Fitzsimmons, later Presser, seeing them as people who were always on the golf course with the employers, or with Nixon, and were selling out the members, but they never linked up with each other.† We had a hodgepodge. There was a group that tried to form TURF, Teamsters United Rank and File. It lasted about two months, but it was interesting. I started contacting these guys and talking to them and learning from them. So when we formed TDU, with some of these people who had been beat up, we had some younger people like me that had confidence. I remember one of the older guys in Cleveland came to me and he said, "If we didn't have you, we wouldn't know how to spell our leaflets right." People were ready for change, even standing up under threats of violence. Presser allied with Lyndon La-Rouche, and hired people to intimidate and use violence, and put

---

*Frank Fitzsimmons was head of the Teamsters, who wound up in prison for corruptions of one sort or another.
†Jackie Presser was in the Fitzsimmons tradition.

out lies about people's families, follow them to their homes, threaten their children.*

We didn't have any rights that worked to our advantage. We had to begin at the grassroots. There wasn't any alternative. We were going to tell the truth to the people. We were not going to tell them we've got a million members when we got a hundred members. People would say to me, "Hell, they don't know there were only thirty people at our meeting. Let's say there were three hundred." I'd say, "The thirty know how many were at our meeting, and they're the most important people to us." So we started building at the grassroots, starting to learn from each other. Throughout the country. We told the truth, but we always looked bigger than we were. Fitzsimmons always thought we had big funding behind us. Hell, we didn't have crap. When they had the national bargaining, we knew so little about what was going on, we had our members sneak into the hotel, root around in the trash cans, and pick papers up. That was our information-gathering network.

The fear factor was very big, but people overcame it and they did join. We were survivors. After a few years, people would say, "Damn, they're still walking around with all their arms and legs attached." One day in our Local in Cleveland, the head of the Local sent some goons down and roughed us up. We went to federal court and filed for an injunction against them. They were shocked. No one had ever done this before. They had always scared people off. Hell, we were talking to the media. We got an article in the *Plain Dealer*. The judge issued what was called a declaratory injunction. People were starting to see these guys are standing up! In truck driver talk: those guys have got balls down to the floor. So we started to grow. Barely. We were up against constant attacks: "They're all employer-funded," "They're all communist," "They're funded by the Rockefellers," "They're funded by Russia." And the threats of losing your job. That was the biggest thing, the threats on your job. Those things happened. This continues today. But we have fought them, we overcame them.

First of all, we operated openly. The mistake that dissidents had

*LaRouche had been involved in quasi-fascist and anti-Semitic activities.

made in the Teamsters was being secretive. I argued for TDU to operate in the open. The employers are going to find out about you. The people that aren't going to find out about you are the rank and file. We're going to put ourselves out there. We're going to take that chance. If they come after us, they're going to have to do it publicly. It was tough, it was slow. There were a number of times when we barely survived.

To give people hope, you gotta show some wins. Whether you're in the civil rights movement, or you're Cesar Chavez, or you're TDU, or you're the environmental movement, you gotta have some wins. They might be small, but you gotta show you've got 'em. In our Local we got the right to elect our stewards. We didn't have that right before. So if someone would say, "You guys never win dog shit," I'd say, "Well, we won the right to elect stewards. If you get involved, we might win something else." Sometimes we could even win things in court, because they had gotten away with doing illegal things. They had taken advantage of people having no rights, and they had gone too far. We started to build support.

The key for us in TDU is faith in the members. You're going to have hope that ordinary people can do extraordinary things, because if they can't, there ain't gonna be no hope for the change we're interested in. We started out to change the union, and we ended up changing ourselves. That is the key to TDU. I've been told many times that working people, they don't care about democracy, they just care about an extra dollar an hour. It's a bunch of bullshit. We proved in TDU that working people do care about having a say in their work, a say in their union. And they'll fight for it.

Today, we have some conservative elements, right-wing elements, really, running our union. We have a union leadership that's running around supporting George Bush. Drilling in the Arctic National Wildlife [Refuge] is one of the top political issues of our union. They're supporting the TIPS program to turn every UPS [United Parcel Service] worker into a spy. When they deliver your package they're supposed to peek around your house and see what the hell's in there, what you've got on your computer screen, see if it's in Arabic.

That's difficult for us, having the old guard in power. In the nineties, we had a reform administration in our union. One of the real high-water marks in our movement was 1991 when the Teamsters rank and file—the first time they ever got to vote in a secret ballot—elected the entire reform slate of Ron Carey, who threw open the doors and invited thousands of members into the headquarters. Thousands of people poured into the Capitol Hill building. That laid the basis for the labor victory of the decade in 1997, the UPS strike that showed that part-time workers could unite with the full-time. The American people, in poll after poll, seventy-five percent of the people, identified with the strikers. We took on the biggest transportation corporation in the world and won every demand.

Years and years of planning went into that. We had to end the division of part-time labor at UPS: the majority making McDonald's wages, while the full-time delivery drivers were making good union wages and benefits. The union leadership took up that fight in a big way: that our corporate society today produces too many throwaway, part-time, casual jobs and too few good-paying, family-supporting, family-benefits union jobs. That caught the imagination of the average American. Yeah, that was a high moment that still lives on. The old guard, they may want to roll back our rights, but they can't put the genie back in the bottle, as one of our members says. It's not the old Teamsters Union of silence. There is a lively democracy within our union.

You look around at what's happening now: we have a depressing atmosphere in this country—of individual greed, of corporate logos, of Fox TV. I live about thirty minutes from a university town, Ann Arbor. When I go there it's depressing. You see the college students. They wear grunge and it's a fifty-dollar shirt with a logo. They drive SUVs. I wonder what kind of hope we're breeding. But then you see positive signs on the campuses. I'm always looking for the hopeful signs.

The small victories keep me going. Three years ago we had a wildcat strike—when the workers go on strike in defiance of the corporation and the union. It was at IBP, Iowa Beef Processing, which is owned by Tyson, the largest chicken, pork, and beef producer in the world. These are immigrant workers, ninety percent from Mexico, some from El Salvador at their plant in Pasco, Washington. TDU sent a full-time organizer for one month, for the whole strike. Hoffa came in, seized control of that Local, and placed it in trustee-

ship to deny the workers the right to vote.* They were deeply discouraged. The last day of the strike they said to Hoffa, "You sold
us out, but we're taking back our Local." They had a press conference, these meatpacking workers from Mexico. Hoffa said, "There
won't be any election." Fortunately there was a TDU. We kept them
going, we went to federal court, we got an injunction against Hoffa.
When there was an election, our people swept to victory. They've
transformed that local. They're reaching out, they're drawing in workers from other food-processing plants in eastern Washington. Maria
Martinez, the leader of the strike, is now a nationally recognized
leader. Things like that give me hope.

Immigrant workers can be a positive, enlivening force in the labor
movement. They bring in a new culture, a different tradition, a new
fighting spirit. When we go into a strike, the first thing we do is have
a family day. Make sure our families come down to the picket line.
In Pasco, they laughed, they said, "Hell, every day is family day here.
This is a Mexican strike. Are you crazy?" The picket line wasn't a
boring picket line of people marching back and forth. It was somewhere between a sit-down strike and a Mexican fiesta.

You've got to nurture these struggles. Almost everything big that's
ever happened has started small. Here in Detroit, the sit-down strikes
at General Motors, 1937, started small. They never encompassed a
majority. They were a minority, but they excited the majority. These
are sparks that set off others. The immigrant workers learn from the
longtime truck drivers, and the longtime truck drivers learn from the
warehouse workers. . . .

Labor has to be willing to take on bigger issues. To see itself as
fighting the corporate culture of greed that many Americans are fed
up with. Two days ago I read in the *Wall Street Journal* a huge article
about Europe, the United States, and work culture. The writer of the
article never got it, the irony that came through. His whole theme
was that Europe was falling behind because they're working so much
less than Americans, hundreds of hours per year less. In Germany,
the average worker gets nine and a half weeks off per year. In France,

*James Hoffa, son of the late Jimmy Hoffa, elected the national president
of the Teamsters shortly after Ron Carey, who was the first president
elected by the rank and file, was disqualified.

they're shortening the workweek, so you can take Fridays off if you want to. American workers are working more hours than they used to, and therefore, the writer said, America will produce more than the EU per worker. The clown writes further: *Surprisingly, the European workers are clinging like hell to this and they're not gonna give it up in a global era.* I'm thinking, *No shit, Sherlock.* When I was a truck driver we worked Monday to Friday. That was it. We didn't have to work weekends. How many blue-collar workers today can say, "I take my weekend off automatically"? They're yelling about family values, but you can't spend your weekend with your family if the boss doesn't want you to. A few years ago, when we were fighting forced Sunday work, one of our members wrote a letter to the CEO and said, *I've got to be in church every Sunday.* The CEO wrote him back, *A true Christian can practice anytime he wants.* So now the CEOs are going to give you religious advice. The labor movement should take up issues like this. We need more time off. We need our weekends off. *To strengthen our family values.*

What's kept me going in bad times is people that I meet that are struggling, that are changing themselves. In TDU, when our organizers go out and travel, we stay in people's homes. Most labor organizers stay in hotels. We started doing that to save money, but if I had a million dollars, I still wouldn't change it. That's what builds a movement, when you start bonding with people. I see new people coming up all the time in the Teamsters, warehouse workers and meatpackers and truck drivers and UPS part-timers that sort the packages in the middle of the night, those that are willing to put in their own time, that are willing to risk a lot, and fight as a democratic group, not where greed is king but where solidarity is king.

Roberta Lynch

"When I was a teenager, I read something by the Greek poet
Cavafy:

> When you set out for Ithaca, ask that your way be long / But
> when you arrive at Ithaca, don't expect to find jewels, don't
> expect to find treasures / Ithaca gave you the journey, Ithaca
> gave you the journey / Without Ithaca, you would not have set
> out / And through this journey, so wise have you become / Such
> things have you learned.

"I love that idea. What gave me my journey?

"I just turned fifty-three. I am the deputy director for the Illinois
Council of the American Federation of State, County, and Municipal Employees, AFSCME. Also, I'm the international vice president, so I'm on our national executive board. In Illinois, we represent
about a hundred thousand active and retired workers, primarily people who work for the state, for the city, for the county. They work for
local governments. Traditionally, public employees, even teachers,
were not covered by the National Labor Relations Act, and so they
didn't have the right to form unions. They're still not covered by the
National Labor Relations Act.

"What we had to do in every state was pass state collective bargaining laws that give public employees the right to have a union.
There are still twenty states where public employees don't even have
the right to join a union. Illinois didn't pass one until 1983, with
Harold Washington's support."*

I GREW UP IN PHILADELPHIA. Neither of my parents had
gone to college. I'm Irish and Italian, Italian on my mother's side

*Harold Washington, the first African American mayor in the history of
Chicago, was elected in 1982 and died shortly after being reelected in 1986.
He was a strong supporter of labor unions and neighborhood grassroots
groups.

and Irish on my father's. They were not political at all. No one in my family was active in labor unions. My father was a car salesman. I have two sisters and a brother, and none of my siblings are politically active. The most influential thing for me in my childhood was the civil rights movement. Just sitting there, watching it on my television, no real connection. This was 1962, '63 . . . Philadelphia is one of the few places where Catholic schools are free. Everybody went to the Catholic schools. They were big schools, like public schools in a way.

My high school was all girls, sixty-three hundred of us. There were no socially conscious priests or nuns in those schools or parishes when I was growing up. No one was like me, to be this passionately interested in the civil rights movement. When I first started watching, I was thirteen years old, and I was a questioner, a person who wanted to know why, and the others did not like me for that reason. I was a smart kid but not a popular one. I remember one of the nuns calling me up after a class where I had been asking a lot of questions. She said, "One of the greatest sins in the church is the sin of pride. Pride is thinking that you can know the answers to things that are not answerable." So that was my sin in their eyes, that I wanted to know the answers to everything. I remember asking, "Why does the church spend all this money on altars and statues and buildings, when there are so many poor people? Why isn't that money going to help the poor?"

My parents were not very concerned about the poor. They would use terms like *nigger*. They were not mean-spirited or hard people, but they had very ordinary values. Good people. My father would knock himself out to help somebody who needed a hand. Always doing that. My mother is eighty-four, she's still volunteering. She takes meals to the elderly at eighty-four. [*Laughs*] We were taught to be kind, help our neighbor. But we had no social vision.

I wanted to get away from my family, I wanted to see more things. I was very ambivalent. I remember saying, "I'm not going to change. I'm going to come back here and live right here with all of you." I told my old neighborhood friends, "I'm not going to join the elite." I remember when I was in high school, a lay teacher—not a nun— she was young and lively, and called me up after class and said, "You should go to Barnard. You should be in a school for kids that are really smart. I could help you go there." She said, "I looked at your records, your IQ, you should be at a place like Barnard." I was very polite to her, but I remember saying, "No, I don't want to be in a place like that. That's a place for rich people, that's not a place for people like me." In high school, I had read Bertrand Russell. I was completely questioning all the tenets of Catholicism. I read *Why I Am an Atheist*. I would just go to the library and take these books out. I barely knew what they were about. I tried to read James Joyce. I didn't do too well ... [*Laughs*] But even with all my questioning, I chose a Catholic college, Duquesne in Pittsburgh. Why? I didn't want to move too far from my roots. Pittsburgh was close to Philadelphia, a city college, an urban college. And a not particularly prestigious college, right? On the other hand, I was very disappointed when I found out there wasn't any activism on campus. I became part of the first antiwar group that formed.

When I got out of college in 1970, I went to work for the housing authority in Pittsburgh, a kind of social service job, right? I didn't want to go to graduate school. I wanted to be an activist. I wanted to bring about change. I had become at that point very active in the women's movement. I became a socialist. I saw myself as someone who wanted to bring about change in the whole society.

How did I get to the labor movement? I couldn't put my finger on a moment. There was this sense that what all these movements have in common is the search for people to be able to live with dignity. Initially you don't see that in the antiwar movement or the civil rights movement. You're not looking at the role of corporations, the role capitalism is playing. I was like a person sort of waiting to be found by the movement. I had all these inchoate desires to make things right in some way. I didn't know what to do with them. Then here come these various movements. Sometimes I think I'm so lucky that I was born when I was. Certainly as a woman I feel that. Ten years before, fifteen years before, my life would have been so totally different. I came to believe there had to be a more sweeping kind of change. It wasn't just about ending the war, it wasn't just about eliminating discriminatory laws against black people, it wasn't even just about women being able to have certain kinds of jobs or not be abused in certain ways. I'm out of college, I'm still young, yet some-how I wanted to be part of the labor movement, because it seemed to me that this idea of working people coming together was going back to my own roots.

I spent many years taking stumbling steps. At one point I went to work for the telephone company, thinking I could get into a union if I did that. In those days it was hard for outsiders to get hired by unions. I so much wanted to be part of this. I came to southeast Chicago, where the mills were, and I started working for a community group. This was in 1976, when the mills were starting to close down. We were trying to get churches involved with the problems of the mill closures and downsizing. I wrote a book about the decline of the steel industry, *Rusted Dreams*. Then I went to the Chicago Area Committee on Occupational Safety and Health to do political action around those issues. I worked with a lot of different unions. In 1984, I went to AFSCME.

In the eighties, when other unions were losing members, we were growing like crazy. We didn't get the right to organize until 1983, when we passed a collective bargaining law in Illinois. An employer could voluntarily recognize you. But we couldn't organize in the city of Chicago. Mayor Daley would never agree to have unions. We grew by about twenty-five thousand members after that law was signed. The public sector was not losing ground, not losing workers. When you look at most state governments, city governments, they were holding their own, even through that period of the eighties. We were starting from ground zero. Most of these workers were not organized at all. When we came in, people were ripe for a union. It's different now, but in the eighties, public sector employers really did not fight the unions. People say workers don't want unions. Now workers are threatened, intimidated, harassed. It's hard to get a union now. When we came in people could vote on whether they wanted a union without employer interference, and every single group of workers that had an election for a union, every single one, voted for a union. We never lost an election.

I think what changed in the nineties was that corporations in this country became so much more aggressively antiunion. You had this development of an actual industry of union-busting consultants, union-busting strategies, union resistance, union-free environments. It began to permeate the culture that unions are a bad thing. "It's because of the unions that the jobs left the country." "It's because of the unions that workers make too much money, and that's hurting the economy." "The unions have driven wages up." All those ideas actually began to permeate the public sector, too. We organized maybe five or six years ago, two thousand clerical workers at the University of Illinois in Champaign. That university did everything they could to fight us, even as a supposedly liberal, open-minded institution. Look at what graduate students trying to organize are going through at universities all over the country.

We historically represent a lot of workers whose jobs were privatized, particularly in human services. For instance, we represent everybody who works in what were traditionally state mental hospitals. Essentially, three-quarters of them were closed down, and all of those individuals were moved into private care, mostly nonprofit agencies that sprang up. There are now about eight thousand workers we represent in the public sector providing direct care services to people with mental disabilities, twenty thousand workers in private agencies providing that kind of direct care, where they toilet people, change them, all those kinds of nursing-home supportive services. All of those workers are nonunion, and yet they're all totally funded by state tax dollars. All the agencies have agreed that these workers are paid, on average, seven dollars and fifty cents an hour, about twelve to thirteen thousand dollars a year. Our members, who are still in the state centers, make up to twenty-eight thousand dollars a year because they have a union and a union contract. Workers in these private agencies have no pension. Our members have health care. Workers in these private agencies have no health care. If you talked to one of these private agencies, they would tell you, "I wish I could pay my workers more, but the state will only give me this amount of money." So we said we're going to organize the workers in these agencies. We know it's not like negotiating with General Motors. We know these agencies don't have enough money to pay these workers twelve dollars an hour. We're gonna tell the workers this right up front. But we're going to build a movement that will change the politics of state government. Change what happens in the general assembly so that it becomes unacceptable for the state to pay wages of seven-fifty an hour. [*Angrily*] Every one of these nonprofit employers who have no money to spare, right? Every single one of them hired a union-busting firm and fought to keep the union out.

This is how hostility to unions has pervaded every aspect of our culture. So that even these employers who claim that they're humanitarians, they're not for profit, are still taking money that should be going to client care and putting it into fighting against a union.

They don't have the political power, these employers. We're a force that would have the political power to go into the general assembly and fight to get more money. One of these places fought us in court. We won an election, two hundred and forty-seven to two hundred and forty-three. That was the vote of the workers. They fought us for five years. They tied us up in court. You can imagine the amount of legal battles they had. It took us five years and a five-month strike to get a contract at that place. Every single one of these agencies that we've gone to, even with the employers fighting us tooth and nail and threatening these workers—and most of them are the sole supports of their family, most of them are women, very fearful of losing their jobs—nonetheless, in every single place, they have voted for a union despite their employer's opposition.

When we organize them, we tell them, "You're not going to get a raise right away." We tell them, "We're going to have to build a political movement to get a raise." But I think workers want a voice. They want to feel that they matter, and that they are actually a part of the equation in a workplace. It's always there, that feeling of wanting to be heard and wanting to be taken seriously.

On the other hand, there are so many forces that put pressure on people. The labor movement is growing very, very slowly now. There is this tremendous opposition from employers. I think what Barbara's book brings out so brilliantly is that these jobs are so hard when you're physically caring for someone.* A lot of people have to be toileted, they have to be bathed, it's hard physical work. A lot of these people are working two jobs. I talked to a woman the other day, she's a caretaker. She goes and does a second job at a nursing home where she takes people out for social excursions. She works the night shift, bathing people, getting their meds, then she leaves and goes to the nursing home and takes people out. And then she's going to school to get her GED 'cause she never finished high

*Barbara Ehrenreich, *Nickel and Dimed: On (Not) Getting by in America* (New York: Metropolitan, 2001).

school. She was part of these newly formed Locals, and I was talking to her about getting involved in the union, and she said, "I want to get involved, but how can I do it?"

It's not like anyone is rising up, and this is why it's so slow. It can take a year to organize a hundred people. Just to train people, educate them, inspire them, help them figure out how they can do this with their lives, it's a whole process of transformation. And it's what makes it so exciting. Because you see people actually transforming themselves as individuals, which then lets them transform the whole character of their workplace. We've still only organized a fraction of this workforce. We probably represent about four thousand of those twenty thousand private sector direct-care workers.

We actually got one employer who was broad-minded enough to ally with us. Usually, the legislature passes a budget that includes what they call a cost-of-living increase that goes to these agencies and then to these workers. The governor submitted a budget with a one and a half percent increase for them. Not even a two percent pay raise. We said, "This is ludicrous." Some of the employers were saying, "We should get three percent, we should get four percent." Our union went into the general assembly—this had never been done— and together with one or two employers, we created the slogan "One dollar an hour." It's like a fifteen percent pay increase. And we won. We got a dollar an hour added to the budget for those workers.

When you ask yourself: what can counterbalance the enormous concentration of corporate power to influence every element of public policy? To me, it has to be a labor movement worldwide. For individual workers, groups of workers in a particular work-place, the methods of control have become so sophisticated. The way that immigrants are brought in knowing that they can be taken advantage of.

You look at the ability of Wall Street's financial institutions in five years to totally undermine American confidence in Social Security, the most successful social program this country has ever seen! They have actually shattered people's confidence in Social Security. You talk to any young person and they're gonna say, "I don't think it'll be there for me." Who is there that can stand up in the corridors of power except the labor movement? You can pressure Democrats who are pulled by that corporate money, always. Who's going to yank them the other way if not the labor movement? When you look at the global situation, at the tentacles that these corporations now have, they have no allegiance to a nation, they're multinational. No, they're nonnational. They have no allegiance to anyone.

Our job is painstakingly slow. It is just building brick by brick by brick at the same time that these corporations are developing at a phenomenal pace. We're still working with age-old tools, and they're working with tools that we don't even imagine.

There are some people who are what I would call hopeful people, maybe incurable optimists. You might be one of them. I would not describe myself as an optimist. I am by nature a sort of skeptical person. I'm filled with doubts. I'm always looking wide-angle, so yes, gee, that was a great meeting, but where does it fit? How would it really build power? Who's it going to affect?

I would just say I'm a person who is periodically visited by hope. Expectations that nobody predicted. I think that Seattle was like that for a lot of people. And you have students on campuses starting to make an issue that matters to them of globalization, sweatshops. They see not just the sweatshops abroad, but they see a connection to workers in this country. Here is something that comes along un-expectedly, shatters a consensus, opens something up. And when something like that happens, you feel this sense of hope and possi-bility. See, hope to me is about possibility. You feel that things can happen.

I remember back to the Harold Washington campaign. I was a lakefront coordinator. I remember these efforts to build black polit-ical power in the city. People felt it was like rolling a rock up a hill, and here comes the Harold Washington campaign, and it's like an explosion.

You get that sense that history can surprise us, always. It's those surprises that break through the deadening, stultifying consensus that gives people a sense, *Yes! We can.*

Eliseo Medina

I first met him thirty years ago when he was an organizer for Cesar Chavez and the United Farm Workers (UFW). "I am the executive vice president of the Service Employees International Union [SEIU], the fastest-growing union in America."

I WAS BORN IN MEXICO. My father used to come to the United States in the forties and fifties. First as an undocumented worker, then as a bracero, and then again as an undocumented worker. Finally, in 1954, my whole family decided we'd move to the United States. We sold everything we had back in my hometown. We moved to Tijuana, right on the border. My father came across to the U.S. as an undocumented worker who'd work in the fields while we stayed behind processing our immigration papers. In 1956 we got the immigration papers, and all of us, the whole family, moved to Delano, which is a very small farmworkers' town. My father and my mother and my older two sisters went to work picking grapes, peaches, oranges, peas, cotton, whatever there was. The three youngest kids, they put us in school. We'd go to work in the fields on weekends and on school vacations until I graduated from the eighth grade. Then I also went to work in the fields. I was a grape and orange picker until the farmworkers strike began in 1965. I joined in that. It was the most exciting thing I'd ever seen. I was nineteen years old and it was great.

Everybody came to the U.S. because they saw hope and an opportunity to make a new life for themselves. I remember my father and my mother kept saying they wanted their kids to do better than they did. They saw it as sacrificing for their children. So when I went to work in the fields, I was fifteen, I just thought, *This is the way things are, and if we don't like a particular grower, the only thing that we can do is quit and go somewhere else.* I never thought we could do anything other than quit and keep moving on. Until the union began.

I remember going to the first strike meeting of the UFW, which was held on September sixteenth, Mexican Independence Day. This was 1965, when they took a strike vote to actually go out. It was at a Catholic church hall, and the place was *packed*. There were people on the sides, on the walls, everywhere, electricity in the air. Anger, but also mixed in with a sense of hope and power. Oh, it was a *wonderful*, hopeful moment. I'll tell you, I left that meeting two hours later and I was on a high. I had actually not been working for about six months because I had broken my leg. I had about, like, fifteen bucks in a little piggy bank. I'd throw in whatever pennies I had. I broke it the next morning, I went into the union and paid three months' worth of dues, which was three-fifty a month at the time. I was sold, I was ready to go. Two days later, I was at home watching *I Love Lucy* and my mother and my sister came running in. "We're on strike, we're on strike!" I'd never seen my mother so excited as I did that day.

This was unbelievable. My mother grew up in a very sheltered small town, a typical Mexican upbringing, very conservative. But I tell you, there was a light in her eyes. And up until the day that she died, she was solid union.

A lot of us, particularly people who were bilingual like myself, saw on television what was going on in the South, and we thought, *God, if they can do it, we can, too.* So that's how I got involved with the labor movement.

A friend of mine and I went down to the Filipino Hall, which was the headquarters for the union. We understood that there were jobs picketing. Some of the big AFL-CIO unions gave us some money. We had no idea what picketing meant at all. So this old man, I guess he must have been in his sixties, he says, "Come on with me." We get in this car with him, and about four police cars start following us. I said, "Oh, my God." I'd never been in trouble. When I came to this country, they told us to raise our right hand and swear we'd never do anything to violate the laws because they'd deport us. I was scared to death. We get out to this field, and the old man jumps out of the car with his sign, and he starts yelling at the crew of strikebreakers. So we follow, kind of sheepish, looking at all the deputy sheriffs with the guns. For all I knew, they were going to jump us at any moment. Next thing I know, this crew packs up and leaves. And I said, "Whoa." There was just this guy and me and my friend, standing around. He says, "OK, we're done, let's get in the car and go find another crew." We weren't arrested, we weren't

beaten up, and the crew left. I thought, *Boy, there's power to this thing.*
It was the first time I actually challenged authority in this country.
And nothing had happened. Not only that, we had been successful
in chasing off the strikebreakers. So I kept coming back, day in and
day out, and then I became an organizer and I started working for
the union. It became my life. I continued working with the Farm
Workers Union until 1978. When I left, I went to work for about
two years with AFSCME [American Federation of State, County, and
Municipal Employees] organizing the University of California.

When I started working in the fields, I was making ninety cents
an hour. At the end, we actually got the wages in some of those
places up to seven, eight, nine dollars an hour. People had health
insurance, they had a pension plan, they had paid holidays, not to
mention the basics, such as toilets in the fields and cold drinking
water. The growers, for the first time, started treating people with
respect which I thought was a tremendous change. Prior to that, you
couldn't challenge the growers, they were all-powerful. We just didn't
think there was anything we could do. For the first time, people
actually felt we have some rights, we can stand up for ourselves, we
can fight, and we can win. That, to me, was the single most important
accomplishment of the union.

There are anywhere between eight and eleven million undocumented workers in the U.S. Some industries are as much as fifty to
seventy-five percent undocumented workers. If some administration
would decide to deport every undocumented worker in agriculture,
hotels, restaurants, and building service, you would *wipe out* those
industries; there would not be anybody left to do that work. All of
these stores where we get all the vegetables and all of these things,
these hotels, they would be wiped out because that workforce is
critical to them.

When we came from Mexico, driven by poverty, most of us went
into the fields. Many other Mexicans started going into the cities and
began working in hotels and restaurants and in janitorial and construction. Going into the seventies, when there was war in Central
America and death, and hurricanes, a lot of people left those countries and also came to the U.S., some of them because of what was
going on in the country, some of them, like us, because of poverty.
They came, like any immigrant, took whatever job they could, re-

gardless of wages and conditions, anything to be able to survive. But as they began to live here, they also began to assert their rights. I think you've seen over the last ten years an explosion of organizing by Latinos and immigrants. And that's injected a whole new sense of hope and new blood into the American labor movement. Women, Asiatics, they're the new lifeblood of this movement. And young. The people that leave the countries are young. In my old home state, Zacatecas, it's very small. You go to whole towns and the only people in these towns that are left are the old and the little kids. Anybody else that's in between is in the U.S. So you've got all these young people coming to this country, and they have this energy and enthusiasm and they want to move forward. And they also have learned because of the struggles like the farmworkers, and they've heard of Cesar Chavez, and then they help drive movements like the Justice for Janitors movement in the U.S. Mexico, right now, the remittances from people here are the second or third largest source of income for Mexico. In Central American countries, it's number one. Those countries back home, their economies would collapse without the contributions and remittances of people here, but I would submit this country's economy would collapse without the immigrants.

If it hadn't been for the Farm Workers Union, I would still be in Delano. Maybe, if I had been lucky, I might be a foreman at a ranch. Otherwise, I'd still be picking grapes. I got an eighth-grade education. Yet here I am now, working with people who are attorneys and doctors.

Thirty-something years ago, when I was first here as a young farmworker, I heard a labor song, and it talked about how freedom is a hard-won thing, and it said that every generation has to win it again. In the Justice for Janitors campaign we learned from the lessons of the farmworkers and they learned from the civil rights movement, and the civil rights movement learned from what happened in India with Gandhi. It will probably be beyond my lifetime, but if all we've done is to inspire other people to continue with the struggle, that will have been enough.

Tom Geoghegan

He has the appearance of a diffident young college professor, gentle and priestly.

I'M A LAWYER, FIFTY-TWO YEARS OLD, who's living at the beginning of the twenty-first century. I do writing on the side.* To my surprise, I still feel I'm the same guy I was twenty years ago. I've had the same job for twenty-two years with Len Despres, a labor lawyer. He is ninety-four, yet still on the job. His secret is his constant sense of hope.

I do a lot of union-side, civil rights, pension work, kind of oddball cases. It's not really a job, it's a way of creating an identity for myself. I represented Frank Lumpkin and Save Our Jobs at Wisconsin Steel, trying to recover their lost pension benefits when the mill went down.† We won. Today, I've become quite interested in human rights law, just as lawyers like me in the 1960s became interested in civil rights law.

I'm from Cincinnati, Ohio, and I came from an Irish Catholic family, German on my mother's side. Our family was devoutly religious. I still attend mass regularly. My uncle worked for Robert Kennedy. I was very much enamored of what my uncle did. Being in the Justice Department with Bobby Kennedy, working on racial issues in the South. I remember when I was on my eighth-grade school trip to Washington, D.C., I went to the Justice Department the night of the bombing of the church in Birmingham, and there was my uncle in white shirtsleeves on the phone to the U.S. marshals in the South. For a fourteen-year-old kid, that was heady stuff.

I went to Harvard Law School. The glamorous thing to me was not law school but college. It was in the late sixties. There was a lot of political activism, antiwar stuff. I was amazed and astonished not by my teachers, but by my fellow students. The other thing that

*He has written several works. His most celebrated is *Which Side Are You On?* (New York: Farrar Straus Giroux, 1991).

†Frank Lumpkin is a retired steelworker and union activist.

excited me was being on the *Harvard Crimson,* the student paper. There were a lot of kids around me who could really write. The only reason I was kept on the editorial board was that one of the editors told me, "You're the only kid around here who isn't stoned."

While I was in law school, I got involved with the United Mine Workers. I worked with a reform group in the union called Miners for Democracy. They were bucking a guy named Tony Boyle, who had killed Jock Yablonski.* My first boss was Jock Yablonski's son, Chip. That experience changed my life. I was twenty-three. It headed me back to the old childhood ambition, to be a lawyer, fight for the people with their back against the wall.

I was a child of the Warren Court. In law school at that time, we were studying the great decisions of the Warren Court, *Brown vs. Board,* all the way up to cases like *San Antonio vs. Rodriguez,* where lawyers were saying that the equal protection clause prohibited denial of equal protection for people of different incomes. It was a move-ment from racial civil rights to economic rights. It was a very exciting time. Wages were still going up. Equality of income was increasing in the late sixties and early seventies. It was the end of the Great Society. It was still the era of the activist. That's why the idea of full employment was so wonderful back then. Full employment meant the cornucopia. Then the country turned around and went in the other direction. What really has driven the country, in the twenty-nine years since I began practicing, has been the decline of organized labor, which means the increase in inequality of income, which means people dropping out of the process, which means people not voting, which means people giving up, which means resignation. In some ways, it's been interesting because you try to be contrarian.

On the other hand, I *do* feel that recently things have turned around a little bit. I've gotten back a little of the excitement that I had as a lawyer in the seventies.

---

*Tony Boyle was a corrupt president of the United Mine Workers of Amer-ica, who had, with the help of thugs, succeeded Philip Murray, who had in turn succeeded John L. Lewis. Boyle wound up in the penitentiary con-victed of the murder of Joseph "Jock" Yablonski, an outspoken member of the miners union who was challenging the corruption of Tony Boyle's administration, and his wife and daughter.

The big one: there's a new type of law developing, not just in the United States, but in the world, and it's human rights law. We haven't figured out a way to make human rights law part of the everyday law of the United States. But I think that's going to happen. What's the difference between civil rights and human rights? Civil rights: we're all going to be treated equally. Human rights is broader: we all have dignity as a person. We have affirmative rights. We have a right to a job. We have a right to health care. A right to be free from hunger. That's somewhat different from civil rights.

I'm doing two things at the moment. The first one: I've been writing up a list for Physicians for Human Rights. We're trying to set out what are the rights and duties of physicians when they're dealing with prisoners, when they're dealing with refugees. How should patients be treated? What are the rights of the doctor against the state? I've been reading UN treaties, I've been going back to things that came out of the New Deal. The UN resolution on human rights was drafted by Americans who were New Dealers. The stuff that Franklin Roosevelt could never get through the U.S. Senate because of the Dixiecrats, they were trying to get through the UN. When the New Dealers talked of the Four Freedoms and international rights, they knew, of course, that these rights didn't exist in the United States. So the UN declaration of human rights was an end run around the Dixiecrats. That's why the Bush administration people are so upset about human rights—it's our own law come back to us. In Europe and in countries outside of Europe there is the sense of international law as being binding on all of us. The United States refuses to accept that. In the human rights treaties that have been passed, the United States opts out. People are beginning to resent that in other countries. We in the United States are beginning to feel that resentment. But who are the American people? I don't know what the American people, the real American people think. Nobody really does, because most of them don't vote. But among the people that do vote—half are in the top twenty percent of the income structure—I think there is uneasiness, yeah. Americans are beginning to realize at this moment that there's a bigger world, and it's committed to values that we don't have. Like abolition of the death penalty. The United States itself is a human rights experiment. The conservatives in the country are adamant that human rights is un-American. What could be more American than the Declaration of Independence, which is the ultimate beginning of the human rights movement? Now other countries are saying things to the United States that we're not used to hearing. There are some other things that make me hopeful, too. The new immigration and the way in which the United States has become like a little Hapsburg empire of different nationalities. What's really shaken us out of our isolation has been immigration in the 1990s. Here we are in the middle of America, Chicago, a million miles from the ocean, and we're surrounded by the whole world here. Not just Mexican, but Polish and Bosnian and Central American, Asiatic.

The Catholic Church here in Chicago is becoming a partially Mexicanized institution. This is the Catholic Church that was run by the Irish for all these years. Now it's gone south of the border: the local church is becoming poor and Latino. It not only shakes us up, it opens us up to the rest of the world. The Catholic Church here had become very much like the United States, which was closed in on itself. The new immigration has broken the thing open. When things are changing, there's hope.

The reason the term *working class* has dropped out of our vocabulary is partly illegitimate, because people are trying to deny there's class, and partly legitimate, because the old working class is gone. The old industrial working class, it just isn't there. The new working class are people in the service sector, who don't have the kind of bonding the old industrial working places created. The term *working class* applied to steelworkers and autoworkers. Try to apply that to a world where people work at Blockbuster's giving out videos. It's so different that you might as well come up with a new word. When I came into labor, the exciting unions to be part of were the mineworkers and the autoworkers and the steelworkers. To me, they were the cutting edge of the labor movement. Now, the cutting edge of the labor movement is hotel maids and janitors. SEIU and HERE [Hotel Employees and Restaurant Employees International Union] happen to be the unions that are the fastest-growing. The reason you think about labor in terms of hotel maids and janitors is not because hotel maids and janitors are the new face of labor, though they *are,* but because SEIU and HERE have had organizing successes there. That's a great thing. It's a transition moment. Glimmers of light and hope have come from the immigrants moving here.

I feel that the world is becoming a better place, but the big wild card is what the United States is going to do. The extent to which the world becomes a better place depends on the struggle between light and darkness in the United States. I think the world will become a better place no matter what happens in the United States, but it will happen more quickly or more slowly depending on how the battle goes here. You can go to extremes of hope and despair being in the United States. Years ago, when I went to Ireland for the first time, it rained and rained and rained. I was on a bus, and I said aloud to the old woman next to me, "Is it ever going to clear up?" "Oh," she said, "we live in hope and die in despair." She laughed. Where there is humor, there is hope.

LIFT EVERY VOICE

Tim Black

A retired Chicago schoolteacher. Though retired, he is quite active as a lecturer, especially on the subject of race, Chicago's history, and the role of technology. He has recently completed his autobiography.

I'M EIGHTY-TWO YEARS OLD, born December the seventh, 1918. A memorable date. December seventh, 1941, changed a whole lot of lives, and mine was one of those. It was a day the president said would live in infamy. I didn't quite share his ideas because the day would mark a turn in the lives of millions of people all over the world, particularly African Americans, who only started to enjoy a little bit of prosperity after the war began.

I was drafted in August of 1943, right after a race riot in Detroit. I didn't know that not too far beyond that, I would be going into France. During World War Two, I spent time in the South as a GI, with my soldier suit on, having to go sit in the back of the bus, yet knowing that those keeping me in the back of the bus were assured of being able to do that by the possibility of me going to war and losing my life. Some of us made a decision that when we returned, if we returned, we were going to do some things to change that. All of my grandparents were born in slavery. My mother and father left Birmingham, Alabama, where my father worked in the steel mills. We were not poverty-stricken. They came to Chicago to seek a better life for their family, for their children, and to make my father more safe, because he was rather reckless in his behavior in Birmingham. My mother was constantly afraid something was going to happen to him. When we arrived in Chicago, the promised land, things were better. This was August 1919, one month after the race riots. We settled on the South Side of Chicago, where we had relatives and friends who were already there. They gave us a briefing on how you behave in Chicago in contrast to how you behave in Birmingham, Alabama. We lived relatively nicely, though overcrowded, in the city. The boundaries were set by restrictive covenants that said owners of property could not rent or sell to Negroes. Because we knew almost everyone and because we had so many relatives here, it was emotionally very comfortable. Of course, we had the entertainment world of the jazz music, and we had gospel music emerging, and we had a good basketball team: the Harlem Globetrotters. We had the American Giants. It wasn't boring. It wasn't at all dangerous or frightening. We had great hopes. My mother and father had decided that my sister, my brother, and I were going to college. We didn't have any money, but they decided we were going to go. That was the great hope. The dream and the hope that this would be a better life for us than it had been for them.

My father worked in the steel mills and the stockyards, the twenties into the early thirties. In 1932, he was laid off among many other workers. The Depression. He couldn't find another job, except with the WPA [Works Progress Administration]. He refused to go on what he called relief. So he would get up in the morning and walk over to Hyde Park and ask people to cut their grass or wash their windows or whatever was necessary. Very proud man. My brother and I worked in ma-and-pa grocery stores in the neighborhood. All the money that was made came to the house. My mother was the treasurer. [*Chuckles*] She handled all the money. So we were never without food, we were never without shelter. Many of the young men who lived in our neighborhood, their families were professionals. There was always that great hope. No question in our minds that our lives were going to be improved over the lives of our parents. During the Depression, my father worked on the WPA until World War Two, and then he went back to work in private industry.

After I graduated from high school, I went to Xavier University in New Orleans, to play basketball. Basketball players did not have to be as tall as they are now. My brother was drafted first, and I was drafted next. Both of us were refused the opportunity to go to OCS [Officer Candidate School] because we had been involved in organizing workers in Milwaukee—Fur and Leather Workers, an openly radical union. When OCS investigated our background, we were turned down. My mother was heartbroken because most of her friends, their sons, they'd gone to college and they were officers. It was like a competition among parents from the South. A feeling of upward mobility, a feeling of hope.

My father went into World War One toward the end of it. He didn't go overseas, but he had many friends who were gassed in France. His idea was, if we're going to have a war, we ought to have one here on the racist issue. My father was a Garveyite, a Marcus Garvey disciple. A nationalist. He felt the only thing that would relieve the problems of race in America was that people of African descent should return to Africa. My mother was very different. She was an integrationist, a very middle-class woman. But she was no less a race person than my father.

Incidentally, my slave name, Black, comes from the family of Hugo Black, the Supreme Court justice. Hugo Black's father was my grandfather's slave master. My grandfather was Hugo Black's father's personal servant. He was called a body servant. So he had special privileges. Hugo Black and my father continued to have a friendly relationship through their childhoods. When Franklin Delano Roosevelt nominated Hugo Black for the Supreme Court, I said to my father, "How could he do this with an ex–Ku Klux Klansman?" My father, who didn't like white people in general, put his cigar out of his mouth and said, "He'll be all right." I thought my father had lost his mind. But he knew Hugo Black, and history will record that Hugo Black was all right, better than all right. My father smoked cigars and chewed Brown Mule tobacco. My mother and father felt that one of the ways out of poverty, out of segregation, was education and learning how to act among those who had power. That was my mother's feeling, very strong. Her family was from Florence, Alabama, the birthplace of W. C. Handy and Oscar De Priest, the first black congressman after Reconstruction. My father was somewhat ambivalent about hope. In his opinion, white people were never going to give up their control over blacks. My mother felt that if you prayed, worked hard, went to school, stayed out of trouble, everything would be all right.

During World War Two I received four major battle awards. The French Army awarded my whole outfit the Croix de Guerre. It was an African American outfit, all black. The Three-oh-eighth Quartermaster Railhead Company. In Belgium and in Germany, at the Battle of the Bulge, we took the heat, we took the brunt of the attack. Fortunately, most of us survived. We were always with the frontline troops because they had to have our services: the ammunition, the guns, the uniforms, the food.

We were in Marseilles, and I continued to see this racism demonstrated by American soldiers particularly. So many instances. Yet we believed that if we survived and returned home, we would be able to change the system. At one time I had thought very deeply of staying in France because the French people were so much more accepting. I had thought of going to the Sorbonne. I felt the freedom that I had never felt in the United States, but then there was the tug of my family, my mother particularly, wanting her baby boy to return and make something of himself. So I returned home.

What I found was even more intensely overcrowded conditions on the South Side of Chicago. A new wave of immigrants from the South who were somewhat culturally different had come to Chicago. So there was a tension between the new migrants and those who had been in Chicago all the time.

The newcomers were rural, agricultural, and less urbane. They had not had the opportunity to become urbanized. Many of the people in the first migration from the South had lived in cities before they came to Chicago: Jackson, Mississippi; Natchez, Mississippi; Memphis, Tennessee; Birmingham, Alabama; Atlanta, Georgia; New Orleans. They had become somewhat sophisticated. In Chicago, at least, though the numbers were small, they were concentrated, and percentagewise, the early blacks in that first migration outvoted the immigrants from Europe.

The newcomers had never voted. The lynchings were still going on in the South. They did not bring a voting culture, a political culture. Immediately they began to be exploited. A class separation developed between the newcomers and the old-timers. Those of us who had been in the first migration were actually harassed by our parents to go to school and get an education, not so much for the money but for the knowledge and status. It was nice for my mother to say to her friends, "My son goes to the University of Illinois." The newcomers were discouraged by the owners of the land from going to school. They would go maybe three or four months a year, even in a place like Chicago.

When I was teaching on the West Side of Chicago at Farragut High School—this is in the late 1950s—it was not unusual on a Monday to have half my students, my African American students, absent. They had gone to visit their relatives and friends over the weekend, in Mississippi and Arkansas. This was also true of Puerto Ricans, by the way, in New York. Maybe true of the Mexicans in the second migration. It wasn't just blacks who migrated in the second Great Migration. There were the Tennessee, Kentucky, poor whites, what we call the hillbillies. But they were white, so they had that advantage. When I came back from Europe, my mother insisted that I use my GI Bill to go to college. So I finished, and then, of course, she could brag to her friends. We are going to change America, those of us from World War Two. The liberal whites also felt that. When blacks tried to get homes outside the ghetto, after being so over-crowded, they had many white sympathizers. We began to work on things like housing. Outlawing restrictive covenants. The Supreme Court decided restrictive covenants could not be enforced anywhere in the United States. Justice Black read the majority opinion. Blacks began to move into neighborhoods where they had never lived before. I personally started a family in Hyde Park near the University of Chicago campus. Things are happening, yes. In 1954, May the seventeenth, I believe, the Supreme Court issued a decree that out-lawed discrimination in public education, *Brown vs. Board*. I was teaching at DuSable High School. I said to my class, "Boy, it's gonna be good from now on." The hope was there among all the kids. Some of our students had begun to go to schools like the University of Chicago and Harvard, in addition to the black colleges. Things began to change. Schools began to accept blacks in greater numbers, jobs began to be available. And we began to look at our children, the second generation of Chicago people, to set an example for other children. My son went to Phillips Andover at the same time Jeb Bush was there. My daughter earlier had gone to a school out east, to Bennington College. We began to see the possibilities, that if this could happen, it would spread all over.

Those of us who returned from World War Two with the hopes and dreams of a future for our children and our grandchildren came to believe that we'd see the results of the struggle. We have broken the barriers. We have integrated the armed forces. Education is now going to be available for everybody. Job opportunities are going to be available. That was our belief. Some blacks were beginning to move up into the corporate world a little bit. We were beginning to see outreach for black professors in white colleges and universities. So we could see examples of the success of our hopes, dreams. We were optimistic about that. This was the mid-fifties and early sixties. Then, of course, the great march on Washington in 1963, where Dr. King was handed the mantle of leadership. A couple hundred thousand cheering. A great moment of hope.

I was the captain of that train, as you may remember.* A very, very high moment. It reminds me of going into Paris and the thrill of the French people. Walking down the streets of the Champs Elysée the second day of liberation.

The French were singing "The Marseillaise." We were singing "We Shall Overcome." Making those comparisons, the feeling of thrill and hope emerges, that somehow this is going to be a better world, this is going to be a better country. It'll take a little time, but we're going to see it. That was the feeling. And so we returned to Chicago on the train. We continued to see progress with the more fortunate young blacks, a new middle class, but then we began to feel the results of the breakup of industry in so many places—the steel mills gone, the stockyards gone, McCormick beginning to shut down. All of these places that had offered employment regardless of education were no longer available. We began to see the concentration of poverty in public housing, particularly as they break the rules and no longer scatter the housing. The poorest of the poor begin to get concentrated in those high-rise quarters, and so the separation becomes not just racial, but class. Then suddenly, an acceleration of the drug industry; that is, the illegal drug industry, having as their couriers mostly poor young black males from these projects. The separation is growing and growing and growing. And the violence increases. The streets almost empty in certain places in the black community. The white liberals begin to be pummeled as well, but they are still white.

The black youngsters reared in suburbs or places in the city like

---

*The train bringing marchers from Chicago to Washington, D.C. I was on that train; that was when I first met Tim Black.

Hyde Park begin to be accused of simply being admitted because they were black rather than that they were deserving. Young people like my son and my daughter begin to feel a sense of alienation from both their past and the places in which they are. The breakdown of face-to-face communication occurs between the generations because the demands of the new world leave very little time for contact and communication. I believe that the new technology has cut off real heartfelt communication between generations, and also between races.

With the guys on the street, the drug dealers, tomorrow does not exist. For the high-tech people, those in the corporate world, tomorrow is so uncertain, they cannot tell where they will be forced to go. My own feeling is our scientific-technological world has moved much faster than our social-cultural world. Dr. King personified the highest levels of what I'm trying to say. He did not have to be killed in Memphis. He could have been at some board meeting making money. He was one of the first of the national figures to come out publicly against the war in Vietnam, one of the very first. He was condemned for doing so. "You just stick to civil rights." But he had already been condemned for that.

I used to say in my classes, black and white: "How do you stay sane in an insane society?" The community concept is one way— the feelings of security, of trust, of sharing. Otherwise you would think that you're crazy and they're sane. As I look at the breakdown in every institutional aspect of the black community, it is a precursor of the coming breakdown in the larger white community. It was more evident in the black community because it has color. When I see the breakdown in the family, I see the breakdown in the community churches, I see the breakdown in the schools where the teachers have almost no relationship with one another, or certainly with the families of these children. I see it in the commercial institutions that have almost no relationship with the community. There is a breakdown of the spirituality of a community. No one has responsibility for anyone else except to the bank, to the corporation. The nation has no meaning. The corporation has the meaning. So what we see in the black community, we can begin to discern in the larger white community.

Elaine Jones

She is the director of the NAACP Legal Defense Fund. She has an air of ebullience and bonhomie that makes you feel immediately "at home."

I'M AN ACTIVIST, from Norfolk, Virginia, one of three children, the middle child. Older brother, younger sister. My father was a Pullman porter, a member of the Brotherhood of Sleeping Car Porters, the first black trade union. The porters sometimes would come off the runs and sit around my kitchen table, talking about issues. This was back in the fifties. My father got to travel. He got railroad passes to take his three kids to Chicago. That was our first trip out of Virginia. When you're traveling, you have to plan everything, especially if you were black in America. This is 1951, '52. He takes us to the YMCA, because he thinks we can sleep there. A woman at the desk looks at us, three little kids and my father, and says, "We don't have any rooms," without even checking the books! Daddy was crestfallen. He had it all figured out; he knew the Y would take us. So he ended up calling one of his Pullman car buddies, who put us up. I knew I wanted to be a lawyer then.

My mother was a schoolteacher, my father was a country boy who came up out of the south side of Virginia. My mother had come down from the north; she was from New Jersey. So the Yankee and the southerner met. My mother had a college degree. My father was self-taught. My mother's father was a big minister in Norfolk. When he died, they closed the schools.

I knew things were not as they should be. Black people were relegated to the back door, and I had a problem with that. I saw the white and colored water fountains. I would get on a crosstown bus and we had to sit in the back, all of that. I couldn't understand why. Meanwhile, I had self-esteem from my parents. They made me think I could do anything. My father was the cook in the family. He could really cook. At that kitchen table we talked about the world, and we would have to defend ourselves. Our parents would throw out something at one of us, and all of us would jump on that one for that evening. I always wanted to be a lawyer. I was about eight. First, I would see Perry Mason and other lawyers on television using the court to right societal wrongs. The lawyer riding in on the white horse, changing the world. [*Laughs*]

People would say, "What do you want to be?" "I want to be a lawyer because I can change some of these things through the law." As I got older, I learned more about Thurgood Marshall.* My high school teacher was one of his plaintiffs in the teacher equalization case. When he came to the South in his thirties, Thurgood tried to equalize salaries. My high school chemistry teacher, in the fifties, had been one of his clients. She told us about him in chemistry class.

I ended up in court one day. I was in junior high school. I had a toothache, and I went to the dentist with no permission from my parents. He did full-mouth X rays and fixed my teeth. He sent a *huge* bill to my parents. A black dentist. My parents said, "We're not gonna pay this! We did not give her permission to go, and you've done more work than was required." So they came to the door and served the summons. My father said, "I have to go on the railroad. I'm not going to miss my money messing around with this." My mother said, "I have to go to school. *You*, Elaine, have to go to court." I was about thirteen.

I went to the court with a neighbor, an adult. The case is called up. The dentist is not there, but his lawyer is. So the judge asks me, "Did you go to the dentist?" And I said yes. He said, "Did you have the permission of your parents?" I didn't know whether to say yes or no. If I said yes, that would make me look good. If I said no, it would make me look like a bad girl. I thought, *Elaine, tell the truth.* So I said no, I didn't have their permission. And the judge turned to the lawyer for the dentist and said: "Case dismissed." I won my first case! [*Laughs*] I won it, I won it. Oh, I knew that I was going to be a lawyer then, I *knew* it, yes!

I went to Howard for undergraduate school. My mother wrote me in college: *Elaine, I know you want to be a lawyer one day, but I want you to take some education courses, so you have something to fall back on. You might*

*The first African American Supreme Court justice.

have to teach. I said, "Mother, thank you, but..." I graduated, and guess who gave my commencement talk? Lyndon Johnson. It was a Great Society speech.

Stokely Carmichael was in my undergraduate class. My class was a cauldron at Howard. All the Freedom Riding going on. That's why Lyndon came to Howard for the Great Society speech. On civil rights and social justice, LBJ was the right person at the right time. He *knew* more than Kennedy on that, he knew who he was dealing with. He understood those southern senators, he had spent time with them. Vietnam, that's a whole different thing. So I finished Howard, and then I realized I didn't know anything about any people other than black people. My world was too small.

I was twenty, coming out of college, and I don't know anything about the bigger world. When I realized that, I went to the Peace Corps. I didn't want to go to Africa, because I knew I would go to Africa later in life, on my own. I went to Turkey. For two years, I traveled all over. Turkey is situated so centrally. I spent a lot of time in a lot of the Arab countries. I was in Israel a few days before the Six-Day War. I went to Beirut when it was a place of beauty, in the mid-sixties. Different people, and nobody looking like me. I'm the only black person in my unit in the Peace Corps.

Then I decided to go to law school. I applied to Howard and to the University of Virginia. Virginia hadn't had black people, and I am from Virginia. I'll be the first case, the first black woman. They had had three black men. If they don't admit me, we'll sue. It was in 1967. The university is in Charlottesville, a closed community. If I had gone to Charlottesville from Howard, I wouldn't have made it, because it was intense. There were some real racial issues in Charlottesville. People mistook me for the cleaning lady when I arrived in law school. I was in the ladies' room during my first week, and an older white lady came through. She saw me sitting on the sofa and she said, "I know you're taking your rest break now, but when you finish, would you clean the refrigerator?" There were hardly any women in the law school. Seven women total, and me—the black one. We had one place to congregate, that was in the bathroom downstairs. We bonded over the years. Oh, yes. 'Cause we got to know one another. We would meet in that ladies' room. They were having a hard time, too, because of gender issues. I was having a hard time because of gender and race. I was double-duty. I tried to figure out, was whatever I was experiencing because of gender or race? At the end of the day I would listen to them, and when I heard their experience, I knew that was gender, and when I subtracted it, the rest was race.

I have some lifetime friends from UVA, a few, a handful. For the most part, they were Virginia gentlemen: civil, and kept their distance. But I wore my Afro, my Nehru jacket, and my sandals from Turkey as I walked through the school. It was an adjustment for everybody. Virginia took a chance, and I took a chance.

I finished law school in 1970 and I did very well. I was in the upper quarter of my class. For more than twenty years I didn't go back to class reunions or anything. But two years ago, the University of Virginia called me back and gave me the highest honor: the Thomas Jefferson Medallion of Law at Monticello. Monticello!

Here's the hope. I got a job offer on Wall Street. Nixon's law firm! [*Laughs*] Woodrow, Guthrie, and Alexander. Wall Street was paying eighteen thousand dollars a year in 1970. They came to me my third year of law school. I accepted the offer 'cause the money looked so good. But before I graduated, I said, "This is not what I want to do. I don't want to go to Wall Street. I did not come to law school to go to Wall Street. I came to law school to practice civil rights law." After accepting the job, I turned it down. I went to the dean of the law school and said, "I do not have a job." He said, "Go to New York. See my friend Jack Greenberg"—of the NAACP Legal Defense Fund. I came to New York and sat down with Jack, who hired me on the spot. Offered me a job as an assistant council to the Legal Defense Fund when I graduated!

When I first arrived, the offices were empty. There was a bomb scare. I spent the first four or five years litigating death penalty cases throughout the South. This was '70 to '74. I had some good successes. I worked with the lawyers in Alabama. The Ku Klux Klan would come out and surround the courthouse in full dress regalia. This was Cullman, Alabama. It had a reputation. The hope was the law. I felt that we could use the law to get some justice. I believed that. So I was feeling optimistic because I was winning some of these cases. I thought the law is the way to go, that we're a nation of laws. I felt all this.

I went into government for two years. Bill Coleman was secretary of transportation, the second black cabinet officer. I was his special assistant. My project was to get women in the Coast Guard, and so we did: women, white and black. When I left, Jack Greenberg came back into my life. He was the general counsel, the position I hold now. It continues to be a struggle for a nonprofit law firm, because people don't like lawyers. [*Laughs*] For fourteen years, I stayed in Washington with the Legal Defense Fund. We were monitoring Congress, looking at judicial appointments, getting civil rights laws passed. Using the political clout of African Americans to make congress more responsible. In 1993, I came to New York as head of the Legal Defense Fund.

The counterattacks started in the eighties, with Reagan as president. Mr. Bush's policies aren't very different from Mr. Reagan's. We've got problems with the civil rights division. It's very important that the government enforce the civil rights laws that people have died and bled to put on the books. The government is not doing the job. There are African Americans in positions of authority, but the policies remain the same. I'm talking about the Department of Justice.

Now, the basic question is, how much can the law alone do? I still believe in the power of law. We can't ignore the courts. We have to fight. But you have to have community pressure and involvement. There must be public pressure to make people respond. There has to be mobilization. Grassroots. Law is vitally important, but it alone is not the answer. [*Sighs*] It's a struggle, because we're coming up now on the fiftieth anniversary of *Brown vs. Board of Education,* and we have *not* lived up to the promise of that decision. This is *fifty* years later. But I'm still hopeful, because I'm in the courts. We are making some of the same mistakes we've made in the past. Consider the criminal justice system. It's an abomination, the way we are taking these nonviolent black and brown people and penning them up in prison and giving them these *horrendous* sentences for nonviolent drug offenses. And it's a mistake, it's a mistake, it's a mistake. I believe the system can change, but it's only if those of us who understand these issues stay involved in them. That's the only way change comes.

There's a Swahili warrior song that I like: "Life has meaning only in the struggle / Triumph and defeats are up to the gods / So let us celebrate the struggle." I think we can eventually win. Otherwise, otherwise I would not get up in the morning. [*Laughs*]

POSTSCRIPT: Theodore Shaw

He is Elaine Jones's deputy, the associate director of the NAACP Legal Defense Fund.

Twenty years have passed since I've joined the LDF. I think it's important to look at the long haul. I often think about how much better we are in 2002. No matter how conservative this administration, we're better as a country than we were fifty years ago: we're better when it comes to issues of race, we're better when it comes to issues of gender, we're better when it comes to issues of gay and lesbian rights, we're better when it comes to anti-Semitism. But nothing is safe. You can't take it for granted, you can't rest. You know Sweet Honey in the Rock, the singing group? In "Ella's Song," they sing: "We who believe in freedom, we cannot rest." There's so much work to do. Martin Luther King was fond of saying that the moral arc of the universe is long, but it bends toward justice. Very often I try to place myself in a long race of relay. We have to take the baton when it's passed to us, and run as fast and hard as we can, and then pass it on to someone else. This work has given me the opportunity to do that. I couldn't ask for anything more. I'm very hopeful, because to be anything else is to lay down and die.

The Reverend
Will D. Campbell

A graduate of the Yale Divinity School, he had been chaplain at the University of Mississippi during the tumultuous years of 1954 and '55. His sartorial trademark is a black Pilgrim hat and a crooked cane. He is a familiar and colorful figure in many quarters of the South. "I have neither a Genevan gown nor a steepled church." He refers to himself as a "bootleg preacher."

We are in his log cabin in Mt. Juliet, Tennessee (on the outskirts of Nashville), where he does much of his writing and conducts conversations. All of the furniture is old-timey. Incongruously, there is a computer.

"Waylon Jennings often came to this cabin.* One day he said, 'There's something wrong. It's not coming through, I'm not getting the vibes in here.' He points at the computer: 'It's that damn thing there. It reminds me of Johnny Cash and me in the Israeli desert. It was Christmastime. We kept seeing a big light out there. My wife kept saying, "It's the star of the East!" I was spooked. We got right up to it. Here was a Bedouin shepherd sitting in a tent watching CNN on a battery. That damn computer . . .' Waylon made an astute observation on progress. We see variations on this scene in many TV commercials. I don't know what progress is. I'm not sure that's progress. I did just as well on my old upright typewriter as I do with this computer."

IF I HAVE ANY HOPE, it's almost an apocalyptic kind of hope that I can look way down the road, way beyond my lifetime and yours, and see a time maybe a hundred years from now or two hundred, whatever, when an Osama bin Laden and a George W. Bush would be arm in arm, saying, "We've got to save the planet Earth." I was involved in antiwar and civil rights. People ask me

---

*Waylon Jennings is a celebrated country singer; for years, he was one of the stars of Nashville's *Grand Ole Opry*.

sometimes, "What have you been up to all these years since?" I have not been up to anything except trying to survive as a human being. I can tell you what led me into civil rights. I was about five years old, in my granddaddy's yard. We were taunting an old black man, called him "nigger." Grandpa Bundt, who finished enough schooling that he could write his name and make out a check, read a little bit, he called everybody "hon," it didn't matter if it was male or female, boy or girl. He didn't have all these Freudian hang-ups that we have. He said, "Now, hon, there ain't no niggers in this world." John Walker was this elderly black man who had just got out of prison for stealing a few dozen ears of corn. He wasn't answering the kids, just trotting along. Grandpa said, "He's not a nigger, he is a colored man." I never forgot that. When I grew up, I saw how black people were treated, and when I got to the South Pacific in the war and was associating with other people and seeing how the islanders were treated, why, I would always go back to it. I can't explain why. My grandpa, cousins, and neighbors, some of them joined the White Citizens' Council, and the Ku Klux Klan. I was always known as the little preacher because I memorized the Twenty-third Psalm. Aunt Susie would sit me, a little barefoot boy in striped coveralls, in the back of the pew, long before I could read and write, to recite the Twenty-third Psalm—"This is our little preacher"—and everybody was so proud of me. When I went off to war—I didn't have to go, but I did—I was already ordained as a Baptist minister. I went to Wake Forest College in North Carolina, and to Yale Divinity School.

I had a parish in Louisiana, a small sawmill village, the mill and the houses and the church. It was a company town. The blacks lived on one side of the road, the whites on the other. The blacks had their own church. I went there in 1952. The mill owners, who were educated, sophisticated people, thought it was cute. They would go to their club in Shreveport and say, "We got the cutest little preacher. He talks about someday our little children are going to go to school with the little darkies." Miss Rosalie, who really was the pastor—the wife of the president of the mill, a very urbane woman, college-educated, spoke French, played the organ piano, classical music—she told me one time, "You have two things you preach on." I said, "What's that?" She said, "Well, the Negro question, and McCarthy." She said, "People want to hear about Jesus; they don't want to hear about McCarthy." This was at the time of the Red scare. I said, "Well, I think McCarthy is challenging Jesus." [*Laughs*]

Along comes May seventeenth, 1954, and the Supreme Court ruled, as they did, *Brown vs. Board*. Then they began looking at one another: "Does this little preacher know something we don't know?" So the clouds were gathering. After that it was just a matter of time before I had to leave. That's when I went to the University of Mississippi thinking that in an academic setting, even in Mississippi, there would be free exchange of ideas. I was the chaplain for the school. I was called "director of religious life." I was paid by the state. I used to tell these Delta boys who would come in there and challenge me, "If you want to get rid of Campbell, get rid of this seat. It's as unconstitutional as hell. I have no business being paid by the state of Mississippi to be a minister." They didn't want to do *that*.

When I went there, there was a poll taken. Seventy-five percent of the student body said they would not object to a black graduate student coming there. But three months after *Brown vs. Board*, that same poll showed like ten percent. You can trace it to the organization of the White Citizens' Council. Had that not happened, there would have been some murmuring, but people were already saying, "We're law-abiding people and this is the Constitution, this is the Supreme Court. What can we do?" They would have worked it out. But when people like Jim Eastland and that crowd started screaming, "Never!" and organized the White Citizens' Council, that negated *Brown vs. Board*. To this day it still doesn't work. Six-year-old black children always played with the little six-year-old white children. There wasn't anything they could do about that. I grew up playing with black children. Nobody thought anything about it. I'd spend the night down at Leon's house, sleep on a pallet with him. But you wouldn't have that after 1954, and you don't have much of it today.

I would invite a dozen or so outstanding religious leaders to come for a week and speak in chapel and fan out to all the fraternities and sororities and the classrooms and so on. I'd invited a man named Alvin Kershaw. He was an Episcopal priest from Oxford, Ohio, an authority on religion and jazz. I invited him to come speak on religion and jazz. But he got on that *$64,000 Question* TV show. He won thirty-two thousand dollars and said he was going to give some of the money to the NAACP. That's when the pressure was on me: "You've got to cancel this speaker." I refused to cancel. The fur flew. I had no hope there.

I think it was February second, 1960, I saw all of these well-dressed, well-mannered black students seated at these lunch counters, I knew that something was going to change. When you see these kids hit, bit, pulled off, spit on, cigarettes put out on their back. I remember the Woolworth's store. There were two lunch counters, one downstairs and one upstairs. This was in Nashville. Downstairs the police had pulled out and left the students at the mercy of the mob.

I saw an old woman walking up and down between the students seated and the mob that would come up and put out a cigarette on them, spit on a young woman's neck and all. The students just sat, they didn't protest. This old woman, I'd never seen her before, never saw her again. She was a white woman. She said, "I just came in to buy an egg poacher." She'd go up and talk to these young white thugs. "How would you feel if that was your sister?" And they would kind of, "Oh, I didn't mean nothing." Then they'd go back in the mob and someone else would take over. She single-handedly kept that from being perhaps a massacre. Now, upstairs there was a different scene. Only male students were sitting at the lunch counter. I remember this one black fella, looked like he could have been a football player for Tennessee State. I could see this guy's about to break when they were putting cigarettes out on him. And then the mob said, "Here comes Old Green Hat." A fella came in looking like Robin Hood with a big feather on his cap, and he grabs this black guy. He threw him to the floor. Just at that point I heard a *phfft*, you know, the sound of a switchblade knife. But out of the crowd came this white guy who looked like what we would call a preppy today. He grabbed Old Green Hat and hit him, knocked him right on the floor, and said, "You son of a bitch, if you touch him again, I'll stomp the piss out of you." And Old Green Hat said, "Here come the cops, let's get out of here." There weren't any cops, but he'd lost face. I've never been sure which one did the work of the Lord that day, but I think both of them did: the old woman with the egg poacher and the young preppy with the steel fist.

Congressman John Lewis is the bravest person I've ever known in my life and the most truly nonviolent person. He was left for dead, beaten more than anyone else, jailed more than anybody I know. But he goes and speaks and the students say, "Well, things haven't changed, we still can't get a job." And John Lewis says, "Don't tell me, don't tell me they haven't changed. When I was your age and I was a student in this town, Will Campbell and I couldn't ride a cab together to go to the airport. We couldn't go to the movies together. I had to go upstairs and he'd go downstairs. We couldn't go to the F. W. Woolworth and get a hamburger. Our children couldn't go to school together. Don't tell me things haven't changed. Now, if you want more change, do what we did, get out there and march and chant and sing and protest. Whatever it is you don't like. We changed it!" Right now, I feel stagnated. I write rare books. I mean they're rarely bought.* I will go on doing what I've done all my life: complaining, bitching, and saying there's something wrong.

When 9/11 happened, I was in Jackson, Mississippi. I went downstairs. The lobby was just filled with people, and everyone was glued to the television. I saw this little girl pulling on her mother's skirt, and her mother was just hysterical watching the television. The little girl kept saying, "What'd we do?" A little child, when they're punished, they know they've done something bad. "What'd we do?" I thought, *That may be the most profound question, the question that no politician in this country has tried to answer.* The only thing they say is, "What are we going to do about it?" The little girl was asking the right question. We've done a lot. The thousands of people who die every day from starvation. I'm not saying that we as a nation caused it, but we as a rich nation could, by God, have prevented a great deal of it, and still can. And our policies in the Near East, for God's sake . . . I don't know what the answer is between the Palestinians and the Israelis, but I know goddamn well the answer is not to go over there and bomb the hell out of Baghdad.

This word of hope, you keep whetting my appetite to deal with it. I can say I found hope in the little girl's question. That this little

---

*His most celebrated book is *Brother to a Dragonfly*. It was critically well received, though it was far from being a bestseller.

four-year-old was asking the elders, "What did we do?" Hopefully the mother had to think about that when she went back home, around her own hearth with her family, and said, "Little Katie asked a good question: What did we do?" [*Sighs*] Now, let's go eat some barbecue.

Lloyd King

You immediately sense his enthusiasm and abundance of energy. High-spirited may best describe him. You're not quite sure whether he is a dark-skinned Caucasian, a Middle Easterner, or a light-skinned African American.

I TEACH MUSIC, I'm a composer. I'm forty-three years old, married, no kids. Got a little dog and live in Chicago, and life's pretty good lately.

I'm brown-skinned. My mother's white, she's a doctor. My father's black, he's a businessman. They've been married fifty years. When people asked what color I was, I said, "I'm black." I don't think of myself that way anymore. I just say that to please other people. I'm tired of denying my white half. I'm just as white as anybody else is white is the way I look at it, and just as black as anybody else is black.

There was a time when I used to put *other* on applications. Now, it depends on what I want to do. Like if I think that it would be interesting to put *black,* then I put *black*. If I think it'll be interesting to put *white,* then I'll put *white*. If people start giving me shit about something, I say, "Look, I'm white." I have white pride. [*Laughs*] I'm proud of my white ass, yes. I'm no longer ashamed. I have an older half sister, two older brothers, and a younger sister, so there were four or five of us running around.

Earlier it was confusing. It was hard to find a sense of identity. At first it was cool, because when we moved from an all-black neighborhood to an all-white neighborhood, it was nice to be anti-establishment. I was a dark-skinned kid amongst white-skinned people; I had something over them—I knew something they didn't know. So you may get into a fight once in a while, or you may have to put up with racism, but that became part of the romantic battle. I was continuing the battle that my parents had started in the civil rights movement. Later I realized that you could take that too far. I was angry at white people when I was in high school, not really at all white people, because then I'd have to be angry at my own mother, or half of myself. What I was angry at was maybe I thought the world didn't treat me right.

I'm teaching a class at Colorado College, okay, and we're talking about race. One of the kids says, "I'm Asian and this school is all white. These people don't understand Asians. It's insulting to me and it's hurtful, and it's really given me a hard time. I'm discriminated against here." Then this little white girl stands up—she's maybe twenty years old—and she says, "Yeah, you probably have a hard time. But I have a hard time, too. I've been funny-looking all my life. I don't look like the typical pretty kid, and people make fun of me because I have zits, and that's pretty horrible." She had acne. I was thinking, *Yeah, the Asian guy, he's pretty handsome and he's a really talented musician. I betcha she has a harder time of it, that white girl, than the Asian guy, because she's funny-looking.*

Things have improved for me largely due to the fact that now I recognize I'm white as well. It opened up a whole new world for me and made me more comfortable around white people and more comfortable talking about race. We're in this age of political correctness, so that language causes a lot of differences. You see people getting offended over this, that, and the other. Everyone is so easily offended. We're at this funny place where people are sensitive and uncomfortable, and there's still institutionalized racism going on, but I think things racially have gotten way better. As things gets better, though, other problems are revealed.

This is what I say to my students: "Let's pretend there is a world where there is no racism anymore. Are we all getting along, then?" I don't think so. I think we're predisposed to form small communities that understand each other, and we're against those other people that don't understand us. I believe we're hardwired to discriminate. It's in our physiology. We may learn to live together as brothers, but nobody fights like brothers fight. Brothers know how to fight dirty; they push each other's buttons.

When I was a child, I was taught to put my hope in liberal ideas and the ideas of the left. As an adult, I'm more confused. The left doesn't look that much better than the right. I think personal responsibility is very important and it's a sign of maturity. It's very difficult to come by. If you want to find a good place to do battle on the left, to fight the good fight, fight against homophobia. That, to me, is a more dire situation than the racial situation in this country.

Intellectually, I don't have that much hope. I'm kind of a glass-half-empty person. I find humanity is fairly disappointing. We are not as smart as we think we are. From what I've seen of humanity, we shit in our own backyard a little too often. That's toxic, and that could kill us. Of course, we're a bunch of stupid monkeys that learned to talk. For monkeys who learned to talk, we're not doing so badly.

A lot of my friends are on the left and they don't like this notion of globalization. They're protesting in Seattle and other places against the big corporate conglomerates who are turning the whole world into Disney and Pepsi. Here's where I agree with the right. I'm for those big conglomerates turning the whole world into Disney and Pepsi. I don't want globalization to happen at the expense of rare and beautiful cultures, but I think as people get more sophisticated, countries learn how to keep their own identities as they get modernized or globalized. You don't have to throw the baby out with the bathwater. It's a gamble, the future, that's how I feel about it.

Yeah, September eleventh affects me in fundamental ways. It's interesting and disturbing to me how sometimes people get over-zealous about their patriotism. Like suddenly, if you're not displaying the American flag, you're un-American. And then there's all sorts of racial profiling going on, where people like me are discriminated against. For all they know when I'm getting on a plane, I'm the Arab guy. I'm dark-skinned, but I don't look like a regular old American black. I'm kind of something else. They might think I'm Arabian or Middle Eastern or whatever. Dark-skinned people in this country might feel a little bit differently about what it means to be patriotic. I understand how people in the other world feel because I think sometimes America can be just a big white bully, and it's a pain in the butt. The part about the patriotism is complicated for me. It's upsetting that people lost their lives, but it seems easier for my white friends to be all gung ho about America than it is for me.

What happened on September eleventh happened in the name of God. That's very interesting to me. I'm not religious, but right after

9/11, while I'm walking my dogs in the woods, I came up with a song. It's called "Self-Contrail." A contrail is the mist that comes out of a jet engine. I'll tell you the words, I won't sing it. It says:

> *Grant me the ecstasy that I deserve*
> *for strapping the chastity belt on the perv*
> *I'd be who I could be if I had the nerve*
> *to laugh with Allah*
> *to laugh along with God*
> *I lost my inheritance in the family lie*
> *I lost my common sense gazing at the sky*
> *We all lost our innocence when we learned to fly*
> *And laugh with Allah*
> *and laugh along with God.*

The bridge is: "Sweat for the oracle / Piss for the nurse / Spit is a miracle / And blood is the curse." The last verse is hopeful and greedy at the same time. It's personal, kind of self-centered. The song is almost like a prayer, and I think sometimes when we pray we're a little bit greedy: "I want some air to breathe and a piece of land / A place where my love and me can make our last stand / If that's just a bourgeois dream, then I'm just a man / Who laughs with Allah, ha ha ha / Trades shtick with Jehovah, ha ha ha / And kills the Buddha, ha ha ha / And laughs along with God."

It's a fun song to sing. This is why I call pop music the perfect text delivery system. You can send some ambiguous or heavy or critical message, but you can put it in this very sentimental music, and then everybody goes around singing it. You know the saying "Nero fiddled while Rome burned"? I used to say, "What else are you going to do?" What else was he *supposed* to do? It's burning. What are you supposed to do? Stop enjoying music?

Most every day I wake up I feel happy. The sun's shining, I love the people that I'm with. If the world is going to hell in a handbasket, should I be depressed about it? I don't think so.

I went to the theater to see the Gyuto monks from Tibet. They sing from their throats. For eighteen hours a day they do that. And they got embraced by American popular culture, right. Here are these monks who live way in the mountains, very isolated, in Tibet, doing this very spiritual Buddha thing. They're on tour suddenly, and they're playing the Park West. There's this monk in full robes, with a shaved head, drinking a Pepsi. My friend goes, "That's sad." I'm going, "No, that's great." It's like a commercial. It seems bad, like something is getting culturally lost. But here's a man who's keeping his traditions and drinking Coke at the same time.

Mel Leventhal

I WAS A CIVIL RIGHTS LAWYER in Mississippi, on the staff of the NAACP Legal Defense and Education Fund. I lived and worked there from the mid-sixties to the mid-seventies. In the civil rights community in Jackson, there was a group of white educators who taught at Tougaloo, a black college just outside of Jackson. James Loewen, who taught history, told me that every ninth-grader in Mississippi had to take a course in history with the most racist textbook imaginable. He said, "I'm going to get a group of historians together to write a new book. It's going to be a more balanced view of Mississippi's history." He meant a book that talked about the Civil War, about the civil rights movement, about the evolution of the country. He said, "When we get this book written, I want you to help me get it published. And when the Mississippi textbook authorities refuse to publish it, I want you to sue the bastards." I made the commitment.

A year later, he said, "We got a book; now let's find a publisher." We went to twenty or thirty publishers. Every one of them saw it as a sure loser. Why in God's name would they publish this book? We flew up to New York to meet with André Schiffrin at Pantheon Books. We sat down with André to persuade him. The first words out of his mouth were, "Of course we'll publish this book." [*Delighted laughter*] It was the early seventies.

The book was published by Pantheon, and we brought a lawsuit to get the state of Mississippi to put it on its approved list. At first they refused. We brought a lawsuit in federal court, in the Northern District of Mississippi. We got a court order requiring the state textbook authorities to adopt this new history book. The book was not widely used. Getting it on the approved list meant only that teachers could select it. But in a handful of school districts there were black educators and enlightened white educators who used the new book, and the textbook that had been used for fifty years started being revised and updated and became more open because of this book. The changes you bring about may come in gradual and indirect ways. You keep at it.

Everything meaningful that's ever happened in the world, any change, any improvement comes about because of optimism. The pessimists don't get anything done. They're naysayers. You have to see the potential for change. And you've got to see it not in terms of the moment but in terms of the long view, the long haul.

The immediate reason I got into civil rights was the murder of those three civil rights workers in Mississippi—Goodman, Cheney, and Schwerner. That was 1964. I was shocked into action.

One of the most important facts about civil rights workers in Mississippi is we didn't realize how *impossible* it was. You don't think in terms of the negatives. A lot of it's got to do with youth. Without youth we can't get anywhere.

I was twenty-four years old when I moved to Mississippi. I was just out of NYU law school and joined the staff of the NAACP Legal Defense Fund. During the summers when I was a law student, I was in Mississippi working with Marion Wright, now Marion Wright Edelman. We were law partners in Jackson together. She came out of Yale Law School. I was on a march with Martin Luther King, the Meredith Mississippi march in 1966, when Stokely Carmichael began the black power movement. What I remember was how quickly... [*Long pause*] I was with Dr. King in Canton. We'd walked from Memphis on our way to Jackson. We had this meeting because we were about to enter the capitol. I had found out that if we reached Jackson and held a demonstration on the steps of the capitol, it was against the local law. There was a statute that prohibited demonstration on the steps of the capitol. King needed a lawyer; I was only a law student. Early in the meeting, I said, "Dr. King, you should know that if you try to hold this demonstration on the steps of the capitol, you might all be arrested for violating this ordinance."

A man named George Raymond said, "Shut up, white man. We don't need to hear from you." There was always a lot of tension between white and black in the movement; it just had never surfaced this much. Dr. King snuffed it out by saying, "We need him. Let the man talk." I explained the ordinance, and Dr. King said to me, "We're not going to—" Some people shouted, "Fuck the ordinance, let 'em arrest us all!"

Dr. King said, "No, we're not getting arrested in Jackson this time around." He went into the bedroom and called the governor of Mississippi, Paul Johnson. I was standing there with him, and he says, "Governor, I'm meeting here in Canton and my lawyer tells me that you've got an ordinance which says that we can't hold a demonstration on the steps of the capitol. I want to know if you're going to enforce it. Are you going to arrest us if we have this demonstration?" The governor apparently said to King, "We're gonna let you hold your demonstration as long as it's peaceful." We went back to the other room and continued the meeting. There was this real anger that I was still there. Somebody said, "Well, we're finished with you, get out." King tried to calm them down, but I walked out on my own. I was angry.

That was the beginning of the so-called black power slogan. One of the ironies of the civil rights movement, to me, is that while it was going on there was a great concern that America would see the movement as being led by whites, and black people as not really involved. I'll be damned if history hasn't turned that on its head. You look at the historians and the people writing about the movement, it's like no whites were involved. I went to see the movie *Ali*. That wonderful movie illustrates this point. Muhammad Ali was represented in his fight to get his license and his attempt not to be drafted by a black lawyer out of Chicago, a great lawyer, Chauncy Ethridge. Ali lost his case in every lower court. Got to the Supreme Court and it was won. He would never have boxed again had he not won. In his claim that he was a conscientious objector he was represented in the Supreme Court of the United States by a white lawyer, a guy named Jonathan Shapiro, of the NAACP LDF. If you look at the history of the Muhammad Ali case, whether it's a movie or a book, it's like Jonathan Shapiro didn't exist. It's like the only people who were helping Muhammad Ali were black. The lawyer who won the case for him was a white Jewish lawyer on the staff of the Legal Defense Fund.

History is being rewritten to eliminate all the white people who participated in the movement. [*Chuckles*] They're being written out. This is terrible for America, because you're not going to have progress without these coalitions. It was white and black together; we've lost that. There was always an undercurrent in the movement that somehow we had all these reasons why white people shouldn't be involved. There was a fear that black people needed leaders, needed people to look up to, role models. There was a feeling that whites wouldn't be there in the long haul, it had to be black.

We need to identify and honor the unsung heroes. There was a black high school student who had been arrested and thrown off the bus months before Rosa Parks. She was beaten up and thrown in jail, a high school kid. We forget that there was a bus boycott in Harlem in the 1940s. There was a bus boycott in Baton Rouge in 1952. We're always building on the work of other people. Rosa Parks needed people to help her. There's always precedent.

You try to figure out when the civil rights movement began, it goes right back to 1619, when blacks were first enslaved. There were probably civil rights leaders back then. One of the most important aspects of progress is having precedent, knowing that you're not the first to do it. The fact is, Rosa Parks was not the first one to do what she did. People think of the sixties, but the civil rights movement was happening in the twenties, when the nation recoiled from lynching. You lived through the Scottsboro Boys. That was a major event in American history. Lynchings were parties in the United States, they were social events. [*Impassioned*] When you get that low, it becomes the bedrock for an upward movement. The trial of the Scottsboro Boys was in every paper in America. It was a catalyst for change.

The movement is a series of events, building blocks. It's a hope, it's an appreciation that there are others working with you. It's so important that you have people who have a vision of what's a moral imperative. And that leads to change. Race relations in America and human advances in America have always been three steps forward, two steps back. America, in human rights, is in a perennial bull market. You have setbacks, you have regression, you have backslides. Right now, we're in a trough. We're backing up. It took the Quakers of the 1760s and their antislavery efforts to give us, a hundred years later, the Thirteenth Amendment. The Fourteenth and Fifteenth Amendments, which were enacted in the nineteenth century, did not take hold until the twentieth century. You're talking about cycles that run a hundred years. The last up cycle was from the 1930s to Lyndon Johnson's Great Society programs: a notion that we've got to help people based on need. We've got to have a beloved community, which was Dr. King's phrase. America recoiled from that in the 1970s. We are right now in one of those backslides. From the explosion of the civil rights movement, running from, say, '35 to '70, we're now going backwards. The only way we're going to get out of this trough to the next moment in the history of the movement is by putting pressure on, not letting up. One of the most important concepts for advancement in human rights is affirmative action, which at this moment is on the defensive. As long as affirmative action is on the defensive, we can't have progress. Unless you grasp the nettle, you're stagnating. Every advancement in human rights is tied to affirmative action. Look at things that we take for granted today. The 1965 Voting Rights Act barred literacy tests. It barred the poll tax. That's affirmative action. You enact laws that prohibit discrimination. That's affirmative action. The 1964 Civil Rights Act prohibited discrimination in public accommodations. I'm talking about north, south, the whole country. Racism is not a southern phenomenon. Each moment of the upswing, where things are getting better, has involved affirmative action. In the nineteenth century, we had the Freedmen's Bureau. That's affirmative action. When you've enslaved people for two hundred years, you can't just say, "You're free." You've got to have a program that we would call affirmative action. It was the Thirteenth, Fourteenth, and Fifteenth Amendments. In the twentieth century our affirmative action programs were the Great Society programs of Lyndon Johnson.

The downtrend that started in the seventies is going to be with us for another twenty years before we have any real change. The civil rights community is just trying to make sure the backsliding isn't any greater. We minimize the amount of lost ground. That's where we are right now. We're trying to minimize the backsliding.

The next fight is a class fight. I think it's important that Colin Powell is the secretary of state. That's a building block. But the next movement is going to be about recognizing the fundamental needs of human beings. Right to a job. During the last phase of this upswing, Dr. King talked about, everybody has the right to a job. King, after all, died in Memphis, there on behalf of the garbage workers, their rights as much as their needs.

The worst moment in my life as a civil rights lawyer occurred in the summer of 1966. We had a welfare rights program, trying to get people to apply for welfare.

[*With emotion*] If you have a welfare program, you have a duty to find the people who need it. You don't just sit in the welfare office and twiddle your thumbs till somebody walks in. You go out, and you go into the community. That's what welfare is, a right. We had to find the people who needed it because many of them weren't applying. I went into Greenwood, Mississippi. My objective was to search for people who were languishing in poverty and might be entitled to benefits. I went into the poorest community. I knocked on a door and I heard a faint, faint voice, "Come in." I walked in and saw something I had never seen in my life. She was lying on the bed. She was in an emotional stupor. There were three small children in the room. It was a dirt floor. There were roaches roaming around this one-bedroom shack. She would lie there and die with her children. There was no one else. We've got to find these people to tell them of their rights.

Workfare is part of the trough I'm talking about. We say, "The people on welfare, it's their fault. Let's make them work." This woman lying on the bed in a dirt-floor shack is somebody we can't say is worthless. How can we bring her and her children back into humanity? We have an obligation to her. We need young people to do more of what young people did in the sixties and in the fifties and in the forties: to keep America honest. We need to make sure the young learn their history. It's important to stand back and see that the whole world is in a downswing when it comes to human rights. And I'm not optimistic. But I'm not giving up. Can't afford to.

THE PARDON

Leroy Orange

In the year 2001, Governor George Ryan of Illinois declared a moratorium on capital punishment in his state. He was the first governor ever to do so. His decision was influenced by the findings of several faculty members and Northwestern University law school students who proved thirteen men, convicted of murder and on death row, wholly innocent.

On January 11, 2003, Governor Ryan commuted the death sentences of all 167 inmates of the state's death row. The day before, January 10, he pardoned four men awaiting execution, making them from that moment on free men. Leroy Orange was one of those four. Released only three weeks, he enters my living room in the company of his lawyer, Cathryn Crawford.* He hesitates for a moment. He moves about tentatively, as though not accustomed to so much space. His voice is soft, almost matter-of-fact in tone, though at times, when his emotions take over, there are long pauses in his story. There are occasional interjections by Cathryn Crawford.

LEROY: I'm a man who spent nineteen years incarcerated, most of those years on death row. I left one world and returned to another, and I'm trying to figure things out.

The world is so technologically different. The cars are scary. People come off as being always in a hurry. When you watch them, they're really not going anywhere, you know what I mean? They're walking around everywhere with the phone up to their ears, taking

*She had been a Northwestern University law student and was a member of the team that had undertaken the investigation of the original thirteen; subsequently she became Orange's lawyer.

care of business, about to be hit by a bus. There's a threat of war. I don't know if this is a better world. . . .

I'm from Chicago, born at Cook County Hospital. My mother was a barmaid, served drinks. I'm not sure what my father did for a living. My father and mother didn't stay together very long. I didn't get along very good with my mother. She was abusive to me while I was growing up and I didn't understand why. First she served drinks and then she became her own customer.

I dropped out of my second year of high school because my girlfriend got pregnant and my intention was to get work and help support the child. I was sixteen or seventeen. I put my age up a bit to be able to get a job in the steel mills. I eventually quit. I wasn't responsible enough. I more or less relied on my girlfriend's mother to support my son. He's thirty-two now. I'm about fifty, I think.

Attempts were made to force me to join a gang on several occasions, but I never succumbed to it. There were a lot of girls. I made another baby. I met my wife-to-be while I was working in the steel mill. I made attempts at being a husband, but I was just too young to get married. I'd hang out on the streets having what I perceived as fun. I got in trouble once when I was seventeen, criminal damage to property. I broke a window and was sent away to Vandalia Work Farm. That was the first time I ever got in trouble as an adult. I used to run away from home a lot when I was a child, get arrested for curfew, shoplifting candy bars to eat, sleeping in cars, stuff like that. I was in Vandalia nine months. It wasn't very harsh. I was a laborer in the carpenter shop. They make the furniture for the institution.

I was eighteen, nineteen when I got out. I fooled around in the streets for maybe a year. Work on a job for three or four months, then quit. Visit the park a lot, smoke marijuana, the sort of things teenagers do.

I'd get up, say, eleven or twelve o'clock. You'd go to each other's houses, whoever's parents are gone to work. You watch television or make breakfast, call girls over, go to the movies, go to the park.

In the disco era, '77 or '78, it was around that time that I was introduced to cocaine. We used to get high. We thought it was a recreational drug. We started getting high more regularly and going to work much less.

One night I was at my girlfriend's. My stepbrother wanted to make a deal with a guy about a big radio-television component set that he had acquired. I had introduced them. There was some discrepancy about the payment. It didn't look like anything that they would fight over. Everybody was high. So I left them talking about it.

The next thing I know, the police were beating my mother's door down wanting to talk to me about some murders. I was asleep on the couch. They snatched me and threw me against the wall. They took me out in the zero weather barefoot, put me in a car, and took me to the station.

They took me to an interrogation room and handcuffed me to a ring protruding through the wall. Lights out in the room. They put a plastic bag over my head for a few moments, took it off, put it on again. It was impossible to breathe. On a couple of occasions, I felt like I was going to pass out. The second time they done it, I agreed to go along with whatever they wanted me to do. They insisted upon me taking them to the locations of the weapons and telling them the story about how this or that happened. I was unable to do that because I didn't know anything about weapons. So they proceeded to electroshock me.

They pull your pants down and attach something to your cheeks. You hear some noise . . . You remember those little cars, like back in the fifties, you used to roll 'em, get the back wheels wound up, then let them go and they'd run across the floor? You'd hear that noise and then it would shock you. They done it once on my arms, while this guy Commander Burge was talking to me.*

You met Burge?

LEROY: Very intimately.

While officers was holding me, John Burge warned me that I was going to tell him everything he wanted to know before I left there. So off and on through the night, the officers was with these tactics. They were saying, "It happened like this, didn't it? It happened like that." Jerking me around and calling me obscenities.

*Commander John Burge, of Area Two, after an investigation by the Police Department's Office of Professional Standards, was found to have engaged in systematic torture of criminal suspects in more than fifty cases. He was fired. He lives in Florida. He is under further investigation.

When they had the electrical device up between your legs, your genitals, and finally in my rectum, I agreed to go along with whatever stories they was putting out there. For the rest of the night they kept feeding me a story that they wanted me to conform to. At one point they told me that somebody was there from the state's attorney's office. They wanted me to talk to him. Some guy came in with a sports coat on. I went to tell him what they'd been doing to me. As it turned out, it was another police officer. He said, "Bullshit, just as I thought." They was trying to fool me, telling me he was from the state's attorney's office.

It was the most painful experience I ever had in my life. It was put against my genitals. I can't describe that pain. It's not like you bump your head or you hit your thumb with a hammer. It's something that has your body, your body convulses. You grind your teeth together. Particularly when they stuck it up my ass.

You confessed that you killed the guy?

LEROY: No, they didn't get the confession. The guy who said "bullshit" walked out of the room. Another officer was sitting in the room and he came over to me. I thought he was going to hit me. He reached his hands up between my legs and squeezed my scrotum a little bit and assured me that we could go through this all night if I liked. I felt helpless, totally helpless. We went over the story again. Someone told me, "We know just how this guy works. Just go along with him."

When they sent the real state's attorney in, I didn't know who he was this time. I didn't know who was real or another cop. I just went along with whatever he was saying. If I said something wrong, he would redo the question or lead me to the right direction. The only thing I had to do was say yes to the questions he was asking.

CATHRYN: That state's attorney is a judge now.

So you said you shot him.

LEROY: No, I said I stabbed him. That was the confession. I agreed with what they wanted, that I got a knife and had everybody tie each other up, and then stabbed everybody. Three adults and one child. One used to be my girlfriend, and the other two were friends, and her child grew up with my child. My stepbrother confessed to doing it, he confessed to how he did it. He's dead now.

Before I was convicted, I thought it sounded so ridiculous that I would just up and kill my friends. I never dreamed I'd be convicted. It was a joke. The first time I got in front of a judge, I told him what happened at the police station, the torture and all. For the cameras and the people there in the court, he pretended like he cared, and sent me to the hospital. For the rest of the time I was incarcerated, new evidence was to come out where these officers had been doing this torture business all the time. I was trying to win a new trial or a new hearing.

My lawyer was supposed to have filed a motion to suppress the statement, but I didn't have money enough to appease him, so he told me that he couldn't file such a motion to exclude the confession. The judge in the case, he more or less dictated the trial with this lack of respect for my attorney. Along with my attorney's inadequacies, I was subsequently found guilty by the jury.

My lawyer suggested that I allow the judge to sentence me, because he had fucked the case up so bad that the Illinois Supreme Court was going to be after him. So that's what I did—I allowed the judge to sentence me. Death. I was sent to Menard Correctional to await the date for my execution. I was beginning to see life as it really is. I saw the criminal justice system as a black and white issue: if you got money, you can afford expert testimony, or at least reasonable assistance from an attorney. But if you was poor, nobody had time for you. While I was on death row my hopes was pretty low and I wanted to go that route alone.

I had just conceded that I would eventually be executed, so I started studying the Bible and trying to find strength and make peace with my Maker before that time came. In the later eighties, different things started to unravel in the courts about John Burge, and cases started coming out that confirmed what I had said. A little hope started to rise. In 1990, I was transferred from Menard to Pontiac. I started to meet other guys who was on death row, who had been tortured by John Burge. I got excited about that because I was beginning to see how they worked the mechanism. They would have one torture case in this courtroom over here front of this judge, and another torture case in another courtroom upstairs. They just had the cases spread out all over the building. They treated them as if they were isolated incidents. I started telling guys we gotta get our lawyers together and show them that this is what they're doing. Some lawyers had already been doing that, so on our end, on the inside, it was raising the level of hope. An investigator from OPS, the Office of Professional Standards, even came to see me and had pictures for me to identify officers. Right there in the bunch was John Burge. I pointed to a photograph and he said, "That's Commander Burge." Some time after that, it was confirmed that Mr. Burge had in fact systematically tortured guys for more then twenty years. They fired him, but the courts wasn't giving anybody no relief. Around that time, I was granted an evidentiary hearing to see how bad my lawyer had screwed up at sentencing. So in 1998, I came back to Cook County Jail in Chicago, to await the hearing.

The judge did grant me a new hearing because he said my lawyer had screwed up at trial. I figured they didn't want me back at a trial level because now I had very competent attorneys. Law students of Northwestern and Tom Geraghty had been visiting me from 1990 to 1998. When the scandal started breaking, we had high hopes that something would be done. But when you get back to court and the only thing they're going to grant you is a sentencing hearing, you're like, "What about the conviction? A sentencing will do me no good. What about the conviction itself?" Tom Geraghty, and Cathryn Crawford, Angela Coynes, Bruce Boyer.

CATHRYN: There were a bunch of us that worked on his case at different points, law students and lawyers.

LEROY: Unlike the first time, these students and lawyers were fighting the judge every step of the way. Until finally, in one of their meetings, Cathryn Crawford said to hell with it, she's going for the pardon because I deserved it. The next thing I knew, rumors were circulating that I might be one of the guys the governor was considering for a pardon, which was unbelievable. I felt very... blessed... to have something come about. I was all my life living in a hostile environment, but in one day, all the attention was on me, and everybody seemed to be happy for me. It was the opposite of how I felt when I first went to the county. I was at the lowest in my life. Being accused of murder that I didn't commit, thinking I'm going to be executed. And the highest point had to be standing in the middle of the room with everybody looking at me and clapping their hands, and hearing the governor call my name.

There were several dates set for the execution, but you still try to hold on. It's a roller coaster.

You only come out your cell for an hour every day. No cellmates on death row. It's an open cell with the bars up there. Like the old movies. One guy could stand at his bars and talk to a guy three or four cells down. If he wanted to pass something down, he could. I always was friendly with everybody. We tried to get into things that would take our minds off of where we were. To help get through the day. We'd watch television at night, talk to each other, signify, study law. I studied law books, because I'm looking for the connection with all these cases and wondering why these people are ignoring this. It was educational and discouraging, because as you study the law in these cases, it became very apparent that no one really wanted to deal with the Burge issue. I discovered that there are a lot of us here on death row, but the way the courts had it, we were isolated incidents. Why don't we call our lawyers and have them meet and present our cases together?

CATHRYN: Our clinic was primary lawyer for Leroy, but we also worked on Aaron Patterson's case with his lawyers, and then two other lawyers represented Madison Hobley and Stanley Howard. We did start meeting together and coordinating. Tom Geraghty was appointed to Leroy's case by the Supreme Court, but the lawyer that really discovered all of the John Burge, Area Two stuff is this guy Flint Taylor from the People's Law Office. He's a Northwestern alum, and he and Tom began working together.

Did you give up hope at any time?

LEROY: I always figured if I gave up completely, I would just die. You get the hell knocked out of you, you just relax and try to recuperate and figure out what next. My lowest point probably was July twentieth, 2001. It was on my birthday. My lawyer surprised me by bringing my kids to court, but the judge wouldn't allow me to touch them or get a hug or nothin'. That was a low point.

Now I feel obligated to so many. Aside from giving what assistance I can to abolish the death penalty, I feel obligated to help other guys who John Burge has tortured to get out of jail. Find some sort of job, attempt to support myself, and enjoy my kids. And figure my way around what's going on.

How does the world look to me now? I think it's changed for the worse. Observing people's reactions to the governor's decision ... and the way other politicians attempted to manipulate victim family members to destroy the governor's message. You've got a machine that's not working, that kills people ... It just seemed to set up a wave of controversy that I don't understand. Governor Ryan didn't review the death machine in Illinois; a panel of experts in different fields in law enforcement reviewed it. He just decided he wasn't going to be the one to go along with a death machine after it had been proven to be wrong. That's like driving a car with no brakes. But I guess it's OK if you're not in the car. I understand the grief and the anger of those who lost family members. But what I don't understand is how killing someone is going to bring closure. That's not what they're taught in the Bible. The Lord says revenge is his, not for you to seek. A lot of people believe what they believe because the police told them this is what happened. John Burge and his crew lied to the public, just like they lied to the judges in the court. So a lot of people are simply being misled.

What I would personally want to do is talk to at least one youth and turn his life around. Say something that would tip the scales against starting the machine back up. Contribute something positive to society. And make peace.

One more thing I must say. A black guy who first goes through the system, me, for example, saw the system as being black or white. If you're white and you got money, you can get good representation, but if you're black and poor, you're discriminated against. It hurt me to some degree, it gave me a racist attitude. But over the years, those feelings have turned around. Just like there are white people that fight for the wrong causes, there are just as many who fight for the right causes. Somebody like Cathryn Crawford here. I didn't trust her and the others at first because of the experience that I had with the white police and the white judges. I didn't trust them because they were white. I was even wondering if they were sent by the state to help put the nails in the coffin. Over time, it was the same people who I was apprehensive about, and the same little woman, sitting right here, who I didn't trust, who came up with the idea to ask for a pardon as opposed to anything else. Maybe I wouldn't have known that had I not gone through this rewarding experience, and it makes you feel something good about mankind.

TEACHERS

Deborah Bayly

CONDO BUYERS BEWARE. NOISY WHITE TRASH LIVES HERE. It is
a large hand-painted sign, hanging from the wooden balcony of
a two-story house owned by Ms. Bayly and her colleague, Anita.
The neighborhood, on Chicago's North Side, has been blue-
collar and is rapidly becoming gentrified.

She is the principal of Lakeview Academy, an alternative
school—a few rooms in a neighborhood church.

MY FATHER, A PROTESTANT MINISTER ordained in an independent church, started a small school. We were just outside Philadelphia. It was parent-owned and -operated. I was a little kid, one
of seven. Growing up in that family—my six brothers and I—and
being a student in that school played a very important part of what
shaped me. There was a cohesion between what was going on at
home and what was going on at school. It wasn't like a lot of traditional schools where strict things were being taught, with adults
not following their own rules. The people who started that school
were from all different denominations, an ecumenical group. There
was a pretty good Christian philosophy, I think, without a lot of
hypocrisy. There was a very strong ethic in that school and in my
home that all of us were responsible for each other, and that we
were all part of a community. I definitely was imbued with that
philosophy pretty young.

We were living in a conservative part of the country. My father
pushed the school to take black students, way back in the fifties when
the civil rights movement was only just starting. Some people, I remember, were horrified at that idea. But it was something the school
just started doing. My father took a job in Elgin, Illinois, as the
president of David C. Cook Company, which publishes Sunday-
school materials. I graduated from Elgin High School and went to
the University of Illinois in Champaign. The state was giving you

free tuition if you took teacher's courses because there was a teacher shortage. I said, "Great, I'll get free tuition." So I got my teaching certificate. There were some of us who wanted to student-teach in the quote inner city. My student teaching placement was at Marshall Upper Grade Center, in the heart of the black community. We got there in 1968, right after the riots, after King was assassinated. That area was the most heavily destroyed during those riots. It looked like a war zone all up and down.

I student-taught there with a young Irish Catholic woman who had grown up on the South Side of Chicago. We stayed at the Martin De Porres Home. It was one of those graystones, run by an old woman with gray hair and a young black woman. It was for wayward girls who needed transitional living quarters, a desperate need. We just walked to the school every day.

From the first moment I had a classroom of my own, I loved it. [*Laughs*] It was a public school, seventh and eighth grade. We had very, very cynical supervising teachers. There was a black man who carried a loaded gun, got a new Cadillac every year, and told the kids that if anybody touched his car, he'd shoot them, and a white man who had probably started out being very idealistic and had turned very cynical. Both of them should no longer have been teaching. One day some of the kids were talking. I was standing up teaching, but he was there. He would sit up in the front sideways so he could eyeball them to make them behave. We had forty kids in the classroom. On this particular day, the teacher said to this girl to be quiet, or shut up, or whatever. He said, "I drive around, I see what you're doing over at the corner of Jackson and Pullman at night." He basically told her that he knew she was a whore working the corner. This was an eighth-grade girl. I turned to him, I actually did this— I was twenty years old—I said, "Will you please be quiet?" He shut up and he didn't do that anymore. That was a key moment for me. I could see that here was a man who had started out good and lost his hope.

When I graduated, I came back and started teaching in the public schools. I loved it. You can't work with kids if you've lost your hope. I like working with teenagers because to my way of thinking, it's about the last chance people have to make some major changes in their lives. There's always hope for change, but adolescence is the last major period of development, the last good moment to instill hope in them.

It's our mission here to try to bring hope to a group of young people and their parents, who have been disenfranchised by major institutions in this society. If we can restore a measure of hope to these kids and their families then we've done something major, even though there is no way that we can make up for the lost years. [*She indicates some of the students moving about easily, doing their work.*] They're African American, Asiatic, Caucasian—ecumenical. We usually have a small enrollment, twenty or so. When I listen to these students' stories and to their parents, one of the things you hear is that the majority of them did just fine through elementary school. They weren't great students. Some of them had learning disabilities, some had behavior problems, but most of them, you ask them how was school: "Oh, it was fine through eighth, at least through sixth grade." You ask the parents, the same thing. What happened is that they hit high school and the system failed them. They were still babies, and they were thrown into a system that was originally created for college students. They fell through the cracks.

Once they label themselves as failures, trying to restore their self-confidence is going to be an uphill battle. If, by the time they leave us, we manage to get some of these students back to where they were when they left eighth grade, we've done something wonderful. Most of the parents are working class, struggling to make ends meet, many single. Many, though not all, have totally lost hope for their children. They're probably disappointed in their own lives as well.

Laura, Anita, and I are the faculty. [*Laughs*] We're still here. We're the solid, stable staff. I've been at this school twenty-eight years. I like where I live, too—as much as I like where I teach. When Anita and I bought that house, we really liked the neighborhood because it was a mix. There was a Vietnamese and Honduran couple with two young children on one side of us. Mexicans in their fifties, whose sons had just grown, on the other side, a black family next to them, and a poor white family on the other side. It was a total mixture.

Because there were a number of people who didn't work and were on welfare, someone was always around to keep their eye on the neighborhood. I think it made it safer. A man across the street who didn't work sat in his front window all day long and watched. If anything happened, he called the police. People didn't think our neighborhood was safe. We laughed about it. We're a block and a half from the projects, Lathrop Homes. There were little gangbangers nearby, and we knew that.

One of the things I always did was try to learn the names of children in the neighborhood and of the kids who hung out in the alley. When I'd go by them, I'd say hello by name. That had a very powerful effect. Typical teenage boys are hanging out there with their hoods up and their hands in their pockets. They'd say hello back and often look startled. They have nothing better to do than hang around the street corner, and often an adult who walks by them is afraid, and it becomes a vicious circle. All of us should be acting as if the children that we come in contact with are part of our community. But we don't. Either we're not out on the streets, or we're frightened. Actually, most of the kids hanging in my neighborhood have been white kids because it was the poor whites who were still staying in that neighborhood. It's a little more powerful if it's a different race; I understand that. Nonetheless, these kids have been abandoned. As long as the neighborhood was there, and there was a mix of people and we knew each other and spoke to each other, I know for a fact that there was a positive impact on crime. You know that most crimes are committed by people who live within one block of you. As soon as we moved into our house, somebody broke into our garage and stole a number of items. Then I had a canoe stolen out of our garage. We heard the kids over at Lathrop Homes were using it as a sled. It was stolen in the dead of winter.

We got to know the neighbors. One door over was a house where a grandmother had her grandson living with her because the mother had problems. This guy started going to jail when he was about fourteen, and she had a grown son who was in jail for a while. I was certain that was the source of the earlier thefts.

A few years later, we had a young woman staying with us for a while, and she had a little motor bike stolen from the garage. I went over to the son, who was in his early twenties, and I said, "I'm wondering if you could find this motor bike that somebody stole from our garage. It was Edie's and she really needs it to get to school. I was thinking since you know a lot of the people in the neighborhood, maybe you could find it for us." What do you think happened?

We got the bike back. It's the same way you run a school. You don't go to the kid you know did the graffiti and say, "Clean the graffiti." You go to him and you say, "James, somebody sprayed paint on the wall. I wonder if you could take it off." And then James feels like a hero—he's taking it off.

Times change and things change. I'm not a person who looks back too much. If they're going to tear down buildings and put up new ones, so be it. But a developer bought two plots and spent over a year building, and was constantly violating all kinds of codes. Every call that I made to report the code violations, the city did nothing about. Now, this sticks in your craw when people are starting heavy machinery at six o'clock in the morning and waking you up, or leaving a pit and then not doing anything for a year while fetid water is sitting there and everyone is throwing their trash in. The thing that really got my goat was that this developer had the gall to ring my doorbell one day and ask me if I didn't want to sell, and when I said no, he had the gall to ask why not. He was improving the neighborhood. You could hardly enrage me more. That is the arrogance that thinks money makes people better, and I *detest* that attitude. What he was really telling me was, *I'm clearing these poor people out of this neighborhood and bringing in people with more money. I'm improving your neighborhood.* I told him to get out of my face and never bother me again.

But he kept harassing my Mexican neighbors because they were old and they were Mexican. He didn't bother me anymore: *I see this woman is white and middle class and smart, so I'll leave her alone, but I'll keep bothering these ignorant Mexicans.*

Then, my next-door neighbor's husband died. The day the developer found out, he rang her bell. "Now do you want to sell me your house?" She said, "Don't you know my husband just died?" And he replied, "Yes, I do know." [*Pained laugh*] That was July of 2000.

The first buildings in the neighborhood to be torn down and replaced with condos were right across the street from us. Within a period of a year, three of them were sold again. Now it became clear that not only were we going to have people who thought they were better than everyone else, but we were going to have no neighbors at all, because deep down they were transients, building these things as an investment and then rolling them over. And they're all in the same income bracket, all about the same twenty-to-thirty-something age. We've eliminated old people and we've eliminated children. I don't object to change. Life goes on. It is the quality of life.

All these people moving in with four-wheel-drive vehicles, and two of them take up three regular-car spaces. City streets were not built for this kind of density.

These people are flaunting their wealth. Between the pollution and the gas they're eating, and the space they're taking up, they're fine for the suburbs. The suburbs were built for cars. Let them move out there with their SUVs. That was the point of the sign: *Condo Buyers Beware. Noisy White Trash Lives Here.* We hung it the day before Halloween two years ago. Cars were just coming to a halt and people were looking and pointing and laughing. You could entertain yourself by sitting on the front steps for an hour and watching people go by. A plumber came, and he was like, "Oh, man, I'm going to go home and tell my family I worked on the noisy white trash house!" The other thing that fascinated me was that Hispanics have laughed less because they have more of a sense of dignity. My neighbor at first was just horrified that we hung this sign. But then her son and her nieces thought it was funny, so now she just laughs—we're the eccentrics.

At Christmas, I always hang a wreath on the balcony. I took the sign down to hang it. One day, there was a group of boys out on the sidewalk in front of the house, black, Hispanic, one or two white kids. I said, "Hi, guys." They said, "What happened to your sign!?" They were upset that our sign was gone. I had police who came around once on a call and they said, "Oh, as soon as we saw the address, we knew it was the white trash house."

In the meantime, every house on our street but ours and the one next door has been torn down. Establishing roots is very hard and not always possible. People often have to move. When poor people have to move, they have no options. They are simply priced out of a neighborhood. If I move right now, it's my choice. But the poor have no choice. They're moving eight blocks west. I'm thinking to myself, *Boy, your kids are going to pick up and change schools, and in a few years you're going to be uprooted again because you're going to be yuppified out of that neighborhood, too.* But, see, there can be hope even if your circumstances are not the best.

What I find interesting is that people seem to have gotten hope just from seeing this sign. I haven't done a darn thing except to make a joke, but that is something. People need their spirits livened, and there's this person who's standing up to the Man but with humor. There are no happy endings. I cannot really guarantee to any person that their life circumstances are going to be better tomorrow than they are today. I think that faith and hope have a lot to do with each other. Basically, faith is the idea that you go ahead and act on something even though you have no evidence that it's going to happen, and I believe that's driven by hope. The hope is what makes you take the action, and taking the action itself is the important thing. Whether it works or not, I'm not giving up. Hope doesn't die.

I want to say one more thing about hope and what is so important about a tiny little school like this one. Tiny. We have been in existence for thirty years. We have served about five hundred young people in those thirty years. A little under two hundred have graduated. Okay, that's a drop in the bucket. I could be out working the public schools. I'm a powerful person, well educated, articulate, and a certified principal. I could be working in a public school and having an impact on a lot more kids. What I think is important about a little school like this is the same thing we're talking about with my sign. The existence of this school gives teenagers and some parents hope that maybe if they screw up, or if their little brothers or sisters screw up, they can come here. It's the idea that it's here.

To me, symbolism is important. Empty symbols are worth nothing. This school is not an empty symbol. It's a tiny symbol, but a powerful one, even if it only serves a few people. Because at least people think that if they wanted to change, they *could*. Even if they know they won't. Even if it doesn't provide service to massive numbers of people, the *message* reaches massive numbers of people.

I don't know how much longer we'll hold. Money becomes more and more of a problem. But we're here. And as long as we're here, for every extra year, that's another twenty kids who got something good.

Quinn Brisben

He is a retired Chicago high school teacher whose years were spent almost exclusively at African American schools. "I've taught children and grandchildren of my early students." He and his wife Andrea are the only two Caucasians in the community. His appearance is a cross between Colonel Sanders and Santa Claus: "Some of the kids of the neighborhood address me by either name." Though his manner is easily conversational, his sentences, or phrases, all sound declarative. This conversation took place a few days before he was taking off, with several other "troublemakers," for Iraq to "see what sanctions has done to all those kids out there."*

A studious admirer of Wislawa Szymborska, the 1996 Nobel laureate from Poland, he writes poetry, too.

WHEN I WAS A KID, people used to speak about "when things get back to normal," and I said, "When was normal?" For a lot of people, it was before the Depression started with the stock market crash in 1929. But then I talked to people about those times: "No, that wasn't normal, 'cause already we had short skirts, lipstick, and a lot of stuff. The world was going to hell in a handbasket even back in the twenties." Maybe before World War One was normal, so then I talked to the old-time IWW [Industrial Workers of the World] people, and they'd talk about the miserable conditions of being on threshing machine crews and stuff like that, and that wasn't normal, either. I came to the conclusion, fairly early on, that there never had been a normal time, that the good old days never were, the golden age never existed; that you can only go forward. There is no back. So the only thing you can do is try to make the forward as good as possible, and not be too terribly disappointed when you get it.

I worked as a high school teacher, mostly in African American neighborhoods, for thirty-two years, bumping good African Ameri-

---

*On his return from Iraq, he phoned me. "I've come to the conclusion that it's the case of a big bully attacking a small bully."

cans up into the middle class. The result is I finally *do* sort of create a black person with great voting power, and his name is Clarence Thomas, and I don't like it. [*Laughs*] I didn't really expect otherwise. I study history. You are going to get double-crossed by the people you help. This is more or less inevitable. You just keep pushing the next bunch up there until you've got enough new people into the system that you have basically changed the system. Imagine, we now have got a Republican administration and the secretary of state is the most respected person in it, and he's African American. And we've got what looks like, more or less, a permanent African American seat on the Supreme Court. And instead of having two or three African American congressmen, and all of them, black as well as white, crooks, we've got maybe twenty-five or thirty of them, and only half of them are crooks. And every major city in the country has had an African American mayor at one time or another. And there are people in real positions of power, or of influence that I can remember when they were nonviolent students in SNCC [Student Nonviolence Coordinating Committee].

Congressman John Lewis. Ah! This is what I'm looking for. Except now that we've got it, I don't want it. I want *more*. [*Laughs*]

The one thing I know about utopia in advance is, I am not going to be satisfied with it. The important thing is to have fun while you keep working, and do it in such a way that you are true to all your basic ideas.

Sometimes progress does things you don't want. I love being able to shop for books on the Internet, for instance, but the Seminary Co-op, where I walk in to buy my books, has not been able to pay a dividend in the last couple of years 'cause it and a lot of others are going broke.

My wife came down with great news. She listens to NPR while she paints. Jesse Helms was going to *quit*. I've been trying to get rid of Jesse Helms for years. But I remember the people I had in my childhood. I remember Theodore Bilbo. The man was twenty times as bad as Jesse Helms. I've worked with some very difficult personalities in the civil rights movement. One of them was James Meredith. We had a big march after he got shot trying to walk across Mississippi alone. As a joke a few weeks later, we were thinking about drawing straws to see who could get to shoot him again. He was that stub-

born. Which had enabled him to survive at the University of Mississippi. And it's a wonderful thing. He ended up working for Strom
Thurmond. I had a former student who did a wonderful thing, got
a running scholarship out at University of Arizona in Tempe. Good,
upwardly mobile black middle-class Chicagoan. He ended up working
for Barry Goldwater. Barry Goldwater got a bargain—he's a damned
good man. This happens all the time. You just go on from there;
you start over. The thing is, you're never satisfied. You never should
be. The only thing you can do is keep watching yourself so that you
don't turn into your enemies.

I worked with a black woman down in Alabama. She ran voter
registration for the Montgomery Improvement Association. When
George Wallace had tea with Jesse Jackson Sr., Idessa poured. Wallace's wives were either dead or had run off. She presided over this
meeting. This man, in my opinion, was a scoundrel. Nonetheless,
even scoundrels do change, even scoundrels realize that the world
has changed. Most of the world's religions tell you to forgive in a
case like that. Make a little fun of them, but forgive.

My folks were merchants. They had a furniture store. They depended on a farming community. They wanted, eventually, to own
farmland themselves because they were, in a way, Jeffersonian agrari-
ans. They thought that was the only kind of wealth that lasted. By the
time my brother and I were adults—this was in the fifties—we could
see that this was not lasting. You couldn't make a living on a hundred
and sixty acres anymore. I was born in '34. I got married just shy of my
twenty-first birthday in 1955. Their way of the way the world had always been just wasn't going to last. Small independent furniture stores
were not going to last. My mother and father liked the good furniture.
I can remember when World War Two brought prosperity and they no
longer had to sell used furniture. We had a celebration. My father had
a nice store just off the city square. Enid, Oklahoma . . . E-n-i-d. If I
had stayed there, I would have had endless arguments with him. He
was a stubborn man. He never would have moved it out into a shopping center in time. The best thing for me was just to go and try my
hand at something else. My father would have been so terribly shocked
at firms like Montgomery Ward not protecting their own goodwill,
their own trademarks. I can remember when Ford and Firestone were
people's names, and they protected the integrity of those names. Now,

no one protects the integrity of those names. I'm terribly shocked at the decline in capitalist morality.

When people tell me that they are conservative, first question I have is, what do you want to conserve? If you want to conserve the Bill of Rights to the U.S. Constitution, I am with you. If you want to conserve the English language to the point where high school kids can understand Shakespeare plays, I am *very* much with you. Decide what it is that you want to conserve. We have got to make some alliances with some very conservative people. José Bové, that French peasant who bulldozed the McDonald's in France so he could preserve his little Roquefort cheese operation, he's a hero.

When I was a kid, my folks and I used to go to Pawhuska, Oklahoma. Pawhuska is the center of the Osage nation. The old men of the Osage tribe would sit on the town square and comment on everything, especially the weird customs of the whites. Sometimes you'd make remarks back. I used to be fond of very bad-smelling cheese that I would eat in sandwiches. They would sometimes make a friendly remark, but in a kind of doing-the-dozens way, about that smelly cheese. I'd make remarks back about their notorious preference for eating dog meat.

But Wal-Mart came into that area about twenty years ago and killed the town square. They moved everything out to one of these big stores at the edge of town. All the little businesses around the town square—like my parents' furniture store—they all folded. The old Osage could not sit there in the parking lot of the Wal-Mart. That was private property. They demolished a *public space*. Furthermore, my favorite smelly cheese has gone. It was called Liederkranz, and they made it up at a little place in Wisconsin. Kraft Foods bought Liederkranz. And then Philip Morris bought the whole deal. They own Miller Brewery, they own Kraft Foods. Somewhere along the line, some bean counter decided that they shouldn't be in a business that small, making so little profit as making Liederkranz cheese. One of the few things that a good bacteria has done for the human race in the last couple of hundred years is that Liederkranz cheese, and they *lost* the formula. It's just like in the old days when they were enclosing the commons, back in England. The people who are being pushed out are the ones who have traditional ways of doing things. Excuse me if I indulge in an old cliché, but the first real social revolution in the twentieth century took place not in Russia but in Mexico when Emiliano Zapata's followers tried to restore their traditional way of life, and the village boundaries of common land, against the followers of Porfirio Díaz, who called themselves scientific men, *Scientíficos*. It was a revolt against progress that wasn't progress for most people. In our coming revolutions, we've got to be on the side of that guy with his Liederkranz cheese. We've got to be on the side of the Zapatistas in Chiapas who want to preserve their way of life. We've got to be on the side of the town square. We've got to restore the commons. Looking forward a good deal, but also looking backward to see what it is that we don't want to lose.

I'm nearly sixty-seven years old. You're ninety. We personally are not going to have to worry about much anymore. It's the young people who are going to have to worry. At least we can set them some kind of example and point out some mistakes we've made that we don't want to make again. I wish I could get myself back to 1967, '68 and yell at people, "Don't you dare make fun of a hard-hatted workingman again. Don't you dare make fun of a cop, who, if he's honest, is barely making a living. Those are people that should be on your side, and you've got to find ways to talk to them." We all made various kinds of mistakes, and more than that, we made compromises that we had to make.

I worked for the Chicago Board of Education for thirty years, and they were a bunch of crooks. I'm sorry I had to do that, but I'm not sorry that Andy and I were able to raise a couple of nice kids in reasonable comfort. I had to do something. I suppose I could have been saintly and renounced sex and family life. [*His wife laughs.*] I never was up to it. She knows that.

My grandfather had a Ford dealership in Pond Creek, Oklahoma. He thought that machinery was going to erase a lot of social problems, that once they got the self-propelled wheat combines perfected, you wouldn't need these thousands and thousands of hoboes going across the land in threshing machine crews every year that were the heart and soul of the IWW in that part of the country. He says we can do this in such a way that *everybody* prospers. But according to my grandmother, one of the last things he said, sitting on his porch watching the traffic go by, was, "I'm beginning to miss the smell of horse manure." He was beginning to realize that depending on that technology was having unforeseen consequences.

Right now I'm working with groups of disabled people. Why the hell, if you don't have the energy to do more than four hours' work a day, can't they construct a job where you work just four hours a day? I just finished a visit with an architectural designer in Ann Arbor, Michigan. He's got a thing that he holds in his mouth and taps. He's quadriplegic. Why the hell can't you construct a job to use that man's enormous talents? Once you do that, you'll establish the principle that instead of adjusting the person to fit the job, you adjust the job to fit the person.

We may have to start from square one on labor unions again. They have to have as a perspective not just higher wages, but *we're going to control our own jobs.* The IWW, the old-time socialists, are going to be the classics for a movement like that. Trade unions have sold out for some short-range gains. I'm not sorry that out in our neighborhood there's a lot of bungalows that were bought by steelworkers. But I have yet to hear anybody who worked in the rolling mills say that he wanted to pass that job down to his son and his grandson. That was damned hard, dangerous, dirty work. But the thing is, now we start again, we start with the people at the computer terminals, and say this time, "We sold out for a few more cents per hour, and we sold out for a five-day week, which eventually they took away from us again. We settled for half a loaf. This time we don't settle for half a loaf." You gotta have roses along with the bread.

I was in jail in August of 1964. In a southern jail. I went down there recently. The ACLU [American Civil Liberties Union] had launched a suit. That jail amounted to cruel and unusual punishment. They won, and Lowndes County, Mississippi had to tear it down. There's a word called an *oxymoron,* you know, where a statement contradicts itself. The right wing is full of them: "military intelligence," "business ethics." My favorite oxymoron is "revolutionary tradition." That's why hope never dies. I suggest we keep building on this revolutionary tradition, and that we keep on with our hope even though it's only going to be shot down now and again. Most of the things that we hope for don't come about. That's not because we hope for the wrong things, it's just because we're human beings, and, well, if a man's reach does not exceed his grasp, then what's a heaven for (as they used to say in the good old days of dead white males)? You set yourself up some realistic parameters so that you don't get too disappointed when something goes wrong, and you just keep on reaching.

Part III

EASY RIDERS

Andrew McNeil

It was a flight from Lincoln, Nebraska to Chicago. There was a four-hour delay. There were only five passengers: myself, my companion, Steve Robinson; a young woman, busy with her laptop; a young woman dozing fitfully; and a blond, ponytailed kid with a whisper of beard. It was cold at the airport, Nebraska cold. A couple of kids in battle fatigues and rifles at the ready were standing guard, having a slightly hard time of it, what with the delay and the temperature. During the flight, the ponytailed kid was reading a book. In Chicago, as I slouched toward a cab stand, the kid accosted me.

As he remembered it: "That's when I grabbed my book out of my bag and jumped in front of you." He flashed the cover at me. It was Will the Circle Be Unbroken? Delighted, though half asleep, I scrawled a full-page inscription. He told me his name and his work—a bike courier. He was on his way home to New York. After he disappeared somewhere into the vast empty corridors of O'Hare, I cursed myself. I knew I wanted him in my next book—just a hunch—but I had neglected to get his phone number. Damn. After an absurd series of missteps, much like Peter Sellers's hapless detective, Inspector Clouseau, I found him.

I'M THIRTY YEARS OLD. In New York City for a little more than a year, I am a bicycle messenger, a courier. I ride around all day with a big bag on my back and a walkie-talkie radio to talk with my dispatcher. What he does is he just fires off the different pick-ups and deliveries. When we talked the other night, you used the word *searching* to describe some people of my generation. That's what I spend most of my life doing, is experimenting and searching. Being a courier, especially, is an incredible experiment and a search. I'm like a hyperactive mailman. Most of the guys are pretty much new to the country. When I started out on this messenger job, I thought I was gonna be a fish out of water, possibly in a little bit of trouble. There's some bad-ass-looking guys out there. But they all got one thing which is nice. You can wear anything you want. It's mostly black guys in New York. The people who deliver food frequently are Chinese and Mexican guys. The people who deliver envelopes and packages are primarily black guys. It's one of the easier jobs to get, but it's a difficult job to do. You've got to learn the city quick. Everything's about deadlines and speed. There's no greater comfort than in meeting tons and tons of strangers and finding out that time and time again, it's everything you hoped they would be and more. They're similar to me and they're generous and they're helpful. I think we need to be afraid of grizzly bears, not people. If I had a kid, I probably wouldn't encourage that kid to go hitchhiking around until I felt like they were strong, but that's not how I did it. You've gotta go find out.

When you peddle your bike all day, your blood gets pumping, and you're an elite crew because it's kind of a war zone with the cars and the people. And when you see someone else who's doing their bike and negotiating the situation, you've got instant camaraderie. You see them at a stoplight, there's just an immediate connection. You talk about the weather, you talk about whatever. That job can crush you, but once you get on top of it, it really lights you up. And then there's days when the weather is unbelievable, thirty degrees and raining and about as miserable as it can get, and it's freezing and wet, and you see those guys and you've got that and you're sharing it with them as well. And people talk, people talk, they talk a lot of slang.

I don't think I had a single bad encounter. I stopped at one point because there was a black guy outside of a rental car agency, having an argument with his girlfriend, but also shaking her up a little bit. I stopped my bike, but I couldn't really figure out what to do. I don't know if I could fight or what. I thought, maybe if I'm just near them, that'll make that guy uncomfortable. Nobody wants an audience for a domestic dispute. So he starts yelling at me and I've got a big space helmet on, it looks like a motorcycle helmet. I made maybe like a little bit of a storm trooper impression, but I didn't do anything. Now, he's coming at me.

Suddenly, another messenger guy I've never met, short little black guy, stops right up, gives me the biggest toothy grin ever, and wants to get involved. He sees what's going on, like, like we're going to get this guy. The little guy came up and he and I together stood there, and then the little guy talked the right talk and made it stop. You get to do some creative complicated handshake and a big wave, and "See you later, dude." That's what I meant by camaraderie.

I got very lucky in the family department. I could not have a more loving and attentive mother and father. Most of my life when I was growing up, my father was working, I don't know the nature of it, but I always think of it as businessman. He climbed the ladder. My mother was very active in the community as an artist, and she's partly responsible for two different historic preservation districts.

I went to public school in Camden, New Jersey. Very large class. Five hundred in my class. I was pretty intimidated through most of high school. I went to five colleges, from Washington, D.C., to Alaska. Wesleyan University in Connecticut, that's where I graduated. I always wanted to study psychology, and that's what I did. After college, I worked in special education for a while.

In New York, I worked at two different start-up companies, and I lost my shirt both times. I just moved from Hell's Kitchen to Avenue B in New York. It's the East Village. For the next month, I have a curtain for a wall. There's three of us in a two-bedroom place.

I'm just very driven to pursue my own interests. I'm not envious of my friends, a lot of them successful, who are very tied down to more serious, more demanding work. I feel a little bad sometimes for these people carrying around a bit of an anvil. I have a lot of time to pursue my interests and that's what I do. I certainly have got money shortages that are often crippling, but I'm too self-involved to be envious! [*Laughs*] It's up and down.

I bounce around. You might say I'm rootless. It keeps me motivated. I feel alive and charged most of the time, but rootlessness can wear you out, because I end up losing touch with people, and short of money. It's no joke, that's a problem. I often felt that I was born with a lot of privileges, and I was born into a country where there's a world of things to do and it's almost a crime for me not to give it a shot. Why not try it? In the future, I'm looking to stabilize a bit. Teaching psychology, I hope, in my older age.

What was I hoping for as a kid? [*Laughs*] I hope to really, really love someone for my whole life. I hope for a family. I hope for a chance to be myself as much as I can. I think that's why I bounce around. I think it brought more hope to me, the fact that I've been able to find ways in my life to try what I was curious about. It makes me more and more hopeful.

The low moments are since I move around so much. I go months where I'm not in touch with people that I would like to be in touch with. I'm not always lonely, but I just feel there's an emotional isolation to really doing what most of the people I love aren't doing. I've got to readjust and really tune in to my friends and my family when I see them, otherwise we might not have a lot of things in common.

There's a great lightbulb feeling when I get that next shock of inspiration. And it's a blissful streak. It must be pure hope because I don't have a single thing I could put out here as evidence that it's going to work out, but I feel it will.

Michael Oldham

We meet on a corner in Uptown, under the El. A bicyclist, he is in colorful attire. His helmet is especially dazzling. "That's a G-i-r-o. You pronounce it like hero. *Made in Italy. The bike clothes that I wear, it's made for riding. If you're sweating and perspiring a lot, it breathes."*

I'M FORTY-NINE AND A RADICAL. Most people think that I'm odd and different.

When I was a lot younger, I didn't want to be like all my male relatives. I'm Irish. English, Scotch, and Welsh. That's what my dad told me to tell everybody when they asked what nationality am I. So my relatives are hot-tempered. They're easily flared up and they're prejudiced. Didn't like blacks or any other nationality except their own. A lot of that was in me, but I didn't really want to be that way. My father's family were Masons.

My dad was a regular blue-collar worker. The last thing he retired from, he delivered juice on a route. We moved out of the city when the white flight started in. That would have been at the beginning of the sixties. We moved to Des Plaines, then all the way out by Golf Mill before Golf Mill was even there. We bought a little house for sixteen thousand dollars. I lived out there most of my life. Because we moved, I was always a year older than everybody in class. That's another reason why I didn't fit in. The area out there wasn't your typical suburb where all the houses are the same. Everything was far apart. So any friends that you had were far away. I was an only child, too.

My mother rode a bike to work, so she inspired me to ride, too. She used to clean people's houses. People like you. My family was a lot like Archie Bunker's family. My mother was like Archie's wife. She went along. Anything that had to be said, my dad said, just like Archie Bunker, only it wasn't funny at all. My dad had no sense of humor. My father was the kind of guy that started real early in the morning, like four or five o'clock, and would come home after work about three o'clock, lay on the couch, read the paper, fall asleep until dinner, have dinner, go back on the couch, fall asleep until it was time to go to bed, and then get up early. Whenever I'd ask him something, he would yell at me, "Just go look it up in the dictionary or encyclopedia." He didn't pay any attention to me. I grew up on my own. I would skip out of school as often as I felt like. The only thing that I liked was art. I got straight A's in art all my life. I graduated from high school in 1971, moved into the city, away from my parents. I was real scared of the city. It's the deep, dark place. I had to start changing, because I had to put up with all the city people. I had to start thinking different about people and not being prejudiced, putting up with people that I'd never been around very much before. That was really hard.

The protest times started big about 1967. I'm getting closer and closer to eighteen, and I'm getting really scared along with the other guys my age that we're gonna go and get killed, 'cause everybody was getting killed then. So what we did was decide not to go because we all believed it was an unjust war on the other side of the world.

I was real into bike riding, and none of my friends liked bike riding. I would just ride a long distance and hang out by myself. I'd meditate, try to figure things out in my life, because I'm getting closer and closer to eighteen.

There was a record store in Evanston. That's where guys my age were, guys worried about the same thing. All the latest rock-and-roll records, Beatles, Led Zeppelin, Pink Floyd. We were radical hippies. Oh, yeah, growing my hair out. This was when we had the big rallies downtown. We all wore black and made coffins and marched. All working-class kids. Their fathers didn't care about 'em or nothing. Their fathers were World War Two vets. They would want you to go to war. But the war they went to was a good, just war. Not Vietnam. But they don't know that. To them, war is war.

I was very lucky. I never got drafted. I always went out and got the mail from the mailbox because my dad wouldn't get up off the couch. All of a sudden there it is, from the draft board. I opened it up and I didn't have to go. My number was very close. I had no hope at that time. I didn't know what to do.

Now it's 1972, '73. Bad winter. Couldn't get a job 'cause the economy was real terrible. Finally got a job delivering auto parts.

I did that until I met the Jesus People in '74, after the sixties were over. Everything was dying out and there was no causes left. That's when all of us just split up.

They were real down-to-earth people, just like me. They were hippies, just like me. But they were a missionary group in Uptown at Faith Tabernacle. They lived in the basement. I'd see them all the time, and they were always telling me, "Why don't you just come by and have dinner, come and talk? Don't be afraid—just see what happens." The other guys that worked in the auto parts store, they always made fun of them. "Ah, them dirty, goofy, hippie Jesus People, you don't want to go over there." But I worked up the guts enough to go see 'em. I remember driving up to the building, pull the door open, and there's a whole 'nother world inside. They're all going around real happy and real fun, and having dinner and talking and everything. It's like a family. Another hippie commune is what it was like. Born-again Christians. At that time, the Jesus movement was real big all over the world. So I went, was born again, got saved, went home, and thought about everything I was doing. The next weekend I just moved in with them. Being born again, it's just accepting the way that the Lord wants you to do things, instead of your own way. That's exactly what I needed, because I had nothing going for myself. I had no plans, no nothing. If I wouldn't have made that change in my life, I would have just done drugs and stuff like I was doing, and ended up who knows where.

At that time, they printed a little magazine they handed out on the streets. That's what we did to get money. We never had very much money. Eating was no big deal. The Lord managed to provide everything we needed. We lived on bare minimals, but we really depended on God to help us. We just depended on getting change from people on the street. We would go out to the airport and talk to people, or just walk around anywhere in the city where there was a lot of people and ask them if they would like to talk about the Lord. Because at that time, the economy was so bad.

I still consider myself part of the Jesus People, but I don't see the people at the church anymore. Right now, I'm more or less just searching my own self. I'm going through another change, is what it is. I like going through changes. In this world, everything that happens, death and plagues and war, that's the way this world is supposed to be. This isn't heaven. It never was meant to be heaven.

This is our test in life: if we're gonna choose to live for Him and His ways, or if we're going to choose to live our own way. There's nothing He can do about that, because he gave us the ability to make a choice.

My hope lies in what happens after this. It's not even a hope, it's an absolute positive knowledge that I'm going to be with Him after this is over. Because I've accepted him into my heart, I'm born again. I know I'll be there, no matter what. Hell is what you choose if you don't choose God. That's the tricky part that a lot of people don't understand. God doesn't send us anywhere; we send ourselves there.

I feel a lot more peace in my heart about a lot of things now. The gift of understanding, I guess you could call it. It's the understanding that where heaven is, that's where God is, that's the actual real reality. This life here is the crummy reality. This one isn't meant to last. It started with the Garden of Eden, where everything was perfect, and Adam and Eve were absolutely perfect, but it degraded from there. And we're seeing the end. We're close to the end. We should really feel honored to see this point in reality. Because we're closer to the end than anybody else in the past has ever been. This will all be gone, and the devil will be gone, and all the evil will be gone, and there will be nothing but good.

Dr. David Buchanen

He is thirty-one.

IN THE SUMMER, SPRING, AND FALL, I bike to work. In the past, I used to see patients on bicycle, out in San Francisco's Golden Gate Park. I would bike out there with medicine and supplies. Every week I had a clinic in the park. My patients were homeless people who lived in the park. There was plenty of business to keep me busy. This was 1997 through 1999. Most of the patients I see today are in Chicago homeless shelters around the city. Sometimes I ride my bike to the shelters, but once I get there, we have a traditional clinic set up. I'm employed by Cook County Hospital, and I work in a lot of different places. I also do teaching and research on homeless populations.

I grew up in western Pennsylvania, in a little town named Beaver, forty-five minutes outside of Pittsburgh. My father was a science teacher in the high school, and my mother was a social services administrator. When the steel mills were closing down, there was a lot of unemployment in that area, up to fifty percent. So in the mid-eighties we moved to Evanston, Illinois. My dad got a job as the head of the science department in the high school in Evanston. At an early age, I remember my mother taking me to these evenings where they would have people with mental illnesses come, sort of a night out for people with mental illnesses, and I would help people out. We would play games and have dances, and so that idea of volunteerism was put in at a very early age.

When I was growing up, I had no idea what I wanted to be. I was very good at math and science. I ended up going to MIT [Massachusetts Institute of Technology] because it just seemed like the place to be. Once I was there, I got interested in economics, but I really wanted to get out in the street and do something. I honestly had never thought about going to medical school up to that point. I was kind of at a crossroads. At the time, I had no idea what I was getting into. [*Laughs*] It turned out to be quite a lot of work.

When I was applying for medical school, I thought I would be a

shoo-in because the person interviewing me was in the social medicine department. It turned out that she had been beaten down from
years of work within the medical profession. I told her about my
dreams and ideas about providing medical care free of charge, about
seeing all people regardless of their ability to pay. Her comment was,
"People will try to stop you from doing that." The way she said it
ended our conversation. [*Laughs*] It wasn't a point of discussion. She
felt that I was very naive. That was at Harvard. [*Laughs*] I understand
where she was coming from. Going through medical school is a very
intensive process. There's something that they call the hidden curric-
ulum. Going through the process of becoming a doctor removes
certain parts of you. I remember very well meeting my classmates at
the beginning of school, and feeling like I'd never been with such
incredible people with such a range of experiences. By the end of
medical school, everyone looked the same. You're expected to work
eighty hours a week, and you don't really have time to experience
other things in the world. So eventually, the things that you used to
care about on a daily basis start to fade into memory.

But my own hopes were still there. Sometimes, on certain days,
though, my goal was just to get through the work I had to do. It
was hard to think beyond that, honestly. Only at times when things
were quieter was I able to recollect my vision of myself as a doctor.
Another disappointing crossroads for me was having an adviser in
medical school who advised me against going into a primary care
training program. Primary care is focused on outpatient medicine,
general practice, closer to a family doctor. Primary care is the first
person you would see if you were sick. The adviser suggested that,
because of the feeling in the academic community, the valuable thing
to do would be to specialize and become a cardiologist, or a critical-
care doctor, or a pulmonologist, a specialist. For me, I knew that if
I became a pediatric surgeon or something, I wasn't really going to
be able to follow through on the kind of dreams that I had. I chose
to go to a residency that was focused on primary care, at the University of California, San Francisco, even though my adviser recommended against it.

One of the things that I set up for myself was going out into
Golden Gate Park a half day every week on my bicycle with medi-

cines. More than anything, that really provided the inspiration for me to continue with my original idea of being a doctor.

Usually, if you work in a clinic, people come to you. Whereas if you're doing outreach in the park, you go up and offer your services. It's a different kind of playing field. I found it exciting work. But I was excited, too, about coming back to Chicago after my training was over. My home is here. I always had a dream of working at Cook County Hospital because it has the reputation for doctors interested in more than just patient care, but in the care of whole communities, and public health. It started out as a dream, as a hope, and now, doing the work on a day-to-day basis is different because there are a lot of details I couldn't have imagined. San Francisco had a lot of homeless people who had traveled there from other areas, who decided, "If I'm going to be homeless, I might as well be in San Francisco." They were all certainly poor, and they had a lot of health problems that related to poverty, but there was a certain energy there, back from the days of the sixties, and all the things that happened in San Francisco back then. On a warm sunny day in Golden Gate Park, I would come upon a crowd of a dozen homeless people, all sitting together, and it looked like they were having a good time. I don't think anyone chooses to live on the street in Chicago, especially in the winter. The total number of homeless people in Chicago is a lot higher, and their situation seems much more desperate.

Ten years ago, homelessness was in the newspapers. It would be front-page news that the number of homeless people is growing. Now, no one seems to notice or care that this is happening. I feel like society's come to accept homelessness as something that can't be solved. There are many places in the world that don't have this problem. It's upsetting to me to know that there is an alternative— support for public housing—and people have decided to forget it. Real, true concern about affordability is an alternative. Certainly national health insurance. Homeless people die at rates three or four times higher than the rest of us. The current trends in policy around homelessness are to criminalize the daily activities of homeless people. If you sleep outside, that's a crime. You can be put in jail just for not having a place to stay.

People get to be homeless in lots of different ways. As a doctor,

I see more of how people's medical illnesses lead them to be homeless. There are lots of routes there. Unfortunately, the biggest demographic area that's growing among the homeless is homeless families. One of the things we do at Cook County is have homeless people come and talk to the doctors in training and tell their own stories, what their experiences have been like on the street, and their difficulties in getting health care.

I remember this one woman. She was raising five of her grandchildren because her daughter was addicted to drugs and couldn't care for her kids anymore. She was sixty years old, five kids, and she's on TANF, Temporary Assistance for Needy Families, a new welfare program. Now, there are time limits on how long people can get assistance, for five years. Hers are running out and she is being told that she has to get a job, despite the five kids, the oldest of whom is nine. She has very minimal job skills. Like many of the African American people in Chicago, she grew up down in the Mississippi Delta, and only finished eighth grade. The kind of money she could make by working wouldn't even cover the cost of providing the child care for her children. So she's in a shelter and it's hard to see how she could get out of that situation in any way that's being proposed by any of the politicians. She would like to work, but the thing is, she has five kids.

Today I work on a public policy planning group called the Chicago Continuum of Care, with a lot of the executive directors of homeless service organizations—shelters for abused women and SROs. Our goal is to end homelessness in Chicago by 2010. I don't know whether we'll achieve it. But it gives me a lot of hope just to sit in a room with that many talented people and decide not to focus on one little change in legislation, but on an end to homelessness in the city. One of the greatest pleasures in life is to have a dream of something you'd like to do and to be able to live that out. I do. I'm a lucky man.

ANYPLACE I HANG MY HAT

IS HOME

René Maxwell

"My name is René Maxwell, like Maxwell House Coffee, good to the very last drop, and there ain't nothin' wrong with the last drop." He is fifty-two years old and lives in a row house in Cabrini Green, a "notorious" public housing project on Chicago's Near North Side. It was in the process of being demolished by the city at the time of this conversation.

I WAS BORN AND RAISED in the Ida B. Wells housing development on the Southeast Side of Chicago. When I was in high school, I was a wrestler. I had a chance to wrestle with one more notable than me, the famous Mr. T. I was on the same team as him.

My mother was like a homebody person. My father worked to take care of the family; he was a butcher. There were eight of us children. We lived in Ida B. Wells because it was low-income housing. It was decent, it was safe, and it was affordable. The idea with public housing was that you would stay there up until you can do better, get on your feet, and then you would move out so that someone else could come in and go through the same process.

I got involved with the Coalition to Protect Public Housing in 1997. At that time, I didn't have any idea that the Chicago Housing Authority had a transformation plan, which is really, a lot of people say, Negro removal. I never thought that the City of Chicago would implement a plan that would displace poor people out of their communities. I kind of held back for a minute because it's hard to believe.

The coalition is a watchdog group for homeless people and for those who live in public housing. The Chicago Housing Authority, in shifting residents around from one project building to another, leaves them hopeless, you know? It seems like the hope has been drained out of their bodies.

The Roosevelt Hotel was a transitional hotel that housed men and women for very little rent. They closed it up about two years ago, and right now they're rehabbing it into a high-price rent place, like $895 a month. That's the minimum. There were a hundred and seventy people living there when they closed it. They are now homeless. They drifted off just like ashes in the wind. We never had a tracking system of where these people might be.

I was involved in what we would call a tent city at Millennium Park. We stayed there overnight and then we took it down. Some of the people who were evicted stayed in those tents. We wanted to spotlight what's happening right here in Chicago, right under the nose of our good mayor Richard M. Daley.

Some of these people might have went under Wacker Drive, living under the drive. Some of those hopeless people who joined us, they're beginning to speak out. Instead of being silent like they were before, hope has brought a voice to them. Now they're making a hundred-and-eighty-degree turn to where they're doing things to help themselves. Later today, I will go back to the West Side of Chicago, to the Rockwell Gardens, a public housing development, and begin to set up a meeting with the residents. One of the lawyers from property law will come and speak to them about the hundred-and-eighty-day grievance notice that they can file so they won't have to move into housing that they don't choose to go in. I know I'm going to stay on the forefront of it all until they have somewhere to live.

A lot of the time, we hear certain things that is going on in Cabrini Green. But there are things that happen that we never hear of it. Jackie Taylor is one of the playwrights that Chicago has today. The Black Ensemble. She was born and raised in Cabrini Green. You have Ramsey Lewis, came out of public housing, Cabrini Green. Curtis Mayfield came out of Cabrini Green. Residents who live in Cabrini Green are just like residents who live anywhere. We have— the great majority—decent, hardworking people. But Cabrini Green is where the developers want that land so bad. Where we sit at right now, that land is worth billions and billions of dollars. It's close to the Loop and the Gold Coast. The Gold Coast is one of the richest communities in the city of Chicago. It's millionaires and yuppies. But it's a fear because there's African Americans that live maybe half a mile away. The developers are talking about condominiums starting at $425,000, just one unit. And we know that no one who lives in the Cabrini Green community can afford nothing like that.

When I leave out my apartment every morning I just see a mixed-income community. I see where we got the rich people inside of it—a whole circle of condominiums—and I just feel like we're right in the center of that community. The developers have built a community within a community. There's an outer shell and we're the inner shell. [*Chuckles*] And they want to see the inner shell go. And they don't care whether we are fellow countrymen or not. They're thinking about that big dollar sign.

There used to be right there on Division and Orleans a Little League baseball field where African American youth used to play. Now, if you go over there, they're building condominiums on that very same land. We're trying to find other programs for those kids who have been overtaken by the love for money. [*With fervor*] Sometimes you have to ask yourself, how much money is enough? You own islands, you own condos, you got places all across the United States. You're not through? You mean, you don't want to see anyone progress other than yourself? Where does the buck stop at? We must continue to fight against the greed. Really and truthfully, you can't take anything with you.

Dierdre Merriman

"I'm an immigrant from Ireland, who is disabled, a recovering alcoholic, and has a mental illness. But I have a dang good attitude."

It's a single room, bathroom attached. The building has about a hundred apartments. The security guard would not allow me in unless she came down. She appeared in the lobby, seated in her wheelchair, greeting me effusively while leading me to her apartment. All sorts of books scattered about: Alex Haley, Stephen King, John Irving . . .

IT'S NOT THE BEST. But it's home. This is my little cave. This is my place I can go where nobody can come in unless I say so. It's my security and I love it. I love to read. I've read since I was a little girl. My mother always told me, "As long as you can read you'll never be lonely." This is my sanctuary. Everybody lives here, all kinds, all races, all addictions, all types. There are drug addicts in the building, drug dealers in the building, alcoholics in the building, recovering people in the building. This floor and the floor below is part of a program that I'm in. I can only live here for two years. The idea is to get you on your feet, to learn how to live independently again. For the last few years, I have been either homeless or in a rehabilitation center for my alcoholism. The rest of the tenants are just independent people who pay regular rent.

I'm from Dublin, Ireland. When I was a little girl, my parents were both drinking alcoholics. My husband died when my children were one and three. Two years after he died, I was ready for a change, to start a new part of my life, so I came over here to live. I was drinking at the time. Big time. All my family were worried about me and nagging me to watch my problem. I decided that it would be much easier to go to America because I could drink in peace.

My brother was already in Batavia, a suburb of Chicago. I was thirty. I kept drinking, and things went from bad to worse. Finally, I lost my children. My brother took them, thank God. I ended up out on the street for about two years. Summers and winters I spent under plastic until the cops would move me on, and then I'd find another place to live under plastic. I stayed in shelters and things like that. You make friends when you're homeless. You have a certain circle of friends. One day, one of our friends came into a settlement and he took us to a hotel to stay the night. That was the night my neck was broken. My boyfriend stomped on the back of it.

I had no feeling from my neck down; I was quadriplegic. By the time I left the rehabilitation centers, I was able to walk with a cane, but they knew that that wouldn't be for very long. I went to live with a friend, and they were all drinkers, too, so that was cool for me. We all drank together every day. For about a year, that's all I did, was drink and look at television. Finally, I don't know what possessed me or why—I have no answer to this—but I was at a party where beer was free. Free beer! That's an alcoholic's dream. But for some reason that day I decided I'd had enough. This was over a year ago. I went to the emergency room and I told them was feeling suicidal. I had attempted suicide about three months before that. They admitted me, and I went up to the nut ward for about two weeks. I've never had a drink since.

My children are now living back in Ireland with my brother. They're sixteen and eighteen. I hadn't seen them or spoken to them for over six years. We now are in communication. I'm in contact with my whole family, who didn't know if I was alive or dead. We write back and forth, and we call each other. I'm going to Truman College, studying psychology and journalism.* Right now I'm doing creative writing, and theater, and psychology. I want your job! I want to be like the next Mike Royko, only better.† And I will be, too. I'll be rich and famous someday. I know it.

I write about me. I always write with humor; I can't help it. I'm a positive person. My life was very miserable as a child, because both of my parents were drinking alcoholics. I had to be responsible for my three brothers and my sister. I never had hope as a child. I straight went into drinking, so I never had hope then. No alcoholic has hope. I didn't realize until you brought it up to me that since I've been sober, that's exactly what I have, is hope. There's nothing

*Truman is a community college in Uptown.
†Mike Royko was the most celebrated and widely read Chicago columnist.

I can't do now. I'm in charge of my life, I know what I want, and I'm prepared to do whatever it takes to get it. I couldn't do any of that if I was drinking. I was a registered nurse when I left school. I qualified for nursing in 1977 in Dublin. But I was drinking at the time.

I wasn't that far progressed in my disease. For some alcoholics it takes a long time. I married a great guy. He was a patient of mine when I was a student nurse. He wasn't an alcoholic—he never drank more than two pints. I didn't like him at first because he was so full of self-pity. He didn't like me because I was so bossy. He had cancer and had had a colostomy performed and he was hopeless. Everybody was encouraging him to feel sorry for himself. He was only eighteen, and everybody was saying, "Oh, poor Winston, poor Winston, that's terrible to happen to a boy so young." I was eighteen, too. I felt that is the most stupid attitude to take with this kid. He's never going to learn anything that way. When I found out they were sending him home the next day, I took him to the bathroom and locked him in with me and said, "Now, you're not going home till you change your own colostomy bag." He had never even looked at it. How was he going to function that way? I told him he couldn't leave the bathroom until he looked at the bag and changed it. When he did, he was like, "Is that all it is?" I said, "That's all it is." I next saw him at my graduation dance. He was with another girl, would you believe. He looked fantastic. After that, we dated exclusively. We had just had our second child when the cancer came back, and he died a year later.

In the beginning the marriage was fine, but I was drinking more and more. When you're an alcoholic, you don't just drink because you're unhappy. You drink for any reason. If you're an alcoholic, you drink 'cause it's raining, you drink 'cause it's not. You drink 'cause the sun's shining, you drink 'cause it isn't. You drink 'cause it's daytime, you drink 'cause it's nighttime. You don't need an excuse. I went to hell in a handbasket. I was drinking more and more and more, and that's when I came over to America. My drinking was so bad, and I was mentally ill, too. I didn't know that. I was so sick in my alcoholism that I thought my life was a challenge. You got up in the morning and the challenge was to get enough money together somehow to have enough for beer and cigarettes. You met the challenge of the day. I thought that was great. Now I hope to be a well-known writer. But the condition is reversing itself, which I knew it would. That's why I'm back in a wheelchair.

I went everywhere on a cane; I can go anywhere on a wheelchair. I was down in the South Loop this morning. I took the bus.

I don't really want to be rich, but I want to have enough money that I don't have to worry about paying the bills, or I can buy something if I want to.

Social Security, disability—it's just enough to live on. The last thing I wrote was about the five people I would like to be if I wasn't me, not five particular people, but five roles in life. A pathologist. Tigger out of *Winnie the Pooh*. He's totally manic-depressive, but he's always on the upswing, he's always going around maniacally happy. He has nothing to do all day, and if ever there's a problem, it always works itself out in the end. I like his joyful innocence.

I get up and go to the café for breakfast, the Inspiration Café. It's a café for people who are up against it. The food is always free. You go in and you can have breakfast seven mornings a week. You can have dinner four nights a week. From Monday through Friday, you can go in and warm up, you can hang out, you can have coffee. There are case managers there. Everybody has a case manager. They will help you find housing, they will help you find work. I'm going to be on the board of directors there pretty soon. There's a spot coming open soon, so they asked me if I'd be willing to take it. I have a lot of responsibility. Last summer, I took a volunteer course for forty-five hours. Now I'm a state-certified rape victims' advocate.

I still have some friends back in St. Charles.* They're still drinking alcoholics, and I don't think they know what to make of me. When I moved into Chicago first they were very, very worried about me because they felt I had no street smarts and no savvy, and I'd be eaten up and spat out by the big city. By the time I came in here, they had me terrified. I was scared to death. They kept telling me, "You'll be knifed on the street, you'll be robbed," and all the rest of it.

I've had a lot of adventures. Everybody in the neighborhood knows who I am, and they treat me really well, black, white, dope dealer or not. I was walking with my cane to the café one morning, and this man tried to rob me. He went to grab my shoulder bag, and

*An old community thirty-five miles west of Chicago.

I said—I don't know what possessed me, but I got right up in his face and I said, "Do I look stupid to you?" He stopped dead and looked at me. I said, "Look at me, I'm a cripple. Do you think I'm going to carry any money around so you can have it? Don't be ridiculous." All the people came out of the buildings, homeless people and everybody, and he ran away. And they go, "He didn't hurt you, did he?" And I'm like, "No, he didn't." And this one black man said, "Nobody better mess with you, we all know who you are. You're the clean white lady with the cane." So that's who I am in the neighborhood, the clean white lady. They keep an eye out for me.

The human race is a strange mixture of everything. You have some of the nicest, kindest, sweetest people, who have absolutely nothing, and some of the richest, richest, richest people who wouldn't give you a red cent. And then you have some people who have absolutely nothing that are horrible, some rich people who would give you the shirt off their backs. The ignorance of some people amazes me, the kindness of others blows me away. You have to take people as they come. If you have expectations, you're gonna be disappointed. I try not to judge people.

If somebody had told me a year and a half ago that I would be where I am today, I'd have called them a liar. I have come through so much and fought so hard to get where I am today, to where I like myself, I like my life. I have not maybe everything I want, but everything I need. I have never, ever in my life been able to say I was content, and I am.

You said you like yourself. That's a big one.

As a kid, I never liked myself. I always thought there was something wrong with me. Now I like myself, and I'm confident of who I am. Even if I don't get rich writing, there's always a sugar daddy, you know. . . .

Do you have a special friend?

I don't have a boyfriend. I don't need one. If Prince Charming comes along, that's cool. If he doesn't, that's OK, too. It doesn't matter. I'm sufficient to myself. It took me forty-two years to get here. I actually enjoy life. I love life. Life is so much fun. I'm full of hope today, yes, I am.

Alderwoman Helen Shiller

Uptown is probably Chicago's most multicultural community. Before World War Two, it was a middle-class neighborhood. Since then, it has become a way station for new arrivals: Appalachians seeking work after the mines ran out, African Americans, Native Americans, Latinos, Asians, all more or less residing here, as well as a reasonably energetic artistic enclave. Many have settled down, making it their permanent residence. Though transients still call it home, there is the undercurrent of tension between upscale young couples in the process of gentrifying and the neighborhood old-timers. Developers have found a mother lode in this community. Thus, the battle is joined.

She is serving her fourth four-year term as the alderwoman of Chicago's Forty-sixth Ward. It is, as usual, a busy day at the office: "We are the heart of Uptown." The telephone rings constantly. Her three-year-old granddaughter scurries in, out, and under cluttered desks. On one wall is a large photograph of the late Mayor Harold Washington and herself. Below is the caption Bringing the Dream to City Hall. *On other walls are woodcuts of blacks and whites, a portrait of Martin Luther King Jr., and a huge poster:* An Untold Story: Jewish Resistance During World War Two.

UPTOWN IS A REALLY DIVERSE AREA. Since the Second World War, it's been a place where people have come who had nowhere else to go, who were displaced. In the twenties, it was housing for actors who needed a place temporarily, a small place. There were a lot of very large houses. A lot of six-flats built in those days, during the forties, were converted to smaller units. Six-flats became twelve-flats or twenty-units. After the war, a lot of veterans came here. People also began coming from different countries, of different racial and ethnic backgrounds. Many of the Japanese who were interned in California came here. After the Korean War, a lot of Koreans came here. In the fifties, black people came up from the South and got jobs in the steel mills on the South Side. There was a small but very vibrant black community up here, as well as many poor whites from Appalachia escaping the poverty at home.

Many of those displaced said they just didn't want to be displaced anymore. As the city made development plans for this area to change, the people who lived here said, "We're going to stay and be part of the changes." So gentrification here was a longer time coming. But it has come.

Single people, young couples. People who have money. You have a division because you have people who have been here for a long time, who have fought hard for improvements, to be put on the map, to get city services. Once that happened, it became attractive to developers. So housing became much more expensive. People with more money have moved in, and there's often a divide. There are also many people who really want to be in a diverse area and love this community. I have my supporters and I have my detractors.

I was a student in the sixties, engaged in the civil rights movement, anti–Vietnam War protests. I'd come from New York to attend the University of Wisconsin. It was an exciting time. A lot of active students wound up in different cities and communities as organizers. I chose Racine, Wisconsin. I spent three years there. We had developed a legal clinic and we had a whole health program, but the city was too small. I had, of course, heard about Uptown in Chicago, and the challenges. So I wound up here in 1976.

I waited tables. I did photography, took pictures for attorneys. Ultimately we started our own print shop in order to print our own newspapers and magazines. Originally we were called the Intercommunal Survival Committee. Then we formed a broad community group called the Heart of Uptown Coalition, which involved thousands of people in the community. I ran for alderman of this ward in 1978. I was terrified. I was very shy, afraid to speak to more than five people at a time.

I won the primary, but not with fifty-one percent of the vote. We had a runoff and I lost by two hundred votes—to a machine-backed candidate. We were bringing fresh ideas, but we were not experienced in fighting the machine on election day. I swore I'd never run for alderman again. There was so much racial baiting that it was terrifying. I was called names. In one building on Lake Shore Drive, they said I was married to a Puerto Rican in jail for murder. In another building, that I had five black babies. My posters had black paint all over them with racial epithets. It was very disturbing.

In 1983, I did not run. The next time around, Harold Washington was running for mayor, and I had been very active in encouraging him to do so. But there was no way I was going to run for alderman. Instead I agreed to coordinate this ward for Harold's mayoral campaign. My campaign in 1979, about which I was so upset, paled in comparison to the campaign against Harold. I still have a copy of the cartoon the police were circulating about him—just horrible stuff—but he won. It was so unexpected. I learned my lesson. What was I complaining about? What I learned was that had we just put a little more effort into it, we actually could have had an aldermanic candidate.

I ran again in 1987. There were several reasons for doing that. The machine alderman who won in 1983 had a chief of staff who was engaged in racial organizing. There were white gangs up here. One of them he helped organize into a consciously racially white-power gang. They hooked up with both the Klan and the Nazi Party. They recruited the son of someone from the Black Lung Association. He was illiterate and did not know what a lot of the stuff was he was being recruited to. When he found out, he said he was going to quit. They told him they'd kill him if he quit. He quit anyway. He was dead a week later. The head of this group, his fingerprint was found on the gun. Because he was a juvenile, he only received six months' time.

Harold was mayor, and he was harping on me to run for alderman. There were a lot of things happening in the community, but people weren't getting any services. People who were living in rental units were being threatened by condominium conversions when we had no protections at all about that, not that we have many now. We were on the quick track to displacement. I decided I had to run. The council had gone from twenty-nine to twenty-one against him to twenty-five to twenty-five. Harold needed that twenty-sixth vote. That was 1987. I ran, I won, and became the twenty-sixth vote. So for the first time, he could finally get some of his appointments made. I've been elected three times since then. The next election is 2003. I think I'm fine in this ward.

Chicago has become overall a less and less affordable city for people. It's more and more expensive to live here. And our community expresses that as well. People are being ejected from the community because they can't afford to stay here. It has been happening citywide as well. We continue to have a problem with homelessness. We have an extraordinarily small rental community of housing where we're losing more rental units all the time. They're converted into condominiums, or they're torn down. When Harold was mayor, it was hard fought for. Under the mayor before him, the ratio of money the city controlled for housing was three dollars of city money to every one dollar of private money. Harold turned that around. So when he was mayor, every single dollar of city money leveraged three dollars of private money, which meant we were building more and more rental units. In the last ten to fifteen years, less housing was built that's rental. It's becoming more restricted in terms of your income. Some people have gone back home, wherever that may be. Some have gone further out in Chicago, and some even into the suburbs. They go wherever they can go.

When I first became alderman, there was a developer up here who felt very threatened by me. He hired a publicist to really go after me. Anytime I talked about development without displacement, they would ream me. They went to the press and got some of the most vicious editorials published. Over the years, I worked really hard at making sure that there was some balanced development up here. We've been able to preserve a lot of units of housing. We've been able to turn around most of the housing that was affordable and that was in really bad condition. Plus things have changed. I don't want a community that is just poor people and rich people. We need the whole breadth of people in between. We have to find a way that people who work in the community, the teachers, the social workers, the clerks, are also able to live here if they so choose. I have this discussion with virtually every developer: "Come here and help me figure it out." Some have come up with great ideas that we've actually implemented. Others look at me and say, "You're nuts." Some just brush me off.

The real problem was going through the eighties, *truly* a period of time when people were encouraged to be selfish. Young people were really "Me first is OK." We're facing some of the ramifications of that today. We have to bring back to people their own humanity.

What they say, in effect, is, "You're not good enough to be here. No more low-income houses. More than twenty percent of *you* is too much." Give me a break. When you say you're doing housing for people at or below the median income, that's *half the city.* [*Her voice rises with passionate indignation.*] For someone to say, "No more than twenty percent of you should live here" is to say, "We want to live in an exclusive community *and you don't fit.*" And you think people don't know that's what's being said to them? They do.

My faith is in the young people who grew up here. We have a whole generation of young people, in their late twenties and early thirties, who have been involved in community activities since they were very young, who themselves have put together a whole summer education program. They do summer school with kids. They use it as a way for the college students to be teaching and getting experience, while working with high school students. And that's been going on for seven, eight years. Many of them have now become teachers, and so the struggle has been to find ways for them to work in the schools in the community. And they're doing it. But their hope will be extinguished if they are prevented. It's like anyone. They have to be allowed to realize that dream. They need to struggle with it and learn and they'll make mistakes. These are young people who have so much heart for the children in the schools because they're their younger brothers or sisters. They themselves almost didn't make it through school; they each have their own story. They're now teachers, and they're struggling to put it together and to put the children first.

They're really quite amazing. I have a lot of hope because they have a lot of hope. This is not easy. This is not a romantic thing. This is very hard, concrete, day-to-day struggle: with yourself, with your families, and in the schools, with the kids and the bureaucracy. To be able to figure out how to make something work and do something different. I think that they can show us some things in the system that we haven't figured out. We have to give them a chance to do that.

A PRIEST AND TWO EX-SEMINARIANS

John Donahue

He is the executive director for the Chicago Coalition for the Homeless.

AS A YOUNG MAN, I was at the seminary, St. Mary's, in Mundelein. Monsignor Jack Egan, Father Leo Mahon, and Father Pat O'Malley came to talk to us about the priesthood. Monsignor Egan was organizing on the West Side, Father Mahon was organizing in the Latino community, and Father O'Malley was organizing a priest union. O'Malley wore gray uniforms and construction boots, identifying with the working class. I got it. For me, ministry is organizing.

I became a priest. I worked at Visitation from 1965 to 1971. I was an Irish kid in the middle of a changing neighborhood. Puerto Ricans and blacks were moving in. The pastor was racist, and he didn't want me to work with the Puerto Ricans and the blacks. I remember sneaking out to march with Martin Luther King in Marquette Park. I began to work very intensely with the Puerto Rican community. The Puerto Rican kids didn't know if they were American, and if they went back to the island, they weren't really Puerto Rican. They called them New Yorkinos. Nobody accepted them. So they got involved in the independence movement for Puerto Rico, and the stopping of the U.S. Navy bombing in Vieques, a little island. They bomb there for training. It's become a big issue these days. These kids were working on that issue twenty-five years ago.

Some people who are better off have the luxury of losing hope. But poor people never lose hope. They can't afford to. That's the only thing they can hold on to, and that's where hope springs eternal. Some people say, "How can you continue to work with the homeless and the poor?" That's where I get my energy because they never lose hope.

I was standing on Halsted Street after a policeman shot Nelson Rivera. Four kids stole a car. Nelson, a little Puerto Rican kid, was riding in the backseat. When the cops chased them, they all got out to run, and a cop shot Nelson in the back and killed him. He was fourteen years old. So all of the Puerto Rican kids organized. The Latin Souls and Emerald Knights, these gangs wanted to kill the cop for killing Nelson. So I went out on the street with my collar on, to talk to them, right? One of the ways they were going to get a cop to come into the neighborhood was by throwing a brick through A&A's Lounge, the Irish bar. I was trying to stop them. They threw the brick over my shoulder through the window. The Irishmen come out of the bar and see me standing with the kids. One of the women comes up and spits in my face and calls me a Puerto Rican–lover. So I figured, *I better find out what that means. I want to be a Puerto Rican–lover.* So I went to Puerto Rico, and I learned Spanish, and I worked there for six months in the mountains in a place called Borinquen. It's the native, indigenous name for Puerto Rico.

Cardinal Cody thought I was nuts.* Some of those kids fighting to stop the bombing in Vieques were my altar boys at Visitation. They went to jail. They were among those pardoned by Bill Clinton just before he left office. When you talk about hope, who would have ever thought that under an agreement now with Puerto Rico, they have to stop the bombing in Vieques within five years? This began twenty-five, thirty years ago. Leo Mahon, the priest who was organizing in the Puerto Rican community, started a Chicago mission in Panama. He suggested I go there. In 1971, I went to Panama. I was a priest and the vicar until 1979. This was during the time of Omar Torrijos, when Noriega was the intelligence chief. While I was there, I lived in a squatters community in Panama City, San Miguelito. I squatted with the squatters. I made my own shack, built my own outhouse, bathed with rainwater, no electricity, and began to organize the community for land rights, et cetera. I had buried eight children

---

*He had been Cardinal of the Chicago Diocese and was regarded as somewhat on the conservative side. He was succeeded by the liberal Cardinal Bernardin.

in two months from dysentery because of the water in the community. We didn't have clean water. So we took thirty women down to the national water works, to the decorative fountain, a thing they'd show tourists, and we had them wash their clothes. I was picked up, arrested, and the bishop had to come and release me. I had a personal meeting with Noriega. He threatened to throw me out of the country. Noriega had engineered the death of a fellow priest, Hector Gallegos, in 1971. He was killed because he was organizing a cooperative of coffee pickers in the mountains. They were picking coffee for a rich landowner who would pay them on credit, and then they would have to buy in his company store.

Hector Gallegos began to organize these campesinos to plant their own coffee. At the first meeting, he said, "OK, everybody empty your pockets. Put whatever money you have on the table." They came up with eighteen dollars. And with eighteen dollars, they bought a hundred pounds of salt. They never bought salt at the company store anymore. The next thing they bought together was cooking oil, and they never again bought cooking oil from the company store. Then they bought matches. So the cooperative started. Last summer, I went to Santa Fe, Panama, that's where Hector Gallegos worked. Now the campesinos grow their own coffee, have their own factory, run their own business, and they put the rich landowners' supermarket out of business because they have their own supermarket in town. They have five stores in the mountains. That's going on now. After thirty years, the cooperative, with one thousand three hundred members, does two million dollars' worth of commerce in a town in the mountains of Panama.

Now, here's the connection with the homeless. A guy who was in a shelter in Northampton, Massachusetts, Ron St. Pierre, a homeless heroin addict, fell in love with his case manager, and she straightened him out. They started a coffee-roasting business with homeless people. It's called Café Habitat in Northampton. Last summer, I took them down to the cooperative in the mountains of Panama, and they're now importing the coffee, roasting it, and packaging it, and I have here for you a package of Coalition Café. [*He hands me a neatly wrapped package.*]* The homeless people are now selling the coffee in

---

*It tasted great—as good as Starbucks any day. Better.

Chicago, and we're going to develop out of this a café where we'll have poetry readings, homeless telling their stories and serving people *great* coffee—the coffee from the cooperative in Panama. In 1979, my wife and I had started this cooperative in Panama. She's Panamanian. At forty years old, after so many years of resisting the urges to be in love, I fell in love with Icela Patino, who lived in the squatters' community. My wife and I married, and we came back to Chicago, and while in Chicago I started the Uptown Comité Latino.

I'm still a priest, but they don't let me exercise as a priest because I'm married. I have five Irish-Panamanian kids. I'm not practicing as a priest, but my ministry, remember, is organizing. My job is organizing *hope*. There are people in the community who have lost everything, even hope. But there are people in the community who still have hope. That's the last thing they lose. I'm organizing the hope for change.

In Panama, I was on Betito Guardia's radio program, and people were calling in. They were calling me a rebel priest, a guerrilla priest. One person said, "Why don't you go back to Chicago and work with the poor instead of causing trouble in Panama?" That always stuck in my head. That day the National Guard came to the station and at gunpoint shut the station down, took us out, and arrested Betito Guardia, who had to go into exile.

When I came back to Chicago, I started organizing Central Americans in Uptown for jobs, housing, and immigration rights. We won a thousand jobs in the park district, we won apartments in the Pines at Edgewater, and we won, with Harold Washington as mayor, Ordinance Eighty-five, which threw the INS, the immigration service, out of City Hall. In 1987, Chelin—that's my wife's nickname, little Che—she and I and our then three children moved back to Panama. I went to work for the Jesuits in the rain forest, working with the Native Americans to protect their habitat from the big logging and oil companies. In 1989, the U.S. invaded Panama and went after Noriega but killed a lot of people. My family was on the outskirts of Panama City in a community of resistance. I had come to Chicago to bury my father at the time of the invasion of Panama. I saw Panama burning, and I didn't hear from my family for a week. I went to Miami, and on January first, 1990, I got on a plane back to Panama. I saw the devastation from the invasion. My wife's brother had been killed. My son, who was two years old, when he saw a parachute drop in our community, ran out saying, "Papi, Papi," thinking I was coming home. It was U.S. troops parachuting into the community, and they ran through the houses with guns looking for the enemy. Who was the enemy? We don't know.

By then we had five kids. The Jesuits were paying me three hundred and fifty dollars a month . . . We decided to come back to Chicago again. On July tenth, 1990, we came back. I searched for a job. There was an opening as a director of the Chicago Coalition for the Homeless. I was interviewed three times, the last time by twenty-three people. There were just two of us left. I walked out onto Wabash after this hourlong interview, sweating, and a bird shit on my shoulder. I went to the first bar and said to the bartender, "Let's have a drink, I just got a job." He says, "How do you know?" I said, "Because a bird shit on my shoulder." By the time I got home, they were on the phone saying, "You got the job."

In 1980, the Pope was coming to Chicago to celebrate mass in Grant Park. We were seeing more and more homeless people in the parks, in O'Hare Airport, in the Greyhound station, Union Station. So Les Brown, of Travelers and Immigrants Aid, gathered Catholic Charities, Salvation Army, Travelers and Immigrants Aid together to prevent anything untoward happening to the homeless who were sleeping in Grant Park where the Pope was going to celebrate mass.

But it also coincided with Reagan's Make America Strong: increase the military budget fifty percent, decrease social programs over ninety percent. And especially decrease public housing. That was the beginning of the end of public housing. That began modern homelessness.

In the eighties, when the coalition started, a homeless person was a man. In the nineties, it was a woman of color. In the millennium, children, just like at the turn of the nineteenth century. In the new millennium, the average age of a homeless person is nine years old. This has to do with welfare reform and the demolition of public housing.

For the first years, the coalition demanded shelter. And then we said, "Wait a minute, we're institutionalizing the problem. We have to fight for affordable housing, jobs that pay a living wage, universal health care." And in the nineties, we were able to gain great victories at Presidential Towers. We forced them to open up the doors to homeless people. We were able to get the city to build new single-room-occupancy hotels, like the one your mother ran many years ago, the Wells Grand. We have been able to convince the city that we don't want more shelters, we want housing. We have a statewide campaign called It Takes a Home to Raise a Child. In 1999, we were able to convince the state legislature to pass the Homeless Prevention Act. And this year, we will have prevented over ten thousand families from becoming homeless.

In this current atmosphere of corporate greed being exposed—poor people just want to live in dignity—the hope is that honest and caring people in America will have the guts to change a system that has been so unequal.

My father was a fireman for thirty years, and on his days off, he worked at a music shop delivering televisions and furniture. One day, with his partner, Elmer Cantor, who was a black man, they were delivering a television set in River Forest, and when they got to the door, the woman asked Elmer to take off his shoes, but didn't ask my father to do that.* My father said, "Elmer, this television's going back on the truck. She ain't getting it." I always remember that. I said to my father one night before he died, "Are there any regrets you have?" He said, "Well, I wish I could have told the firemen at the firehouse that I loved opera."

*River Forest is an upscale suburb, west of Chicago.

Jerry Brown

He is the mayor of Oakland, California. In 1976, 1980, and 1992, he was a candidate for president.

I'M A GUY WHO grew up in San Francisco in the '40s, in the '50s. My father is a guy who went into politics about the time I was born. I'm from a traditional middle-class family. My grandmother was very anti-Catholic, though my father became a Catholic later on in his life. I attended St. Ignatius High School, a Jesuit school, then went to a Jesuit college, Santa Clara. After a year, I entered the seminary to study for the priesthood. I took vows of poverty, chastity, and obedience.

I'll tell you why I went into the priesthood. It was in a search for God, a search for the mysterious underneath part of life that is not encountered in everyday existence. I wanted to get at the roots of faith. So I went to the seminary. After being there three and a half years, it just struck me that the stories, the dogmas, were not something that I could literally accept in the way that I had as a child. The obedience, the particular way of life of the Jesuit order, just didn't grab me as it once had. In January of 1960, I left the seminary and went to the University of California at Berkeley. That was before Vatican II, before the great exodus of priests and brothers and nuns. I guess I anticipated by a few years what later became a great rush out of seminaries, out of Catholic schools, out of what had been this great support of the immigrant Church. Nevertheless, even though there were questions in my mind, there was a deep truth in what I learned in the Jesuit seminary.

I showed up in Berkeley just at the beginning of student activism, very much a part of the ferment that I grew up with. Yet between the seminary and Berkeley and Yale Law School, I developed a certain critical way of looking at things that disinclined me to any particular ideological niche. So I have a skeptical eye. At the same time, I have a bedrock confidence in the way our society is organized, in the way I was brought up. It gives me a certain hope, although my critical intelligence tells me that we're in one hell of a lot of problems in the contemporary world.

I'm never satisfied that where I am is where I always need to be, a feeling reinforced in the Jesuit order because the vows of poverty were meant to emulate the friars, for instance, of Assisi, St. Dominic, the Apostles. This was a way of life in contradiction to the world. This was what they taught: the cross represented a contradiction. Even though there's the Roman Church and all that wealth, young novices are taught the pursuit of a nonmaterialistic world, to transcend the selfish. That call certainly has remained with me. I don't have the right words, but I do think, and I feel, that the material world is not the ultimate resting point for the human mind.

In the sixties, there was a sense of reform in the air. We were going to end poverty. The country would end segregation. We would advance to a more enlightened state. And we would do that through government. We would transcend mere profit. Subsequent years brought about a growing skepticism that's still with us. So there was a transition from a belief in government and public interest to this powerful doctrine that the market, buying and selling, is the principle that will make everything work at the end of the day. That's the dominant ideology that we live with in America today. That's our new religion. That's our mythology.

Oh, they were very hopeful days, the '60s, and of course I started reading the dissents of Justice Black and Justice Douglas, the great defense they made of the Bill of Rights. Since I was ultimately going to law school, these subjects very much interested me. That was a different mood than we're in today. We still have perhaps more injustice than ever, so hope is not as easy to come by as it was in those heady days when we, I certainly, felt we were on the edge.

Starting with the assassination of Kennedy, the mood changed. Even while Lyndon Johnson called for the eradication of poverty, some of the magic had already begun to disappear. Then came Nixon, the Vietnam War, and Watergate. Then it was Afghanistan, the Iranian embassy takeover, and of course Reagan. It was the market and the Evil Empire. That's pretty much where we still are, only now we're engaged in this conflict.*

We're more vulnerable since 9/11. We know we're going to have to work with other countries. We can't go it alone. Our whole eco-

---

*This conversation occurred shortly after 9/11.

nomic system is now dependent on global transfers of products, of capital, and what they call services. We're embedded in the lives of other people in other countries. Fortress America is over. We're definitely being *thrust* forward with greater material wealth, greater military power, greater information processing. Still, billions of people are hungry, and the threat to the global environment is real.

Oakland has been getting more prosperous and receiving immigrants from all over the world. The visible change is evident. Still, there are disparities. That's something we try to deal with, neighborhood by neighborhood. What I find as mayor, it's not abstract, it's block by block. It's just people living their lives. They don't live their lives in ideology. They live their lives by what they face every day. Very few people generalize, or stand back and look at the big picture. It's getting rid of a drug dealer on the corner, or creating a group to watch out for the neighbors, or working to fix up a local school. All these things build community life. At the same time, the media, national entertainment, advertising, brand shopping—and work that people have to do—occupies a lot of daily life, so people don't have much energy left over to organize their neighborhoods or work on civic issues. But there are thousands of people in a place like Oakland who do just that: they find the time.

Though in some poorer neighborhoods there is a fair amount of crime and blight you don't have in middle-class neighborhoods, there is a vitality, a lot of life on the streets. Yes, kids are hanging out on the corner, and yes, dope deals are coming down. Yet, in some of these neighborhoods, there appears to be more human vitality. In the middle-class and certainly the affluent neighborhoods, there aren't that many people on the street. People go from their house to their garage to their car with the windows rolled up, then they go to a store, and then they come back to their house. And they're literally *garaged* in their space. You find a lot of emptiness on the streets. People aren't sitting out on their steps waiting to talk to their neighbors. You get some of that in coffee shops in some of these affluent areas, but the poor are pulled together by necessity, by habit. Without romanticizing their position, because God knows they have a lot of hardship, there seems to be a level of humanness, in some respects more sophisticated, more advanced, than that of some affluent people almost in fortresses behind their walls.

Many of the poor are not working, so they're on the street. It isn't good. Yes, many of them are hustling. And yes, there's a breakdown of the family, and yes, the kids get caught up in the cycle. And yet at the same time, there appears to me, an outsider, to be a humanity there that has to be respected. It gives me hope that human beings can flourish wherever they are. We don't have to wait till the millennium to be fully human. The programmed lives of the professional, of the more secure, have definite benefits, and yet there's a loss, too—a loss of autonomy, a loss of being in charge of one's own place. That's why religion and ritual can take people to a level beyond shopping and office work, which is often repetitive and trivial. That's why men in war have such profound experiences and are drawn so closely together, and why when there's a disaster, it pulls people together. In some of these lower-income neighborhoods, it's like a continuing disaster that pulls people together, while at the same time fostering a lot of antagonism and anger.

What is going on in low-income Oakland in some ways is being replicated in our country because we're under attack. Now our forces are fighting back and killing, and so we're seeing the drama of war, which takes people to a certain level beyond the mundane, the predictable, and the programmed. If you don't have the power, your whole life is under such pressure. The simplest thing becomes such a major thing. Just to keep your house together, food, medical care, making sure your kids are OK. Those become big issues that don't even exist for the half of the population that has the money. We don't fight in Oakland with tanks and with flamethrowers and airplanes. But we have a lot of disputes among different groups, who have their own filter on reality.

I sense that America is still the land of a lot of possibilities. We have a lot of openness here. We're not as cramped by a past: *My father did it, so I have to do it.* There's a lot of room for innovation. That leaves space for more understanding of our human predicament, and the urge to act, to do something about it. In a city like Oakland, where we have eighty different languages in our public schools, all different races, ethnicities, religions, and political ideologies, somehow we're holding it together. That's hopeful. Why can't we do the same with the world at large?

Ed Chambers

"I'm an organizer." The executive director of the Industrial Areas Foundation, he succeeded its founder, Saul Alinsky. He has been with the IAF since 1956. He's known as Big Ed, with the build of a football linebacker.

"We were poor shanty Irish. My father came over to this country when he was twenty. Ill-educated, he could barely write. His sister got him a job out on a railroad in Clarion, Iowa. He was smart. He married a schoolteacher, my mother, and they had five kids. We were all raised during the Depression, in poverty. We got cornmeal mush three times a day. My dad was making a dollar a day working for the Catholic Church, gathering corncobs from the farmers. It was burned in place of coal for the school."

I FAILED AT MY FIRST CAREER, studying to be a priest. They threw me out of the seminary for arguing in English and asking too many questions on theology. What really got me clipped was talking about the laity having a say-so. So I'm hitchhiking to New York because I don't know what to do with my life. Here I am an idealist—hoping for an afterlife, but now confused about this one—who believes in the world as it should be and isn't. This was about 1953. I hitchhiked from Clarion to the Bowery in New York looking for Dorothy Day.

I'd read about her. And during college, I took a year off and bummed around Europe asking questions, meeting the French priest-workers. They were the priests who took off the collar and dressed as workers and got to know the working Frenchmen. They got crushed eventually by the Vatican. I heard of Dorothy Day through them and through reading the *Catholic Worker*. That's where I met Ammon Hennessy.* Dorothy gave us an assignment to go down to Wall Street and sell the *Worker* for a penny a copy. I got on one corner and Hennessy got on another corner. The only trouble is Hennessy would get into arguments with the suits and I was selling

*A colorful, somewhat eccentric disciple of Dorothy Day.

225

the copies. I was serious. I'd call out: *Catholic Worker*, penny a copy, "*Catholic Worker*, penny a copy." So I'd sell the three dollars and forty cents' worth of papers in two, three, four hours. Coming home on the subway, Hennessy would say, "Here, Ed, take the papers," 'cause he had sold maybe ten, and "Give me the money." He'd turn the money in to Dorothy. He'd say, "Oh, we had a great day. We got four dollars and whatnot." She'd always look over his shoulder to see who actually did the work, and give me the nod.

Dorothy Day was a saint. She taught me to kneel when they started playing "The Star-Spangled Banner" during the fifties, during Mc-Carthyism. She was arrested for kneeling during the cold war, when we were supposed to be in bomb shelters. Dorothy was drug off and thrown in jail. She taught me courage and hope. Well, Dorothy Day was an authentic Catholic. I had run up against other Catholics, but I never had the same kind of feeling as when I was in her presence. She didn't talk a lot, but she had a lot of expressions that didn't have to do with words. The way she looked at you, the way she listened to you. The way she would nod: *I know who sold the papers*. That sort of thing. Then I got a message from the government that I no longer had a four-D deferment from the seminary; I was going to be one-A for Korea.

At the time, I'm living in a Catholic interracial commune in Harlem. It's blacks, whites, men, women. The women lived in one slum part of the building, and we lived in the other. We got paid six dollars a month for handing out old clothes to winos. Suits and whatnot. I did that for two years. I lost my idealism and began to learn about the real world.

Dorothy was an inspiration. She was the one person who would say it was OK to be a conscientious objector, because I had decided I was not going to go kill Koreans. I was a CO. But Catholics weren't recognized as COs. I was told to take the physical by my atheistic Greek lawyer. He says, "You gotta take the physical. We gotta prove that you're not crazy." So I went to the Brooklyn Navy Yard. They took us into a huge room, there were about three hundred and fifty of us, and they threw a document in front of us and said, "Sign this and then you can get a meal on the government." I looked at it and it's a loyalty oath. And the list of the organizations. There'd been a few of them that I had attended. I refused to sign. They said, "Wait a minute, wait a minute, everybody signs this." They called the MPs over to make sure I wouldn't run away. I'm scared. I was twenty-four. All of a sudden, a redheaded Irishman comes bounding out from the back room. He hollers, "You're no goddamned Catholic." He's a sergeant. And I say, "I'm sorry, I'm not going to sign." "Well, we'll see to that. Guards, we're going to go up to Captain Rodriguez." I remember the guy's name. The sergeant came bursting into Rodriguez's room. He said, "Excuse me, Sergeant, you can wait outside." Rodriguez and I were alone. He said, "Would you like a cigarette?" I was getting the soft treatment. I said, "No, thank you, I don't smoke." "Well, you know, nobody likes this sort of thing, but I wish you'd reconsider here." And I said, "I'm very sorry, sir, I object to this, and I'm a Roman Catholic, and—" "Well, Roman Catholics aren't recognized as conscientious objectors. Why don't you say you're a Jehovah's Witness or something?" I said, "I'm not!" I said, "I'm sorry, I can't, sir, I'm a Roman Catholic." He said, "Well, that's all right. We'll meet you down at Fort Benning when we induct you down there." I said, "Am I really free to go?" So I skipped the free meal, I was so happy to get out of there. Anyway, I beat them on a technicality.

Dorothy Day wrote about me in the *Catholic Worker* and stood beside me and gave me encouragement. My pastor back in Fort Dodge, Iowa, retired chaplain from the Marine Corps, when the draft board called him up, the assistant priest overheard the conversation. He said, "Chambers, you got Chambers? That son of a bitch! Arrest him if you got him. He's un-American." [*Laughs*] I'm twenty-six, and I'm getting an education from the African Americans in Harlem. I got to know black people the hard way. I was handing out these old clothes and shoes, and this guy kept coming back for a pair of shoes. He said, "They stole them on me." I says, "I'm gonna follow this guy." So I give him a new pair of shoes, and I follow him. He turns around the corner, whips the shoes off, gives them to the guy standing there for a bottle of Sneaky Pete, cheap wine. I said, "Oh, so that's our interracial justice. We're subsidizing the winos." I said, "This doesn't make any sense. I want to help some of these poor ladies, these ADC [Aid to Dependent Children] mothers." So I started organizing tenants associations. This was before I met Alinsky. A commie organizer, a black guy, saw me working some of his turf, and he said, "What are you doing, whitey?" I said, "I'm trying to help the mothers with the sick kids get some heat and hot water." This is January. He said, "Well, I don't mind that, but you can't work my turf." So he gave me some blocks that he wasn't working.

A lady come in with a sick kid to Mr. Friendship—they call you that—"I need a handout. I got no heat, no water." I says, "Lady, if you got no heat and no hot water in that five-story walk-up, nobody else has either." She says, "I know that." I said, "I'll tell you what I'll do. I'll come by tomorrow, around three in the afternoon. But you gotta have a couple other ladies in the apartment with you. We'll sit down and figure out how we can get some heat and hot water." I knew a handout wasn't what she really needed. She needed some power against the landlord. I went there early and started ringing doorbells and knocking on doors. Some would open, some wouldn't. And I'd tell some of the ladies, "Come up to five-B at three o'clock to figure out how we deal with this landlord." So I learned by trial and error. I learned not to do things for people, but to get people to do things. I'd put on a shirt and a tie, get a taxi, and myself and six ladies would go up to the housing court, the no-heat, no-hot-water court, and I'd pretend I was a lawyer. I'd say, "Your honor, these ladies can explain it better than I can." Then I'd slip in the background. I got away with that for about four or five months during the wintertime, the cold months. The judge finally caught me. He found me in contempt of court. I said, "Your honor, I never said I was an attorney. I just came up here with the ladies . . ." They pleaded their own case.

The slum landlord would say, "What part of the room did you stand in when you took those temperature readings that you're claiming was fifty-five?" The woman would say, "Well, sir, I'm standing in the center of the room." I taught her that trick. My atheistic lawyer helped me a lot. I'm growing from a guy of idealism, I'm growing in smarts about the streets, the world as it is.

Then I got lucky. I had a phone call from a guy I'd never met, Nick Von Hoffman. Nick said, "We've heard about your good work in tenants associations in Harlem. Would you like to work for Saul Alinsky?" I was reading his book, *Reveille for Radicals*. It resonated with something inside of me.

It was another kind of idealism he talked about, a new kind of language, a nonchurch language about hope and about the future. I knew that's what I was now about. People in the community having the power to do it for themselves, that's the iron rule. Never do for others what they can do for themselves. Never, never. So I bused out to Chicago. Saul took me to the Blackstone Hotel and gave me a steak dinner and hired me.

He sent me to the asshole of the world, Lackawanna, New York, a suburb of Buffalo. It's U.S. Steel Company, thirty-two thousand employees. Lackawanna is the slum. Again, I'm too idealistic. So Von Hoffman was assigned to train me. He gave me a list of about thirty-five Polish names, which I couldn't even pronounce. He says, "Go see these people, do one-to-ones with them." My training lasted three and a half days, and Nick flew back to Chicago. Next time I saw Alinsky I'd built an organization and we were going to have a founding.

Trial and error, same thing that had got me through in Harlem, now was getting me through in Lackawanna. I had the First Ward, which is right beside the plant. The First Ward was about thirty-five different nationalities. I'd never met people from the Middle East before, I'd never met people from Africa. I mean, this was the poorest of the poor. Many illegals at that time. They'd have the low-paying jobs at the steel plant, the cleanups, and they'd do the dirty work.

When I got yanked out of Lackawanna, I was called back to Chicago by Saul and Von Hoffman again. I was assigned to the Southwest Side. I thought, because I was a Roman Catholic, that I'd get the Catholic parishes to organize. Saul said, "No, Chambers, you're going to do the Protestants. I want you to organize the Protestants." He said, "I'm afraid you'll start that theological talk with the Catholics, and that won't work. You gotta deal with those guys pragmatically." That was a learning lesson.

Dorothy Day in the Bowery, and in Saul Alinsky, in Back of the Yards, Chicago, I had heroes. That's one of the great lacks going into the twenty-first century, the lack of heroes. We're in bad shape as a country. We're suffering from the collapse of both political parties. They're bought out. They're owned by corporate America, lock, stock, and barrel. The media is sold out. The corporate dominant culture, which is driven by the market, the bottom line, sells out everything.

Sure, there are people out there, but there's so few. We should have six hundred professional organizers, and we've only got a hundred and twenty. I got Saul to found the Training Institute before he died, so that we'd have some organizers besides Von Hoffman, Chambers, and Dick Harmon. I'm talking about 1968, after I went to Rochester for Saul, and built a black power organization called FIGHT, Freedom, Integration, God, Honor, Today.

One of the things you gotta learn in this business is that all organizing is constant reorganizing. There was a powerful group on the South Side called the Woodlawn Organization, led by a great man, Bishop Arthur M. Brazier. But it went the route, and today it's a twenty-two-million-dollar economic development corporation. That's fine, that's pretty good, but in terms of citizens organizations, it's weak. These organizations that aren't constantly reorganized become part of the establishment and the status quo. Saul saw that happen to him in Back of the Yards, and it was a pain to him. I said, "Saul, you gotta go back in there and disorganize it and reorganize it."

Joe Meegan had taken it into politics and soft money, and so it soon became corrupt and one of the most effective organizations anywhere in the country for keeping Negroes out of the neighborhood. Irony, yes. You've got to build and rebuild these things.

If I thought we'd only have a hundred and twenty organizers, I don't know if I would have done the last thirty, forty years. So in a sense, I'm a failure, too. As a refounder, I've done better than Saul has. Saul only had two organizers, and he was burning us to death, jumping us from one city to another. We would have been cinders in another ten years. Except now I've got an institution, but do you think the foundation world will give me four million dollars to start a university in and around these ideas and concepts? *No.* They want to fund something they can control. I have a challenge. I'm seventy-two.

I refounded Saul's start. Saul had a great start and had most of the universals down, but we had to institutionalize in 1968, '69, or it all would have died with Alinsky. There are a couple changes I made. I saw that women could do this work as well as men, and so we started inviting women in and training them. Saul said, "You can't be married and do this work." Today, most have families and raise kids. Half of our hundred and twenty are females. Black and white and brown, Latino. Yes. That's the success part of it. The nonsuccess is, why aren't there five hundred or a thousand? I pay decent salaries. I have tried to make this a professional organization, a profession like medicine is, a profession like teaching is. A profession like journalism is. That I've accomplished. But it's very hard to talk young men and women to come in, particularly those who have a high degree of native intelligence, who have anger, and who will commit themselves to a struggle that really has no end. It's hard to get young men and women in this culture to drop the markets-driven vision.

I'm a little bit discouraged, but I'm not quitting, I'm not giving up. I still got the hope that the next refounder of IAF can take it into a better future. The purpose of life isn't truth; the purpose of life is meaning. The struggle of meaning that keeps you going, and a hope that you are about to get something greater than anything you've got. If anything keeps me going, it's building the future of these institutions on a broader base, so they can take on corporate America. That which you possess isn't as great as that which you are about to possess.

What keeps me going is that I realized, sometime in my forties or early fifties, I couldn't just dig down inside myself and pump it out like in my thirties. Then I realized that I got my energy for this work from other people, so the self must stay in connection with others, new others, others that have more talent and more vision and more power than you have. That energizes you and keeps you going. Without that, you will ossify. You can call it what you want. You can call it community, you can call it necessity. You've got to be in relationship with real people. I try to stay in touch with everyday, ordinary citizens. I don't need celebs. The big power, you can't have a relationship with. They don't want you, they don't need you.

THE DISCOVERY

OF POWER

Mike Gecan

I'M AN ORGANIZER with the Industrial Areas Foundation.* In
the thirties and forties, most people knew what an organizer was.
There were labor organizers and citizen organizers. Saul Alinsky was
making *organizer* a well-known word in America. Today, most people
think it has something to do with your desk or your laptop.

I'm an old-fashioned organizer. I organize leaders and institutions,
primarily in cities, to identify things they want to change and then
go change them. We use it and get the inevitable reaction from people who have power.

Most of my work the last twenty-two years has been out east, with
the IAF. I started in Chicago for a few years, then to Baltimore, and
in 1980, my wife and I moved to New York. We're usually invited
into a place like East Brooklyn. Often we're asked by local leaders
and churches and congregations that are badly off. East Brooklyn is
a large area that's among the poorest in the city, historically. Alfred
Kazin wrote a memoir about East Brooklyn called *A Walker in the
City*, way back in the late sixties. I was at Yale. I borrowed a car and
I drove to Brownsville. I walked the streets he described. About
eleven years later, I found myself working there. About twenty years
later, we found ourselves rebuilding the whole place. We built a citizens organization.

I was born on Ferdinand Street in Chicago, on the West Side. My
parents were what used to be called working-class people. My dad
was a construction worker, bartender, plasterer, security guard, all
through his career. My mother worked in a toy factory. I went to

*His recent book is *Going Public* (Boston: Beacon Press, 2002).

Our Lady of the Angels school, the one that had the big fire. I was in that terrible fire. Ninety-two kids were killed and three sisters. December first, 1958.

Most of my first lessons in power were as a kid in that neighborhood. We grew up in a world where power was present everywhere. If you walked across the street to another neighborhood, the Polish area, you got beat up. If they walked across the street, we fought them. My neighborhood was Croatian, Italian, and a little Irish. The Cook County Democratic Party was very powerful. If you wanted a job, you had to pay. You had no recourse because everyone was participating in that way of doing business. If you were a bartender or a tavern owner, like my father, you had to pay the mob to stay in business. If you wouldn't pay, you got punished in various ways. Your place got firebombed, you could be beaten up, you could be killed. The role of power played in every aspect of our lives.

There was the power of the Roman Catholic church in that neighborhood. It was the most powerful. It was a mixed power. Sometimes it could save your life: if you were a kid who needed to be adopted, if you were sick, if you needed a social life, if you needed education. At other times, it could ignore you and harm you, or at least put you in jeopardy. For example, part of the lesson of the school fire was a lesson of negligence, of an institution that did not attend to the needs of a school, put its children and its staff in jeopardy. We paid a terrible price for it. It was an institution that took for granted the loyalty of its members—for instance, the working-class families of the West Side and the South Side. When realtors began to block-bust and panic-peddle, the church often did very little or nothing. Literally hundreds of thousands of hardworking families lost money and equity and hope, and were driven out of neighborhoods. Hundreds of thousands of hardworking African American and Hispanic families were sold homes at more than their value. So we had an institution that could have played a tremendously important role, both in protecting the interests of its own existing members and the interests of the new black and Hispanic families, and for the most part did not.

I think I was aware as a six-year-old, seven-year-old, eight-year-old. I think I learned about power in my gut and in my heart, and in my eyes I saw it, felt it. I saw people abused, saw people hurt, saw people broken, saw people killed. Before I knew what the word was—power—I knew it existed. I grew older and went to high school, St. Ignatius on the West Side. It was the greatest place I could have gone. The scholastics and priests took us to civil rights actions and into black churches, which I'd never been in before. I began to see a whole different kind of power, constructive, and I began to think about it. The way I learned about power, I think that's how I learned about hope—first viscerally, seeing it, feeling it, observing it, and beginning to put the words on it. You can't think about hope unless you think about power.

I went to Yale on a scholarship and majored in literature. I wanted to be a novelist. Home from college, I read in the paper one Sunday morning about a group in Lawndale, an African American community, working with contract-buying home owners. I called up and asked if I could work there that summer. They were black, so they couldn't get mortgages at that time because of redlining. So they bought homes on contract. If you're on contract, you don't really own your home, you don't get equity till you make your last payment. The contract is written to enable the contract holder to take the home away from you if you're late, if you fall behind, if you get sick.

Jack Egan was working on this, along with a group of leaders in the neighborhood.* They were organizing home owners to go after the mortgage bankers and those who sold them these contracts, and to get those contracts renegotiated so that they were more equitable. Eventually they succeeded. I saw in their work a way of using and building power that was positive and constructive, and able to reverse some of the things that had damaged people. The important thing was not that it was just positive, but that it was successful. It wasn't just like a token or moral pause. This was a group of people who were savvy and canny.

My father was a great fellow, World War Two veteran, landed on Omaha Beach, nearly killed in the Battle of the Bulge, a very courageous guy. But he didn't understand why I was doing some of these things. My mother was a working person, but also a reader. She'd leave great books around the house—Dickens on the table—

---

*Monsignor Jack Egan was a bone-deep activist, who was a familiar figure on picket lines and rallies for peace, civil rights, and labor.

for my sister and me. You wouldn't pick her out as a university-type person, but she was a very intellectual, very broad-minded person. She was nervous about what I would do because it was dangerous, but she was always very positive. My parents were mixed about it but never discouraged me. They were never disappointed by what I did. The longer I organized, the more they seemed to support it. The negative reaction I got was from some of my friends in the neighborhood. I remember one Sunday, I was invited to a Bears game by a friend. Those were the days of Gale Sayers and Dick Butkus. My friend, who was African American, and his uncle and father drove up to our house one Sunday to pick me up. We went to the Bears game, had a great day, and came home. My parents invited them in for a drink. This was a tough, working-class, all-white neighborhood, 1966. That night a cross was burned on our lawn. I remember my mother going out in the neighborhood to try to find out who the hell did this. We didn't find out for many, many, many years, but eventually we did. Even then, my parents never said, "You shouldn't have done that." My neighbors next door never said anything. Never. No one ever said a pop, no one ever said a word. My parents were nervous, but they never said stop, and I never did.

During one of the Marquette Park marches during the civil rights period, Martin Luther King was hit by rocks and bottles. I got there late, I parked my car and started to walk toward the march through the whites who were pelting the marchers. I looked in everybody's face and they looked like me. There was blood lust in the crowd. They wanted to kill. I was afraid. As I was walking through the whites, I knew I couldn't get to the march. I was too afraid to march that day.

I had to wrestle with my own fear that day. They were me. We were the same people. They were working people, crazed by their ferocity. I don't know what the lesson is except, watch out for self-righteousness and watch out for demonizing others, because sometimes people who hate aren't so different from you. If anything, maybe it sobered me up about how difficult it was going to be to do these things.

This was a kind of formation, and much of it was accidental. People get the idea that you form yourself very deliberately politically, but I think people get formed accidentally with a lot of help, and a lot of detours, and a lot of being late and you see something because you're late, not because you're on time. People teach you different things. A lot of people think you learn from books, but most of my political formation was from direct experience and good people.

By the time I got out of college, I wanted to try two things. I spent several years trying to be a writer. The other thing I thought I would like to do was something called organizing, but I didn't know what it was. It wasn't a career. I literally picked up the Chicago papers and looked for a job in organizing. I got one with a little group on the Northwest Side called the Northeast Austin Organization.

The organizer is a talent searcher, he's like a Hollywood producer. He's looking for not just the one star but all kinds of talent. And if you find the right talent that you can train, almost anything's possible. Talent, in a sense, is people who have relationships with other people. It's not so much the talent of speaking, although that's important; it's the talent of relating, a person who understands how to build trust. That's not necessarily a charismatic person. The people who hit the beach on Normandy were not a bunch of charismatic twenty-year-olds, right? They were people who trusted and believed in one another. The organizer sometimes has to be wary of the charismatic person.

That's my life. I'm a talent scout. If you can find the right mix, it's like putting a great play together, a great production. You find the right talent, the right crew, the right team, the right players. The second thing is that you win sometimes. Not every time, but you gotta *win*. The performance has to be great sometimes. And the re-action has to be loud. You *have* to win.

So I just went on to CAP, the Citizen Action Program, and from there to IAF. Ed Chambers was reorganizing organizing. He had a couple of insights. One was that you had to build organizing through institutions. You couldn't just organize with people around causes, because if the cause lost or won, the thing would evaporate. You had to have some kind of institutional base. His second big insight was to have a systematic training of leaders. Just as with actors and actresses, you have to keep working at that craft. It's not just you wake up one morning and you're going to sing an aria or you're going to do *Hamlet.* You gotta work at it. You gotta get good at it. You gotta practice. Ed understood you had to have training that was top-flight.

These people deserve the *best,* 'cause they're doing the hardest kind of work that you can do, with very skimpy resources, against great odds. You've gotta equip people so they have a shot. The third thing is you had to be able to pay for this, and the institutions had to pay some dues. These were very significant themes in organizing, and they ran against a more movement style of organizing. Not that movements are bad, but they were more built around charismatic leaders. There's always a tendency to look for the most charismatic person, because that in a way solves your leadership problem—but only in the short term, not in the long term. And not to do much training. And not to worry so much about money.

I had this background that told me that if you don't have top-flight trained leaders and a strong power base and your own money, you're gonna get creamed. Because the other powers have it all. They have institutional bases, like the old Cook County Democratic machine. They have a money stream. They have their own training system, by the way, even though you might think it warped. They have a way of forming people. People are trained to operate certain ways, and they do, and they're pretty good at it. You can't counter institutional power with good intentions, or with charisma alone, or with wishful thinking. You have to build your own institutional power. And you have to hit hard. I love to fight and win. As a young person, I'd seen my people bullied, taken advantage of, abused. As a kid, I had no way to do anything other than observe it and feel it and remember. As I got older, I found work that enabled me to punch back. If you throw a punch at me or people I work with, we're going to hit back. I made a lot of mistakes, but the satisfaction was seeing what happens when people are able to defend themselves, and punch back when others come at them. It's not all nicey-nice, you know. People come *at* you, they take things from you, they take your life!

Real estate interests do it, bad school systems do it, mayors do it, governors do it, presidents do it. It doesn't make 'em all bad or evil. They have different interests. It's OK, provided you have the power to *stop* 'em, and to turn 'em around, and to teach 'em some things, and to maybe reverse it sometimes. If you have power, all those things are possible. If you don't, you gotta hit the road, or you gotta get very passive, 'cause otherwise you'll go crazy.

I vividly remember Ed Chambers driving me around the East Brooklyn area before I was hired—block after block, devastated, abandoned, burned out. It was intimidating and a little frightening. Ed said, "What an opportunity!" [*Laughs hard*] There was a little Italian pocket in one part of East New York, still, but I'd say it was ninety-five percent, ninety-eight percent African American. It was the worst of times: September 1980. Shooting everywhere. Burning everywhere. The establishment's prevailing theory was something like benign neglect, you remember that? It meant, "Don't throw good money after bad in these neighborhoods, they're dead." I'll tell you how dead it was: there weren't stop signs, there weren't any one-way signs. There weren't any more street signs at all. The place was being demapped. If you wanted to find Mr. Gonzalez's house, he'd tell you to go five blocks to the abandoned building and make a right, and then you go to the abandoned lot and you make a left, et cetera. That's OK if you're an organizer, but it's not good if you're an ambulance driver or a cop. These were places that were falling off the map of America. East Brooklyn was just one of them. There are still many places like that today. Ours was not the job of a civic group to do a few things to maintain the community or stabilize it. It was too far gone for that. Our job was to see if we could find a team that wanted to rebuild the place. That was a much bigger challenge than anything we ever attempted before.

I did what an organizer does. I did hundreds and hundreds and hundreds of individual meetings. I'd find out who the leaders were and meet them. The group already had twenty active congregations, twenty churches. I'd meet with the pastors, and they'd give me lists of names of good people, and day after day, night after night, I would just meet people.

You're in the midst of hell. You walk into a house or an apartment in a project, and there's this tremendous person. Strong, good people, solid citizens, willing to work, members of their congregations. When that happens you start to have a feeling that, hey, maybe something can happen.

Of course, it's not just an abandoned street anymore, you know what I mean? It's not just a tenement that looks intimidating. It is intimidating, but there's a person in it, a family in it, there's a leader in it. When that happens and you start seeing it's not just five, there's fifty; there's not just fifty, there's a hundred; there's not just a hundred, there's two hundred, and they're all over the place, you begin to have the idea that you can do something politically, collectively.

I don't know if I'd say I was surprised and astonished, I'd just say I was impressed. There was a woman named Alice McCollum, a mother of ten, a single mother, black, lived in a terrible apartment. A lovely person, great sense of humor. That's a big part of life, by the way. Big thing in organizing, mostly missed. That's what the ideologues never quite get. Good people like to laugh, it's not all grim, and it's not all us and them and they're the devils and we're the angels.

So I meet Alice McCollum. She tells her story. I ask her, "Do you want to work on it? Are there other neighbors who would work on it as well?" She says, "Sure." So she pulls them together, and we do the research on what's happening with this local park and pool. We find out that the city sold a contract for over three million bucks. Ninety percent of the money's been spent, only five percent of the work's been done. So you have a person in a difficult situation who's got energy, she's angry, but she's not grim. She's got a following, she's smart, she's willing to strategize on how to address this problem, and then we go address it.

That's just one example of one person, one issue. You multiply that by twenty, thirty, fifty, a hundred, and you start to get a sense of what you're organizing, the spirit of it. You're trying to organize the spirit of action, accomplishment, experimentation, humor. These lousy food stores were another story in this area: high costs, bad meat, bad vegetables, awful abuse by the managers who sit in their pillboxes and yell at the women shopping. This came up in meetings we had in many, many houses. So we trained a hundred people to be food store inspectors. Everybody had a badge and a clipboard and an inspection sheet. We bought weights and measures so that we could see if the meat was accurately weighed. We had no status, you understand, but we assumed the role of food store inspector anyway.

On a Saturday morning, ten leaders went into ten different stores and conducted an inspection. We knew the storekeepers would react, so we called the cops ourselves the week before, briefed them on what we were going to do, and requested that there be a cop car at every store. We had thermometers, so they'd put a thermometer in the cooler and check the temperature. We had a team that would buy all the bad food and a fifty-dollar budget per store.

When our teams went in, two things happened. Everyone else in the store wanted to participate in the inspection. "Hey, what are you doing?" We'd say, "We're just inspecting. We've heard the meat here isn't so good." The other customers would say, "Come over here, we'll show you where the really bad stuff is." And they'd pull out the green meat, or they'd show you where the rats had their holes, or they'd pull out the rusty cans, or they'd show you where the spoiled milk was, or the fuzzy grapes. This would go on for about an hour. The whole store stops. The managers come down from the pillbox and say, "Who are you?" "We're EBC [East Brooklyn Congregations]." Everyone is formally dressed, and they've got their tickets and they've got their clipboards. "I'm going to call the police." "No problem. The police are right outside. We already called them." They're midsize stores, they're not little bodegas. Seven of the ten managers signed agreements that morning to improve all the things our inspectors found wrong that day. They were so happy to get us the hell out of there. Three of the ten resisted. We threw all the inspectors at those last three stores, and they finally gave in. So we were ten for ten. We had this wonderful party for the hundred inspectors. People wanted to keep their badges because this had been a success. About half the people asked the most beautiful question you could hear in organizing: "What do we do next?" The other half went back to their lives and never forgot that experience.

The more experiences people have like that, you don't have to tell them, "Now you got power." They *know* it, they *feel* it. We got all the street signs put in, we got buildings demolished. We did scores of these local issues that were important unto themselves, but the most important thing was what was happening to the people. They were feeling effective and they were having fun, and they were beginning to see that they could do things, and they were getting wild and interesting reactions from people in power they never imagined they'd get.

Ultimately the same organization built two thousand nine hundred single-family houses. Had every park and pool and play area redone. Started two new public high schools. Essentially tackled almost every issue in the neighborhood of about a quarter of a million people. It's not like one little community, it's like a small city.

In the late seventies and early eighties, this area was like the South Bronx. Mayors would come visit it from other cities to see hell. Mayor White of Boston toured the area, and his quote was, "I have now seen the beginning of the end of civilization."

What we say is that we have a civilized rebuilt community. This is part of what I've been doing for the last twenty-two years. It was not without ups and downs. Don't get me wrong—this isn't romantic work. There are days when you think, *What the hell am I doing here?* It is grassroots, but I'd say it has large ambitions as well. I'm really an on-the-ground organizer still. I do what I call old-fashioned organizing. We're trying to see if we can apply what we learned in New York, Chicago, and other places to other cities, many in terrible shape.

My feelings today are mixed. I feel good about what I see happening in many of the places. What I worry about is whether we can get this kind of work up to scale, whether it can be replicated in other places quickly enough. As we rebuilt East Brooklyn, North and West Philadelphia were falling apart. They need to be rebuilt. Trenton needs to be rebuilt. The question is, how can you pick up the pace so that more people in more communities and more leaders go through this kind of experience? That's a big question for us, and an anxiety. Other people have to do it, too; they just can't read about it. So that's a major challenge. We gotta get more organizers.

It's easy to talk yourself into despair. Hope is physical and visceral. I don't think you can talk yourself into it. I think you have to *do* yourself into it. The more people try things, work at things, test things, push the boundaries, experiment, the less we just angst about it, the better.

Linda Stout

She is the executive director of the Peace Development Fund, Amherst, Massachusetts. "We're like a mini think tank for people engaged in grassroots work. Our big challenge is the people's spirit of helplessness. Power corrupts, absolutely, but so does powerlessness. That's the only thing that can stop us. I feel incredibly hopeful that we can turn things around."*

I WAS BORN IN 1954, the daughter of a tenant farmer, and also thirteenth-generation Quaker on my father's side. I lived all my life in North Carolina up until about a year ago. I grew up in poverty.

My mother became disabled when I was six, so I sort of became the parent of the household, taking care of my mother and my two younger sisters. My dream was to go to college and become a teacher. No one in my family had ever gone through high school. My father had gone through the fifth grade and my mother through the sixth grade. When I started school, I began to realize that I was different than the other kids. It wasn't until third grade that I realized I was poor, because at that point I started being called names like "white trash." I never before heard that phrase. I was making straight A's through the third grade. The only complaint my teachers had about me was that I talked too much. In the fourth grade, things began to shift for me when a teacher moved me into the lower class and told me to forget about college, that I was stupid. From then on, I made C's and D's. It was like that message that I was stupid, that I didn't count, I took in. In the ninth grade, we moved and my father started working in a textile mill. I decided I wanted to make good grades, and overnight I started making A-plus grades. I did win a scholarship, but unfortunately, because of financial reasons, I never did get that chance to go to college.

I had been raised to believe in equality, being Quaker, and believing that everyone was the same. And yet once I got out of my own

*Linda Stout wrote a memoir called *Bridging the Class Divide, and Other Lessons for Grassroots Organizing*, published in 1997 by Beacon Press.

family and went to work in the mills and began to see how racism worked and what was happening, I started becoming involved. I had been raised to believe that black people were equal, and growing up, I certainly had friends who were black, because of my parents' beliefs. My mother, I should tell you, was a Baptist who was always singing hymns. She was very progressive for her time. When I was about six, I remember her registering to vote. We walked into this teeny little store. It was wintertime, and so all the farmers were in there. There was a black woman ahead of her registering to vote, and she was reading this piece of the Constitution because she had to take a test. When it was my mother's turn, she said, "I need to take the test." They said, "Oh, Mrs. Stout, you don't have to." Because she was white, see. And my mother said, "No, if she has to, I have to." So I come from a long history of parents who taught me that things should be equal.

Getting out into the world, I realized that that wasn't true at all. When I first got involved in civil rights and the women's movement, I realized that as a low-income person, I spoke differently than most of the middle-class leaders in these organizations. As a result, I was overlooked as a possible leader. Even when I would volunteer to do things or offer to go out in the community and speak about issues, I was always discouraged because people felt I didn't have the right grammar; I didn't speak right by their definition. I never felt like I belonged. I always felt left out. Even if I would bring other low-income people into those organizations, they would soon drop out for the same reason. That's when I began to realize that we had to do something different if we were really going to win, to really make change.

I had been involved in hiring blacks in the first job that I worked at, and got targeted by the Klan. We went underground in 1988 because we'd been so successful we began to get harassment from the Ku Klux Klan. Even though we'd only registered a small amount of people and were doing turnout, we unseated some of the Klan's people—you know, those respectable sympathizers, who we could spot in a minute—off local county seats.

For the first time in the history of that county, we elected African Americans into positions of power. We'd became a real threat in the community to a lot of the very right-wing folks. We began to be targeted by the Ku Klux Klan. A lot of people were hurt; some people left town. Over a period of two years, seventeen ministers moved away. Of course, I felt fear, too. So we went underground for two years. We worked as much as we ever did. We just didn't hold public meetings.

We were secretive about our meeting places, so we developed the most powerful word-of-mouth communications system, better than any e-mail system could possibly have been. In ten minutes everybody in the community would know what was going on. After we came out of underground, we became a powerful force.

When we did come out, the Klan held a rally to protest us. We had to do major organizing even to get protection. It took a call from Ted Kennedy. The marshals came in and took the weapons away from the Klan members. So we were in action again, this time aboveground.

Finally, I moved away from there and went to work for a civil rights attorney in Charleston, South Carolina. There I met a woman named Septima Clark. I didn't know who Septima was at the time because we didn't learn African American history in schools. She was a very famous civil rights leader who had worked at the Highlander Folk School.* When I met her, she was eighty-five years old, and she began to give me guidance. I would come in and say, "Oh, Septima, they didn't like me in this meeting." She'd say, "Of course not. What do you expect? Next time you go, you'll do this and that." She was tough and wonderful.

It was the twentieth anniversary of the March on Washington. I had been trying to get enough money for all the folks in the community that couldn't afford to go. I went to one law office, and the lawyer there said, "Tell me who you're buying me a ticket for." I said, "Septima Clark." He said, "Well, I'll definitely buy a ticket for Septima." So from then on, I went down the whole Broad Street

---

*The Highlander Folk School in Monteagle, Tennessee, was founded by Myles Horton. Here, black and white labor organizers and civil rights leaders had appeared, as teachers and as students. MLK and Rosa Parks were among them. Septima Clark succeeded Horton as the school's director.

row of law offices in Charleston and asked lawyers if they would buy a ticket for Septima Clark. They knew who she was. So I sold a lot of seats for Septima. [*Laughs*]

I became involved at the Piedmont Peace Project with a place called Midway in a county in the Piedmont region of North Carolina. It was a very small black community where eighty percent of the housing was below living standards and people lived without running water. Midway was surrounded by the town of Aberdeen, a more white, middle-class community. Midway's not unusual in the South. We often refer to places like Midway as "the hole in the doughnut," where the town does not annex them into the community because they are poor and they're black. We began working in that community to try to get water and sewer systems. The first thing we began to do is deal with trash because they had no trash pickup, and getting a dumpster into the community. People celebrated that victory. We went on to win battles for block grants, and to get water and sewers and the houses upgraded.

We began to register people to vote and started literacy programs. We had them reading about issues that affected their lives. Talk about change! We reached our congressman at the time, Bill Hefner. He was a very powerful, conservative Democrat who sat on the Defense Appropriations Committee. We were able to change his voting record on peace from zero percent to eighty-three percent.

We lobbied in our own way. We knew where he liked to go to breakfast on Saturday mornings. We'd send one of the ministers in our group to go talk with him, have coffee. We knew where he liked to hang out for ice cream on Saturday afternoons, and we'd send a farmer, a teacher, to talk to him, have a soda.

We had taught folks to link things together: military and domestic spending. We had built a power base he had to respond to. He didn't change because he had suddenly become enlightened. He did it because we had eventually registered forty-four thousand people to get out and vote at the polls. He knew we were a power to be reckoned with. But even more importantly, I think it was beginning to make people understand that you had to go beyond your own backyard, that we had to begin to work with people in other communities similar to ours, and to link with other people on national issues that affected us. Maybe we could win this month this one victory in our community, but how was that going to change things in a system that supports only the wealthy and not working-class people?

If it's just self-interest, we'll never be able to really change what needs to happen. If it's the environment in my backyard, I might clean that up, but it's not going to change what's happening to the ozone layer. Or I might change one politician in my community by registering people, but it's not going to change what the president does.

I think low-income people are very politically sophisticated when they have the information. People understand how the government uses money and that half their tax dollars are going to military, but they don't know how to act on it. That's what we had to bring people together to look at: how could we begin to make a difference?

Midway, like many other towns in our communities, was very discouraged. The people felt hopeless and despairing. As a result of organizing and making changes in the small community, people began to believe that they could really make a difference. More importantly, other communities began to see what Midway had done. We began to build this broad alliance of people. That's the most important thing about the work we did: for people to feel like they could make a difference. I'm talking about all generations. Our smallest organizer going door-to-door was four years old when she started. And we had people who were in their nineties who were going to vote for the first time in their lives. We spanned five generations in our organization.

I used to cry for a couple hours before I'd have to speak in front of a group of middle-class liberals. I was very frightened and felt that I didn't have anything to say that was worthwhile. The first time I ever spoke publicly was in Boston. I had been asked by a peace organization. They had heard of my work. I was very nervous. There was an older man speaking first who spoke for a long, long time, and I'm getting more and more nervous. Finally, when I got up and spoke, because I spoke from my heart and my feelings, despite the fact that I didn't have perfect grammar, people heard me, and they were able to understand what I had to say. When I finished, I got a standing ovation. The older man who preceded me said, "I am honored to be on the platform with you."* I was speaking at Harvard Law School a few years ago. At the end of it, one young man stood up. He said, "What you had to say was very important, but I think you would be more effective if you learned to speak proper grammar." My first thought was to feel bad about myself. And then I said to him, "I speak perfect grammar for my community. You would have a hard time communicating in my neighborhood. People wouldn't understand you." That's what we have to understand, that it's not about one grammar being better than another or one language better than another.

Midway today is a very different community. All the houses have now been fixed up; they have water and sewer. They still are struggling, they're still a low-income community, but children are moving back into the community. It's a community that people are proud of.

During the [first] Gulf War, we took a stand for peace. We were different from what you would think of as a peace organization. Many of our folks had been veterans. A lot of our members were actually reserves. Who goes into the military when there's not a draft? Poor people, people who are looking for jobs and education. The Piedmont Peace Project had more than five hundred people over in the Middle East for this war.

We built what we called a Wall for the Living. We didn't want to build a wall for the dead. We had all the names of our Gulf War veterans on it. We said, "We support them, but we don't support a war that is our blood for oil." We got more coverage than we expected. We were on CNN, in the *New York Times, USA Today.*

A lot of us think you have to have millions of people ready for real change to happen. I know that a small group of people can make significant change for everyone. I have a vision of what it looks like on the other side.

---

*It was John Kenneth Galbraith.

Pete Seeger

Some years ago, Downbeat, *the jazz journal, referred to him as "America's tuning fork." Along with Woody Guthrie, he was the balladeer, who, with Leadbelly and Alan Lomax, stirred up the American folk song revival in the late 1940s and early '50s.*

His pervasive influence among the young was such that it brought forth this whimsical observation: "When you see a kid with Adam's apple bobbing and banjo held chest high, you know that Pete Seeger, like Kilroy, was here."*

He and his wife, Toshi, live in a house he built in Beacon, New York, an upstate town along the Hudson River. He is eighty-two.

His latter years have been devoted to the Clearwater, *as a schooner and as an idea: cleaning up the Hudson River, which had through the years become polluted, "dangerous to all living things." It was the name he had given the sailboat he built that would cruise along the river. Young kids and adults would all be invited to become crew members. Its purpose was to galvanize all the communities bordering the Hudson into action: clearing the river, and having songs and fun at the same time.*

THE IDEA STARTED when I read a book about old sailboats in 1963. In 1966, we had a party on a neighbor's lawn. I sang some songs and said, "Let's build a replica of one of these boats." We simply want to restore the river and make the shores accessible to everybody. Maybe I planted a seed. I didn't know what the hell I was doing, but something wonderful has happened. The water is clear. You can swim in it now. It's not as clear as it will be, but it's safe enough to swim in. The governor, by gosh, has said, "Open up the beaches." He wants to boast that the Hudson is getting clearer. Beaches are very expensive because they're kind of dangerous with

---

*"Kilroy was here" was the graffiti hallmark of American GIs as they passed through foreign towns during World War II.

that tidal current. So we're now starting a floating swimming pool where people can swim more safely.

There's more cleaning to be done. It's still murky, but when we began, the Hudson was literally an open sewer.

We first had a little plastic boat. We went out on it and when we looked in the water, there were lumps of this and that floating by with the toilet paper. It was stinking. And the ghetto of every city was on the water's edge, all up and down the river from Albany to New York.

The good and bad are all tangled up in this. It's so ironic. You know what we started? We started a real estate boom in the Hudson. Now, the ghetto has been moved from the waterfront and they're selling that land at high prices. Thirty years, Cold Spring, three miles from us, was a little town of unemployed people. There was a nice little old house on sale for $10,000, a simple little workingman's house with a slate roof and a wrought-iron fence in front of it. Nobody wanted to buy it. Cold Spring has now become gentrified. That same little house has sold for $200,000. A person who's got a high-priced job may have an apartment in New York City, but he has a house in Cold Spring. The train service is better.

It all started with the *Clearwater*. The *Clearwater* is still sailing. But we started something else, too. In Milwaukee, they heard what the *Clearwater* was doing and said, "We'll do it, too." They've just finished building a Great Lakes schooner. The *Dennis Sullivan* is the name of the boat.

Do you realize our country is more full of such little organizations than ever in history? A lot of it is small business. There are small religious groups, small political groups, small scientific groups, and little ecology groups all over the place. Stop this development, save this. They call them nimbi's. But you know what Lois Gibbs says: "NIMBI, spell it with an *i,* now I must become involved."* The *Clearwater* is just one of these thousands of little things. Now there are a dozen big boats, like the *Lady Maryland* in Chesapeake, the *Ernestina* in New Bedford. They all do what *Clearwater* does.

*Lois Gibbs was a housewife in Love Canal, outside Buffalo, who led in the elimination of toxic waste dumps endangering the town's families. NIMBY is an acronym for "Not in my back yard."

The first time the *Clearwater* sailed, frankly, we didn't know how we were going to keep it going. Where would the money come from? And then somebody suggested we take out schoolkids.

We take out fifteen thousand every year. The first time it was not too successful. They learn a little sailing, they learn a little biology, they learn a little history, and they go back to school with the idea, somebody is trying to do something.

A biologist stood on the roof of the cabin and said [*Mock-yells*], "Kids, I want to tell you something about the river . . ." Fifteen minutes later, he was hoarse. The kids weren't listening anyway. They were looking at this hundred-foot-tall mast and looking at the view. They'd never been on a sailboat before. Now a bus pulls up, fifty kids pile out, and they're immediately divided into five groups. One group goes to the starboard side and learns to put a net in the water and catch some fish. Another goes to the port side and puts in a net as fine as a lady's stocking. It comes up with some green slime. It's put under a microscope, and the kids say, "What's all those wiggly things?" And the teacher, the crew person, who might be a volunteer—like last year, our thirteen-year-old granddaughter—says, "That's called plankton. Plankton is for fish what grass is for cows." Then another group goes to the big stick, the tiller. The captain says, "Push that thing to starboard. That means over there. Now push it to port. That means over here. Now hold it amidships." The kids say, "We're steering the boat!" And they are. So it's an exciting thing. This is now going to happen all over the world. I understand a man in Japan has built a schooner he calls the *Water Planet*. And he's sailing around saying, "We've got one planet of water, let's take care of it."

The *Clearwater* organization hired some experts. The experts got in touch with other experts, and we found out, for example, about PCBs. It's true that you could drink a barrel of Hudson River water and it wouldn't give you a stomachache. But you drink it every day and twenty years later the doctor says, "That pain inside you—you've got cancer." Women should not have anything to do with PCBs because they're what they call teratogenic and mutagenic, and that means they make for birth defects.

I tell people I think we have a fifty-fifty chance for there to be a human race here in a hundred years. They think that's being pessimistic. No, I say, that's being optimistic, because it implies that any one of us might be the grain of sand which will tip the scales in the right direction. Imagine that there's a big seesaw. At one end of it is a basket half full of rocks. That end is on the ground. At the other end is a basket one-quarter full of sand. And a bunch of us with teaspoons, we're trying to put sand in that end. A lot of people laugh at us, they say, "Oh, don't you see, it's leaking out as fast as you're putting it in." Well, we say, "It's leaking out, but we're getting more people with teaspoons all the time. One of these days, you're gonna see that whole basket with sand so full that this seesaw is going to go zoooo-up in the other direction." And people will say, "Gee, how did it happen so quickly?" Us and our damned little teaspoons.

Frances Moore Lappé

She wrote Diet for a Small Planet. *Her most recent book is called* Hope's Edge: A New Diet for a Small Planet. *"With food as an entry point, we want to help people see the world in new ways, opening up possibilities in their lives to express more fully."*

ONE BILLION PEOPLE are living on less than a dollar a day. Over two billion are living on less than two dollars a day. There is the constant terror of hunger. That's where my adult life began, asking the question "Why hunger? What's up with us that we haven't figured out this most essential task?"

I came across a woman named Wangari Masai. Growing up in a small Kenyan village, she ended up becoming highly educated, the first female Ph.D. in biological sciences in East Africa. She became acutely aware of the encroaching desert. Trees were being felled much, much faster than they were being planted. So on Earth Day in 1977, she planted seven trees. Then she began to realize that it would take millions of villagers planting trees all over the country to begin to reverse the ecological decline. So she went to government foresters and said, "There have to be millions of people planting trees." They said, "No, no, it takes foresters to plant trees." That did not deter her. She started a nursery in her own house, growing little saplings. Her husband thought it made for a very messy house. He ended up divorcing her. That did not deter her. She ended up creating a village-based movement of women. There are now sixty thousand of these tree nurseries, run by village women who have planted twenty million trees throughout Africa.

Colonialism teaches people to think of themselves as helpless, to devalue the knowledge that has grown over centuries and centuries of how to sustain life in climates that are challenging. To me, the tree planting is just one step in this reversal of learned helplessness, of people gaining a sense of their own strength. She created what's called the Green Belt Movement throughout all of these villages. Instead of just cutting down trees for firewood, the first step is planting trees so that you have firewood to cook your food. Once this sense of capacity is being built, women are saying, "Look, I'm not just a victim."

The men had always controlled the trees in the villages, so the women didn't have what they needed, even to cook. They had to walk many, many, many miles to get the firewood. That sense of taking control of their own destiny led them to question the export crop treadmill that they were on. They then began to plant the traditional food crops that had been drought-resistant, crops that had been devalued. Our colonialists had been telling them that these crops are lesser, that imported food is better. So these women reclaimed the traditional food crops. In a way, that was an entry into this larger question of power. I visited Wangari. When my children told me I had to do this thirtieth-anniversary sequel to my first book, our common idea was to challenge what we call the dominant mental map, to show that throughout the entire planet, there are these breakthroughs of people saying, "No, human beings are not simply selfish material. We are much more complex, much richer than that." Every place on this planet, people are breaking free.

The most powerful influence on my life was being the daughter of parents who were very courageous. They were never acknowledged for their courage. In the 1950s, in Fort Worth, Texas, as lay people, they founded a Unitarian church. The Unitarian religion was all about democracy: each person being able to follow his/her own search for truth. It was during the McCarthy era. The church was targeted because in Texas at that time, if you were a Unitarian, that meant that you were an atheist, that meant that you were a communist. A lot of people lost their jobs as a result of being members of the church. My bedroom was right down the hallway from the kitchen in this little house in Fort Worth. My parents would have their friends over in the evening, and they'd sit around in the kitchen with the coffeepot perking, talking politics, talking about integration, talking about all the big issues of the day. I just remember what I came to call the hum from the kitchen. It was so exciting. There just was an assumption that the good life was an engaged life. What else is there in life?

My first goal in life was to be a diplomat and to try to save the world through the U.S. State Department, because I believed that our government was trying to make the world better. I wanted to go to other countries and help to improve life there, because that's what I assumed our government was trying to do. I lasted a year. I hated the School of International Development at American University. It was very much "America first." How do we promote American interests? It wasn't at all what I had in mind. I therefore ended up at a small Quaker college in Earlham, Indiana. I graduated in 1966, the height of the conflict over the war in Vietnam. That's when my awakening came, which was absolutely shattering. I realized that the U.S. government is not really representing my interests.

My parents had become very anticommunist in the meantime, and they supported Johnson. So I had to break with my parents over the war. That was very traumatic. My brother and my mother moved to the right politically. My father and I kept moving to the left. Nonetheless, it was never anything that affected our love for each other.

The war in Vietnam was clearly the single most explosive moment of my life. Once I started reading the actual documents—I remember it was a book called the *Vietnam Papers,* a collection of things that the Quakers had put together showing the subterfuge, the deception, how much we were being lied to—I almost had a nervous breakdown. I had to completely reconstruct a worldview.

I came to see the problem as systemic. I wanted to work with people who were suffering the most under the current economic and political system, and so I went to a Quaker organizing school, the Upland Institute in Chester, Pennsylvania. We were trained to stand on soapboxes in Rittenhouse Square in Philadelphia and preach against the war. I left there and became a community organizer with the Welfare Rights Organization in the late sixties. When I think back, that was my first experience of exactly what Wangari was doing in Africa: helping people see their own capacity not just to be victims, but to have the creative capacity to change their situation. My job was to go door-to-door, talking to welfare mothers and drawing them into a group in which they could come up with strategies to change the welfare system. I never thought about this before, but just having someone there, a random young woman—what was I, twenty-three?—listening to them and creating a space for them began to change their sense of possibility. I ended up in a graduate program in community organizing, in the School of Social Work at the University of California at Berkeley. That was '68. But I could not see how what I was doing was really getting to the underlying root causes of people's suffering. I dropped out in the spring of 1969.

I was terrified because I didn't know what I was going to do with my life. I decided to just follow my nose and try to learn, try to educate myself, try to figure out why there was so much suffering in the world that seemed so needless. I started reading. If I just understood why people were hungry in the world, that would unlock the mysteries of economics and politics, because I felt food was the primal need. It links us to the earth, it links us to each other. If we're not eating, what else matters, right? Remember, it was the era in which the newspaper headlines and the textbooks were saying that the earth was running out of food. Too many people, famine was inevitable, humanity was overrunning the earth's capacity. I thought, *Well, are these experts right? Is it true? Is scarcity inevitable because of overpopulation?*

So I set out to answer that question. I found the UC [University of California] Agricultural Library, I hid away and did my research, and learned that the world produced more than enough food to make us all chubby! But we were feeding more and more of that to livestock because people who were hungry couldn't afford to make the quote unquote market demand for it. So because hungry people couldn't afford to buy it, it made perfect economic sense to feed cheap grain to animals, who then turn it into a high-priced product, meat. We create scarcity. That was the realization that launched my adult life. In those first years it was all library research. I just sat there and put the numbers together and realized that there was enough food. So *Diet for a Small Planet* came out in 1971, saying that scarcity is a myth, that we are creating scarcity for marketing purposes. The numbers, the volume of food produced in the world, it was all there for anyone to put together. I did have the hope that if people just had the facts, that would be enough to motivate them. If they realized that you couldn't blame nature, that we were creating this misery and it was all unnecessary . . . That was my initial hope. Through exposing the myth of scarcity, we could reorient the entire world, and people would start to question the whole economic system. Of course that didn't happen.

The book has now sold well over three million copies because there were many people like me. I think that gave me hope. I wasn't alone. That was a source of inspiration, that there were all these people looking for a way to connect their lives with solutions.

Life is engagement, life is struggle. That's what's rewarding. So there's never a thought of giving up. I kept trying to peel away the next layer. The facts, certainly, the facts alone are not going to change things. I came to believe that unless people had a taste of what it meant to have democratic power, to feel that they were real players in the public world, they wouldn't believe that democracy was possible.

In 1990, I co-founded an organization called the Center for Living Democracy. That organization lasted for ten years. Its philosophy was that democracy is not something we have, it's something we do. We started a national news service to infiltrate the mainstream media with stories of regular people who were engaged in their communities, solving public problems.

The Latin root of *power* is *posse,* "to be able." Power just means our capacity to act. I wanted to show people that we all have this capacity to affect the larger world. Our book, *Hope's Edge*—we went to five continents—is a continuation of this same approach, that we human beings are social creatures and learn from one another, that we all live by stories.* We wanted to show that Wangari could be you or me.

Hunger is not caused by a lack of food, it's caused by a lack of democracy. An answer to that is the Edible Schoolyard, at the Martin Luther King School in Berkeley. It's very Wangari-like. You start with the premise that if you allow young people to grow food in their schoolyard, to feed themselves and their peers, they will never look at themselves as powerless, because they feel the power. You feel like a miracle maker, right? You plant seeds and things grow and you actually have food to eat. So children from an early age experience the power, they experience the wonder of relating to the earth. They never will think again that the food grows in aisle three somewhere in the supermarket. The experience of actually working together to learn about science and also to prepare and serve the food, it's happening all over the country.

*A sequel to *Diet for a Small Planet.* Her daughter Anna was the co-author.

This particular garden at the Edible Schoolyard grew out of a conversation with the school principal. Alice Waters has been very much involved.* The kids design the garden, so it doesn't look like an adult did it.

In Bangladesh, there's a banker. He's a great example of thinking in a new way, in order to solve problems. In 1974, right after the war of independence in Bangladesh, he was an economist teaching in Tennessee. He went back to help rebuild his country. It was hit by a terrible famine. Every day, he would walk to teach his economics course, he would literally see people dying. One day he said, "Wait a minute. What does my teaching economics have to do with these people who are dying? There's no relationship? What's wrong here?" He said, "I had to become an ignorant person, drop all of my preconceptions." He gathered students to go back to the village and just listen and look with no preconceptions. He then realized that what was keeping people poor and hungry and causing the starvation was not lack of food, but debt bondage. They were so indebted to moneylenders that they couldn't get off the moneylender treadmill.

He had to completely rethink all of banking and turn all its premises upside down. First he went to the banks and said, "Here are these poor people, they need your loans." And the banks said, "Oh, no, we can't loan to the poor, they have no collateral." He started out just loaning out of his own pocket, microloans, and realized that poor people were better risks than the rich, because they all paid off their loans on time. He went back to the bank and the bankers again said, "No, no." Finally, he said, "Forget the banks, I'll just create something myself." So this bank has now loaned over three billion dollars to over two million village women. People often think of it as just a miniaturization of capitalism, but it's not. It's not just little loans for little people, because the whole premise is rethought. In other words, the collateral is not property, the collateral is trust among people—that people trust one another, that if somebody defaults, the others have to take over. The owners of the bank are not shareholders sitting like fat cats in Karachi. The owners are the village

*Alice Waters, who in the '60s, experimented in the art of cooking. Her restaurant, Chez Panisse, is one of the most honored gourmet dining places in the country.

women themselves, the borrowers. So it's built on a very different premise. Thinking anew.*

My daughter and I went to Brazil because I'd always thought of Brazil as the last place on earth that you would see successful land reform. I knew that most of the large landowners held as much as half of their land unused, but they didn't want to give it up because it was there for future speculative gain. Yet over the last twenty years, a land reform movement led by the Landless Workers Movement has settled almost a third of a million families on seventeen million acres of land.

This is how hope can spread across continents, because one of the founders of the Landless Workers Movement in Brazil said that he was inspired by the U.S. farm workers movement. In the early eighties, when it was against the law even to congregate, they managed to bring farm workers together and begin to claim land that was unused. Then in 1984, at the end of the military dictatorship and the beginning of civilian government, Brazil wrote a new constitution. There's a clause that says the government is required to appropriate land that is not being used for a social purpose, and redistribute it to the landless.

My daughter and I both came to redefine what we mean by hope. We came to see that hope is not something that one seeks in evidence through the grand tally. Over here is the way things are going down, and over there is the way things are looking up, and you figure out which is winning. We said, "No, that's not what it's about." If you look at the trends of the world today, forget it. The trend lines are all down. Hope is something else altogether. Hope is an act, hope is in action. Hope is not something we find, hope is something we become. It took on a whole different meaning to us. The people we

---

*Barbara Brandon, a disciple and biographer of Ayn Rand, wrote: "She taught us how to recognize communist propaganda in movies. *The Best Years of Our Lives* was one of them (Academy Award winner, 1946). She didn't say it was subversive or anybody should go to jail. She thought the public should recognize what it was. As I remember, the banker decides to give loans to the poor without collateral. That was considered virtuous. That it breaks banks, that was ignored. Virtue was to give away other people's money."

met on our journey are the most hopeful people in the world. It's not because they say, "Oh, yes, we're certain that we're winning in this struggle." But simply by their actions every day, in defying all the odds against them, they experience hope. They embody it: they don't seek it, they are it. So that's what we mean by hope and hope's edge. My daughter, Anna, loves to say, "I used to think that hope was for wimps." Hope is not for wimps; it's for the strong-hearted who can recognize how bad things are and yet not be deterred, not be paralyzed.

What keeps me from just total depression in reading the daily papers is constantly being aware that none of the things that we've witnessed would have been predictable thirty years ago. How can I say, no matter how bleak the picture looks, that anything is impossible? None of us would have predicted a successful land reform in Brazil. No one could have predicted that white minority rule would end in South Africa without a bloodbath, and yet it has. Well, gosh, if I had predicted any of these things thirty years ago, I would have been considered delusional. I think that there can clearly be these breakthroughs none of us can predict from the dominant forces that are so evident, because what the media isn't covering is exactly the stories that we've been talking about. The dominant mental map is so out of whack with people's own deepest needs for real connection with each other that it's fundamentally unstable.

The choices are so clear. Even ten or twenty years ago, it hadn't sunk in, the devastation, the ecological devastation, the global warming that we're already experiencing, the ozone hole, the species extinction. This is the first generation to know that the choices we're making have ultimate consequences. It's a time when you either choose life or you choose death. There's no middle ground. Going along with the current order means that you're choosing death. So it's an extraordinary time to be alive.

My next project is about fear. I think what holds us back from acting on this innate hopefulness is fear, and the deepest fear is fear of exclusion, fear of being cast out, stepping outside of the pack. I also believe that in order to act on our hope, we have to be willing to be outcasts. To be hopeful people, we have to overcome that fear. To create genuine community, we have to overcome our fear of losing community. One of the metaphors my daughter and I use a lot is the drop in the bucket. We're just a drop in the bucket, and that's meaningless. But we say, "No, wait a minute. If you have a bucket, those raindrops fill it up very fast. Being a drop in the bucket is magnificent." The problem is we cannot see the bucket. Our work is helping people see that there is a bucket. There are all these people all over the world who are creating this bucket of hope. And so our drops are incredibly significant.

Part IV

IMMIGRANTS

Usama Alshaibi

He is a sound engineer at the Chicago Historical Society, as well as an independent filmmaker. He is thirty-two years old. He had been sworn in as an American citizen a few days before this conversation.

THROUGHOUT MY WHOLE CHILDHOOD, it was from school to school, country to country, language to language, learning Arabic one year, English the next, then Arabic, then English. I was born in Baghdad, Iraq, in 1969. My father is Iraqi, my mother Palestinian.

My father went to the University of Iowa, in Iowa City, working on his Ph.D. in business administration on a scholarship he received from the Iraqi government. I didn't speak any English; I was just at kindergarten age. I ended up adapting to an American sensibility by the time I was in third grade. That's when we went back to Iraq. A lot of families from the Middle East will come to the United States, study, and return home. My father was going to teach and practice what he learned here.

We had a nice house in Baghdad. I have a lot of fond memories of sitting on my grandfather's lap. He was a tall man. He had many daughters. One of them was my mother. My grandfather was Palestinian; he was very proud of that. School was very tough because I had forgotten all my Arabic. We lived in Baghdad for roughly a year. Then we moved to southern Iraq, to a town on the sea called Basra, very close to the Gulf, very close to Iran. During this time, I was in fourth grade. My sisters and I had to have a tutor help us at home, but we were very happy. My parents bought a house, and I had a dog. Then the war started, the Iran-Iraq War. I remember hearing the sirens. When I was a kid, I would always go out in the street to watch the ambulances. But this siren never got closer. It just went on and on and on, this droning sound.

I remember my father came rushing in with all this food. I said, "What's going on?" He said, "We're in a war now." That night was the first time I experienced the bombing, where the ground would literally shake. They would turn off the electricity every night. That's when I started to fear for my life, to think I was going to die. I was probably eleven. I started to not believe my parents anymore. I would rush to the bathroom to try to take cover. We all had to sleep in my parents' bedroom because it was on the first floor. Life suddenly got very, very hard. Eventually we ended up leaving.

My father got a job in Saudi Arabia. My mother decided to take all us kids back to Basra to try to sell the house, and then things just got worse. They wouldn't let anyone out of the country. All of a sudden, my father was in Saudi Arabia, and we were stuck in the south of Iraq. I remember that because the regime of Saddam Hussein was becoming so fascist that they were watching everybody. To discuss the war over the telephone my parents would use the metaphor. They would say, "Our aunt, she's becoming more and more ill. I don't think our aunt is going to make it." That's how they communicated. We had to escape. Finally my mom says we're gonna go to Kuwait, which is south of Iraq. They were not letting anyone out of the country. My mother hid all her jewelry inside the diapers of my younger sister. I remember my mom said, "If the guards, the soldiers, ask you anything, just say 'I don't know.'" She was afraid that they would trick me into admitting where we were going. We took a bus to the border. I remember seeing tanks, remember seeing the desert. I remember the soldiers with guns. They took me aside, away from my mom, and they said, "Where are you going?" I said, "I don't know." They said, "Are you leaving Iraq?" I said, "I don't know." They said, "Are you a dumb kid?" I said, "I don't know." So they laughed at me. My younger sister was crying so much they let us go. My mom swore she was going for medical reasons and would return in a week. We never came back. Months later, half of our house was bombed.

I didn't understand politics at the time. I became very fearful of war. In Saudi Arabia—it's a very religious country—I was going to an all-boys school. I was constantly terrified of nuclear war. I became very religious. Every night I would pray to God not to allow World War Three to happen. That thought consumed me. I was suffering post-traumatic stress disorder. I would sit in class and hear planes overhead and I would want to duck. My heart would race.

The thing that I missed the most when I left Iraq was my dog. We had to leave him. I would cry every night for my dog, but really, I was crying, I think, for a lot of things. I felt safe in Saudi Arabia, but I was dealing with something else, which is religion. I was going to a very strict Muslim school, where I would have to memorize ten to twenty pages of the Koran. If you screwed up a word or two, you would be beaten on your hand. Eventually, my parents lost everything, so we returned to the United States, and all of a sudden I was in seventh grade. It was very hard for me to relate to my peers after what I had been through. I pretended I was coming from a very neutral experience. I would have to say I was embarrassed about being an Arab or from the Middle East.

I remember once in global studies in seventh grade in Iowa City, the teacher made me stand up in front of the whole class and tell everyone where I was from and what it was like. When you're in seventh grade, it's such an awkward age. You don't want to stand out, you want to fit in. I was very shy, just trying to be like everyone else. Not until years later have I become more open in discussing, and very proud of who I am.

My father tried getting work in the United States. We ended up returning to the Middle East. We lived in Jordan. We lived in the United Arab Emirates. Finally, my father bought a house in Iowa City. We were going back and forth, very nomadic. I finished high school in America.

I stopped trying to fit in so much and found a more political and artistic crowd. We had kids from different countries. We had some Jewish kids that hung out with us. The majority of our high school was all white. I would stand out in a class just because my skin was a little dark, or my name was unusual.

Then things didn't work out with my parents and they got divorced. I took off. By the time I was eighteen, I had become even more nomadic, just traveling around the United States, working here, going to school there. I ended up back in Iowa City, and my immigration status ran out. Then the Gulf War started. I had no visa, no right to work in this country. I was working under the table at these very low-paying jobs.

[*Sighs*] It was a scary time. When people would ask me where I'm from, I would say Jordan, not Iraq. I would go out to bars and overhear people saying things about how we gotta kill all the sand niggers. People can't really look at me and tell where I'm from or who I am. It's kind of like I was a voyeur. I was a part of this culture, but I was quiet, because I was afraid.

This was a very scary time. I had no visa. I had no status. I had to go to Omaha, Nebraska, hire a lawyer, and fight to be in this country. My father, who was working in the United Arab Emirates, was contacted by the Iraqi army. They wanted me for the draft, and this country wanted me out! I was twenty years old. I went in front of a judge and fought my case, stating that if I returned to my country, I would die. I got political asylum. Thank God. I will always be thankful for this country because they gave me political asylum to stay here.

Eventually I got my green card, and more of my family from Iraq and the Middle East have emigrated here. A lot of them had to escape or bribe people to get out. They wouldn't let my grandfather out of Iraq. Keep in mind, he was from Palestine, left in 1948, during the exodus, and ended up in Iraq. Here is a man who has been kicked out of his own country, placed in another country, not even his, and he's not allowed to leave. They say he died of a broken heart. He gave me my name. Usama was a great Islamic warrior. It means "son of a lion."

Saddam is a bastard. What he's done to his people, what he's done to Iraq . . . but our interest over there is questionable. It was a very paranoid time for me. As an Arab, I felt my status here was shaky. I never felt grounded anywhere. My family tried to make a home in Iraq; that didn't work. They tried to make a home here in the United States; that didn't work.

After the divorce, our family just disintegrated. I had no sense of home or place. I felt vulnerable. I felt I had to be quiet. After I got my green card, however, I started to be more outspoken. I started to read more, to find out what's really going on. I became active in politics, to try to end the sanctions against Iraq, to be outspoken about what's happening in Palestine and Israel. When 9/11 happened, I wasn't surprised. Already Osama bin Laden had been doing things. The tension with Israel and Palestine was getting worse. I started getting death threats over the Internet: "Die, sand nigger." Anonymous.

There was this great ignorance in this country. Everyone kept on saying, "They're envious because of our freedom, because of our democracy." I said, "No, it has nothing to do with that." "Our country did nothing wrong, our country doesn't deserve this." Of course nobody deserves this, but let's not play innocent, let's not pretend that a million dead Iraqi babies, dead from the UN sanctions against Iraqi citizens, don't go unnoticed in the Middle East. A lot of people that I had developed bonds with through the Internet turned against me. I had anonymous death threats saying, "Go back to your land, we're going to bomb the Middle East and turn it into a gas pump."

I was very worried because the government took three thousand men and put them in detention centers. They weren't officially charged. There was this great paranoia. I really didn't know what was going to happen. I wouldn't be surprised right now if they grabbed me and just started asking me a bunch of questions. Who knows? During the [first] Gulf War, my mother was contacted by the FBI and interviewed. I was being very vocal on the Internet. I started hearing politicians saying, "Just stop anyone with a diaper and a belt on his head." I was hearing people say, "Let's just nuke all of the Middle East and let God sort them out." It felt like *Here we go again*. And then I got paranoid. My sisters were saying, "You should be careful with what you say. They can take your words and they could..." I said, "What do you mean, my words? All of a sudden, my words have become dangerous?" They said, "Well, you're not a citizen." [*Whispers*] "You're right." So again, I was quiet. Because if anything happens, they can put any case against me, they can ship us all out tomorrow. So I waited patiently, made sure I got my citizenship. I remember, I was sitting in court the day of your birthday, and the judge gave this impassioned speech. He said, "This country is a country of immigrants. We *all* came from somewhere else. It is your duty to speak out about your culture, about your race, about who you are." This was the judge. It was a really great speech. I'm sitting with people from a hundred and three countries. I'm getting my citizenship. It's like graduating. I just remember feeling, *OK, I belong somewhere. I'm Arab, I'm American, and I'm on a mission.*

My mission is to give voices to people who have been really afraid to talk. I think there's a great silence among a lot of Arabs and Arab Americans in this country. There's a lot of fear in this. I don't know how many times I hear people on the radio and the TV news talk about the Islamists. It's given an ominous meaning.

I got married to an American girl, and I got my citizenship. Kristy grew up Christian. We're both not religious. For me, it's actually easier to discuss politics when I keep religion out of it. The Koran is filled with contradictions and all sorts of stories. Al-Qaeda, bin Laden, all these guys, they don't represent us. They don't represent the religion, they don't represent our community. I think sometimes of what happened to the Japanese after Pearl Harbor. I hope from this tragedy that there is an interest in what other people feel, instead of having anger and this lust for revenge.

I have hope that my generation of Arabs that grew up here can bridge the gap and incorporate our culture into this country without having to sacrifice our values and our sense of who we are. I think it's a great country: freedom of religion, freedom of speech. These are the things that I'm defending. Civil liberties. When I see people screened for racial profiling, I say, "If you keep letting this happen, eventually it will come back to you." How much of your rights are you willing to sacrifice for "safety"?

I'm thirty-two years old. For the first time, I feel like I belong somewhere. It's here.

"Maria" and "Pedro"

We are in the rectory of St. Pius Catholic church on Chicago's Near West Side. It had been their sanctuary during their early days in Chicago. Now they have a tiny flat in the community.

They are undocumented workers from Guatemala, of Mayan heritage. In addition to Spanish and a smattering of English phrases, her indigenous language is Kaqchikel and his is Mum. From different villages, they met in Guatemala City. They are married. She is more passionate in expressing herself; he smiles easily. He is twenty-eight; she is twenty-nine. The interpreter is Father Brendan Curran, a young Dominican priest.

MARIA: It's very dangerous for us at this time, being here. Very risky. That's what not having papers means to me. At any time, someone could threaten us with deportation.

PEDRO: We came here to find work for the benefit of my people, not only for myself. My mother and father were farmers: corn, beans, tomatoes, in small fields, very small parcels of land. And a certain kind of yeast, to make bread rise. Little seeds. I lived on the south coast of Guatemala in the high heat. Maria and me did not know each other, but we both worked in plantations picking coffee beans. We earned two dollars a day. Sometimes the coffee beans did not have a good harvest, so we would get one dollar a day.

MARIA: In my small village, large families cultivate our tiny fields, raising barely enough to eat to sustain ourselves. So we went to bigger villages for that two dollars a day. My mother had to raise our large family because my father died very young. I never really looked toward tomorrow or the future. I was always focused on the present, on helping my family survive.

PEDRO: We very seldom ate meat. Just a simple pound of meat cost three dollars. My father helped bring me through somewhere in the middle of high school. I went to work as a machine operator for a company in Guatemala City, where they made bathroom tissue. I had to work very fast on that line in order to gain more money. I sent some money back home to my family. The supervisors of the

271

company were pushing people to extreme conditions, where we had to work more than sixteen hours a day.

MARIA: I went to school for twelve years. [*Father Curran interjects: "College level."*] I was able to finish my master's in primary education. In my practice teaching, I had to teach sixty little ones in a rural community. Then I got a job with an organization of indigenous people. I began working as simply a secretary, but my bosses invited me to take advantage of my talents. So they had me out to visit communities. I helped organize indigenous communities around their issues, their problems, and how to make solutions as a community. That is when I met Pedro. His family came to the office in Guatemala City, knocking on the door, looking for a place to rent. At the time I was a general coordinator in the community organization. We invited Pedro and his friend to stay in the office in a spare room that no one was using. There came a time where Pedro had an infatuation for me. He and his friends were scheming for a way to get my attention. They decided to pretend a birthday party is for Pedro, even though it wasn't really his birthday. It was at that party where Pedro told me that he really liked me. After a long relationship, we got married.

First I must tell you how we came to be here. Since 1971, 1972, that was when the violence began throughout the country, but also right in my little area where I lived. The army had heard explosions of bottle rockets, fireworks. It was the guerrillas doing this, celebrating. The army thought that they were bombs, and so they came into the rural village and they killed people in the midst of their celebrations. They accused the villagers of celebrating with the guerrillas, and they weren't. They went about killing people and burning down houses, and burning sheep, burning livestock. The army had already had in mind what they had wanted to do. They wanted to take people out. Through seeing all the misery and suffering that we had been witnessing, and that of our own family that was suffering, I realized it was necessary to set as a goal raising money for the communities, in order to continue to be a helping hand for their suffering in the midst of the oppression. So that's why we came to Chicago. We needed to find funds.

PEDRO: My hope in coming to the States was realizing that my house was made of bamboo. We did not use lumber, we did not use bricks. Maria and me wanted to have a piece of land of our own to cultivate back in Guatemala, and to fix up a house that was made of something stronger than bamboo.

MARIA: And to help the community group to grow. We decided to come to Chicago through the parish here at St. Pius. It was the only contact we had in this country. You won't just come to the U.S. without knowing somebody.

PEDRO: I was hoping to get a car in order to move around to get a place to live.

MARIA: My hope is to be as if a bird, passing only for a time through here. I'm not planning to stay here, I don't hope to stay here. I only want to accomplish the dreams of my community and family that I still keep alive.

PEDRO: What I hope to accomplish is to be able to someday work for myself, not to be working underneath an owner that holds me under his feet. I want to return to Guatemala.

MARIA: There are two objectives of the organization. The first is that we be treated with fairness and with dignity, equally as women and men. The second major objective is to defend the rights of the people—the Cinca, the Garifuna, who came over from Africa, some escaped from the slave ships—and then the Maya, the indigenous people that originated from here. The Mayan people is a huge umbrella of peoples.

We came together in April of 2002. I knew various Guatemalan families, and I got to know Father Chuck Dahm, the pastor here at St. Pius. We needed to find jobs, of course. Father Chuck offered us space. Then we moved to Pilsen. There are many Mexicans here, some Guatemalans, some Peruvians. My landlady told me that day labor might be the way for me to go. When I began, I was getting up before three in the morning, to take the bus. I would have to pay out of my pocket for the bus to the day labor agency. When I arrived at the agency the first day, they did not send me out. I had to sit in the agency office, and then pay my way back without getting a job. I did that every day for a week.

PEDRO: I had the same experience.

MARIA: I would sit there for hours and they would ignore me, completely ignore me. I found out that they would only send out people who had been there for over a year or longer. They were the first sent out to the easiest jobs. People like me would sit in the office, waiting and waiting. Every once in a while, somebody would say, "Look, I've been sitting here for hours. Send me out." Finally, the woman behind the desk sent me to one of the hardest jobs. No one else wanted to go anyway.

PEDRO: When I first arrived, I had to fill out a lot of paperwork. There were over two hundred and fifty people waiting in that waiting room for a job. I noticed the same as Maria. People they knew, they sent right out; people they didn't know, you sat.

MARIA: I would be very offended because they would also make comments from inside the window about some of the workers. The woman who ran the office would call out a guy and say, "Hey, good-looking," and that would be the person that they would call to work.

We never have worked together. They don't send men and women to the same place. They usually send the guys to a place that's really heavy labor. I was sent to Graphic and told to carry huge bundles of paper. Graphic was outside the city. They took us in vans. We had to pay the driver a dollar fifty each way. They didn't like people who had their own cars, so they did not always give a lot of work to those people. I was paid thirty-five dollars a day for eight hours of work. But we did not receive the money at the end of the day. We were paid by the week. It's a day labor agency, you're supposed to get paid every day. I've been told that the work we did usually pays around ten dollars an hour, which is almost double what the workers got.

PEDRO: I was sent out with fourteen others to a candy factory. We had to mix the ingredients. You began with a dusty powder. It got all in the air and we breathed it. We had no masks.

MARIA: We always had to start by going to the agency first, and we would always return to the agency at the end of the day. When we lived on the North Side, we got up at one o'clock in the morning. We left the house at two o'clock. We had to take the buses. We'd get there at four A.M., wait outside until five, when the agency would open the doors. We wanted to get there early to get a good spot. They'd open the doors at five A.M., and then we'd wait. It depended. We'd leave at six A.M., seven A.M., eight . . . We'd arrive home about five or six in the evening. It would depend on when the van arrived after we finished our eight hours of work.

PEDRO: The job I had done at the candy factory, only certain of us would volunteer to do this work. The carts where they made candy were very sticky. The only way to clean them was to put them in the oven so the sticky stuff would fall off. The oven would be over a hundred degrees. The only people who would do that were the un-documented. My shirt, underwear, everything would be soaking wet. I could only be in the oven for about twenty minutes at a time before you had to come back out. We were the only workers who would do it. [*Laughs*] The week after working in the ovens in the candy factory, I was sent to work at a pizza factory. We had to go inside the freezer.

MARIA: In the evenings I would go to the church, very desperate, frustrated about the work. I would be praying to God, trying to sort out what to do.

PEDRO: I finally found a job that was a little bit better, gardening and yard work. I began work at almost nine and work five to six hours and get decent money. I still work there.

MARIA: I now work three days. I baby-sit for a small child. Two days a week I do cleaning. It gives me two days free. It's much better now. I now work from ten in the morning till six at night. At times, I can work with the child and visit with other people in the street. It's much more tranquil than the crazy pace at the factory. When we come home, we eat at a regular hour. It's more relaxed. Life is a little better. We have friends now. We never had friends before—we didn't have time.

My hopes are for my health. And to have a good job. I see hope in that the people I baby-sit for want to give me more hours of work. The family wants me to help them for two or three years, maybe even five days a week. That is a hope in helping me to fulfill my responsibility to my organization in Guatemala.

PEDRO: [*Laughs*] How can I have hope? Tomorrow is my last day on this job. I am losing the job because it is winter. So I have to find another job. My hope is to be able to obtain a turkey so that we can have turkey on Thanksgiving Day.*

MARIA: We want to return to Guatemala. We want to return with enough money so we can contribute to the organization without

*The conversation took place two days before Thanksgiving.

worrying about being paid. The organization has no money to pay us. We are afraid of being deported. When we walk in the street, we worry about somebody reporting us. We worry about meeting someone from immigration. When we sleep, we worry about someone knocking on the door. We always live with this fear.

In Guatemala, I saw great exploitation and prejudice and racism against the Mayan people. Here I see the exploitation is just as grave. We have experienced it in these temporary agencies. People have been exploited or overlooked just because of their color or their way of speaking.

PEDRO: I feel the gravity of being undocumented. I worry about what if my wife is sick again and if she needs to go to the hospital. They'll be asking for ID. I am always afraid of not being able to present the right papers. What if somebody from immigration deports me and she is sick and something is wrong and we're separated? I'm always thinking about it. If I'm driving and I get pulled over, will they ask about immigration? What will happen to me? I never felt that in Guatemala. It's been sad to realize that here, without papers, you are considered nothing.

MARIA: For each of us, it's important to remember that God doesn't have a distinction between people. Whether you have papers or not, we're all equal in the eyes of God. The thing that keeps me motivated and energized and gives me great hope is to remember that God honors me as a person regardless of whether or not somebody else does. Roses before they bloom are beautiful and protected. And when they bloom, we remember that they also have thorns. We often can be the thorns for others and not allow the beauty in other people. But we always remember that God created the roses, and that God created us all equally as beautiful.

A Caveat: Sam Osaki

"A Nisei is a person of Japanese ancestry who was born in these United States. His parents are Issei, first generation. My kids are Sansei, third generation. I have grandchildren and they are Yonsei, fourth generation. We, in many ways, are still strangers to America, although we have been here sixty, seventy, a hundred years."

I WAS BORN in Los Angeles, California. My father had been a dry-goods [store] owner in Little Tokyo, Los Angeles, but with the Depression he was wiped out. So we moved into the truck-farming area called Keystone, and he became a fertilizer salesperson. Many small Japanese truck farmers lived in that area, and of course they needed fertilizer.

My mother was a very religious person. She became involved with the Salvation Army first, and then became a very devout Seventh-Day Adventist. We have a family of three boys and three girls. My oldest brother, Kai, he's a medical doctor. Second is Yoshi, a social worker, he lives here in Chicago. I was a classroom teacher. I became the first Asian American school principal in the Chicago public schools. I was principal at two different elementary schools, and then three different high schools. I've been retired for thirteen years. I enjoyed my career very much.

We were fortunate. We were very poor. Well, everyone was poor during the Depression. I still recall my elementary school experience, and I think about my teachers from those days. I've heard of many instances of discrimination in the schools, especially against the Nisei. At our school, for whatever reason, that was not the case. It was majority white with very few Japanese, and some Mexican Americans, but our teachers treated all of us with quiet dignity and love. I think that's one reason why I've always remained very hopeful for our country, because of those teachers.

When December seventh occurred, I was a seventeen-year-old high school senior. My sister tells me I came running into the house saying, "Japan bombed Pearl Harbor." Of course, like everyone else, we didn't know where Pearl Harbor was. But instinctively we knew that, since the Japanese empire bombed Pearl Harbor, we were in trouble. The FBI, and even President Roosevelt, had been investigating the Japanese American community for years because they anticipated war with Japan. So right after December seventh, the very hour after, the FBI picked up a good two thousand of the Issei generation, the leaders of the Japanese American community, in the business world, the Japanese-language-school teachers, Buddhist priests, and so forth. My father was not picked up on that first round. I guess he was not *that* important. But a few weeks after, the FBI came to our house. Three big, white, strapping FBI agents. They searched the house, they questioned us, and then they took my father away. They didn't tell us where they were taking him. For weeks we didn't know where he was. He finally wound up at the Santa Fe Federal Detention Center. So that left us without a father.

This was still before Executive Order 9066, February 1942. Our good president, Franklin Delano Roosevelt, signed Executive Order 9066, effectively placing all one hundred and twenty thousand persons of Japanese ancestry into America's concentration camps. Two-thirds of the one hundred and twenty thousand persons of Japanese ancestry were like me: native-born American citizens. The wording of Executive Order 9066 does not say anything about Japanese, Italians, Germans, but everyone—Franklin Delano Roosevelt, congressmen, governors, military leaders—understood: it was simply the Japanese Americans. Later on, when they posted signs in the streets, on buildings and telephone poles, it said all persons of Japanese ancestry living in certain areas must report to certain designated areas. Everyone living in the three western states: California, Washington, Oregon. We were so naive. We were just completely naive, and we accepted orders. The FBI came in, we didn't ask whether they had a search warrant or anything. We just simply accepted what we had to do. We didn't ask questions.

At that time, being a seventeen-year-old, I didn't even know the JACL existed.* Later on, I heard that the Quakers, the American Friends Service Committee, had suggested we say no. It's sixty years later, and there's been much controversy in the Japanese American

*Japanese American Citizens League.

community about [how] our JACL and its leaders cooperated with the United States government. When I think of it now, and when I think of the history of our country, beginning with the genocide of the first people, the Native Americans, and later slavery, Jim Crow, the taking of California from Mexico, I feel really that if we had all decided to resist, it would have been just like the Trail of Tears. Our government would have come in with soldiers with bayonets. They would have rounded us up. Conceivably, many people would have been killed.

As Bill Osakawa says in his book *The Quiet American,* we were such a small minority. Since the days of the Chinese Exclusion Act, Asians had never been given any rights; they were just totally stepped on. So we grew up with that. As my parents used to say, it's the nail that sticks up that gets pounded down. I think we were taught to be subservient. We *had* to be.

It was just shocking. I was a senior in high school in Wilmington, California. I was taking a class in journalism. My teacher said, "If you'll write some letters telling about your experience, I can give you a grade and pass you." I still remember writing to the school newspaper and telling them about my disappointment. We had been taught, and we believed in, the Constitution and the Bill of Rights. All of a sudden to have all this taken away, it was such a disappointment. I still remember writing that: just a big, big disappointment.

My father was sent to a separate federal detention center for people who had been picked up early on because they were leaders in the Japanese American community. After the executive order, we were instructed to report to different places—in our family's case, the Santa Anita racetrack. They had not prepared concentration camps, so the government took over facilities like racetracks, fairgrounds, where they had some kind of facilities to house thousands of people. Stables, in our case. They moved the horses out, they moved us in. When I talk to students, I always tell them, "You know what? They treated the horses better than they treated us." Racehorses are worth lots of money, so naturally they're going to get plenty of tender, loving care, they're going to be well fed, treated well. In our case, we were not worth two cents: we were the enemy.

My second brother decided to go with some friends—they were encouraged to volunteer—to Manzanar in California to help build that concentration camp. So it was my three sisters, my oldest brother, my mother, and myself. We drove the car to Santa Anita. You could only take that which you could carry in your two hands. In our case, we just did not have any resources. We didn't own our house, we didn't own much of anything. But many people lost thousands of dollars' worth of property: furniture, automobiles, truck and farm equipment, simply because they were given such a short time to get rid of things. We were at the Santa Anita racetrack about seven or eight months, until they were able to build the more permanent-type concentration camps further inland.

What was life like? It depended on your age and gender. I was a seventeen-year-old and active in sports. So I became involved with the recreation department. There were a lot of things that had to be done to run the camps, and they provided employment for us. We did not have any money, so we were all happy to work for the small sums they paid us. Two-thirds of the camps were young children. They knew they had to keep these young people occupied or there would be hell to pay. We started a sports program: we had softball teams, volleyball teams. That's what I did. I tried to carve out a softball diamond in the dirt, and so forth.

When they built the permanent concentration camps, we were sent to Jerome, Arkansas. This was swampland. The other eight concentration camps, for the most part, were built in desolate areas. One was in Hilo, Arizona, right next to an Indian reservation. I was there about a year.

The way I got out—they had stopped drafting Nisei into the army after Pearl Harbor. A number of them already in the army were arbitrarily discharged simply because of their ancestry. But after some thought, I guess, our government had a change of heart. They decided to form a segregated infantry unit composed entirely of Japanese American volunteers. Of course, that was controversial. People got very upset about it in the camp. You put us in a camp, you want us to volunteer to fight for this country? They sent recruiting teams to the ten concentration camps, and to the territory of Hawaii. In the territory of Hawaii, *everybody* volunteered. They were overwhelmed with the volunteers. They had been discriminated against, but not put in concentration camps. When they went to the ten concentration camps, understandably, there were not that many people who volunteered. Along with four good friends—Babe Okura, Ted Yasanaga, Harry Ora, Iso Masuta—we decided to volunteer for this segregated unit that went on to become the Four-forty-second Infantry. That's the one that served in Europe. We became the most highly decorated infantry unit in U.S. Army history for its size and length of service. Two of my good buddies were killed in action, rescuing a lost battalion in France. They wanted us to prove our loyalty to this great democracy, and I guess we did. [*A cross between a chuckle and a sigh*]

I think about it many times: why did I volunteer? Blacks, for example, they have been fighting and dying for this country since Bunker Hill. The same with the Mexican Americans, with the Native Americans. It was no different with us. We felt that just maybe, just maybe, we had to go out and prove our loyalty so our families would then be able to be released from the camps, and we would have a future in this country. Oh, the irony . . .

I have a great photograph. I didn't realize this photograph was taken. My sister happened to be in Los Angeles visiting the Japanese American National Museum. She sees this photograph up there: "That's my brother!" It's a photograph of my mother and father— he was finally able to rejoin the family in Jerome, Arkansas—and myself in uniform, visiting just before going overseas to fight for this great democracy. Visiting my parents in a concentration camp.

We received great honors, great publicity in the American press. So we were able to come back, receive our discharge, and then, like all other GIs, we had to think of adjustment to civilian life. What are we going to do now? Of course, there was still discrimination in job fields. But at that time, because of the increase in children, the field of education began to open up, so that we could become teachers.

My mother had been a teacher of Japanese in Japan, so she always encouraged us to go into fields of service of people. They always stressed the importance of doctors and nurses, so my older brother became a doctor. I became a teacher.

We faced all kinds of discrimination, even after we had proven ourselves in Europe and in the Pacific. In California, when Earl Warren was governor, even after they released the families from the camps, he still did not want our people to return. There were firebombings, and people were shot while trying to return to their homes in California, Oregon, and Washington.

This is the only country I know. All the friends I went to school with are here. Despite the fact that they put us in camps, I still believed in this country. I think you have to believe, you have to be an optimist. When you talk about the glass being half empty or half full, you have to see it's half full. My mother and father, despite their experiences, were still very positive about this country. They died some years ago.

There was the problem of communicating with my parents. They spoke Japanese, I spoke English, and our communication was limited just to day-to-day living. So I really never had a chance to go into depth with my parents. But they never said negative things about this country, especially my mother, who was always thinking positive. I have always talked to my kids about our experiences. I still remember when I started at Roosevelt University in 1946 or '47, one of the first papers I wrote—for English, I think—was about America's concentration camps. But many families wanted to shelter their kids. They may have felt some shame, that maybe we were at fault. That's the thing that really bothers me. It was our country, the United States government, that was so wrong.

Our kids' generation, they grew up with the civil rights movement and they began to ask us why, even though it's forty years later: "Why didn't you challenge our government?" And that's what started the JACL redress movement. And of course I testified.

We finally were awarded twenty thousand dollars each in reparations. And a letter of apology signed by the president of the United States. It was Ronald Reagan, that's the surprising thing. Of all the presidents, you would think Ronald Reagan would never sign. The story is that when Ronald Reagan was an actor, the Japanese began returning to California and they were having lots of problems. The government decided to try and get some positive publicity. So they had Ronald Reagan along with General Stilwell present posthumously a Distinguished Service [Order] cross to the sister of, I think it was Sergeant Matsuta, so there would be some favorable publicity. Someone reminded him of this when he was asked to sign the reparation bill. That brought back some memories. That's the story I hear. True or not, it's a good story.

Because of what happened to us, I thought it was very important for Japanese Americans to stand up now for Arab and Muslim Americans—that these are Americans who are not to be treated any differently from others. They are to be treated with dignity, respect, and equality. I think that's such an important issue right now. For us to speak up, especially us Japanese Americans, because we have gone through that. We read of a number of Arab and Muslim Americans who have been picked up and not been allowed to see their attorneys, being held for indefinite periods. We really have to be alert and vigilant and see that our government does not repeat the mistakes of the past. But I'm really very hopeful. Americans are beginning to realize that there are a lot of people in this world other than Americans and Europeans.

We have always been so self-centered. We think the world whirls around us. And there are billions of other people. I think it's great when you walk the streets and you see different shapes, different sizes, and they're beautiful. That's what America has to see. People ask me, do I feel bitter? When I see something on TV where an Arab American or a Muslim American has something done to him, that really brings up the anger. I like to take out my anger and bitterness in a positive way. I speak to many student groups to let them know the truth about America. For the most part, American history is written by white males. The young have to begin seeing things from a little different perspective. I want America to live up to its promises.

YOUNGLINGS

Mollie McGrath

She is petite in appearance. She speaks in a casual, throwaway fashion.

I'M TWENTY-FIVE. I grew up in Wisconsin Rapids, a mill town. My dad is a dentist, my mom is a grade-school teacher. They're Republicans. I remember in sixth grade I told my teacher he ought to vote for Bush. I was just a regular kid.

It was a rocky road for me between high school and college. I was a cross-country athlete and pretty good at it. I was a really good student. Towards the end of high school, I got really fed up with that sort of life, like I started to question it, I guess. I was anorexic, and towards the end of high school, I was in a hospital for anorexia and depression. That probably was my way of breaking myself off from my family. The hospital wasn't that helpful, but it was my entry into the world as an independent person. I moved around. I lived in California for a while, couldn't even find a job, and then I decided to go to college, to Madison [the University of Wisconsin], because it was easy to get into and cheap since I lived in-state.

I was a very angry person. But I took one women's studies course and I really loved it. It was a channel for my anger. It gave me an explanation for what had happened to me—not just that women are exploited, but the whole way the world was working. I started to reach out to people. I was sick of sitting around in my classes, and people talking but not doing anything. I got active in a pro-choice women's group. And then, right around that time, the antisweatshop campaign just came up, sweatshops as links to the people that produce garments that have school logos on them. For me that was a working-class issue that connected with women's issues, because the majority of people in the global garment industry, just like back in the 1900s, were women. I was working a lot with the student government. They made the antisweatshop stuff their whole campaign. I started going to meetings, organizing press conferences, and we had a sit-in in 1999 to get a code of conduct for the university to make sure the university only licensed with corporations that would accept this code of conduct, that it would give a living wage to people. It was very exciting. Now lots of universities have them.

As I got more and more involved, it became like a mission. I got the Wisconsin state AFL-CIO to take me to Seattle. We got there right in the middle of all of it. We were there to protest the WTO, the World Trade Organization, but to me it was more labor and environmentalists really coming together to articulate this position against globalization. The WTO is not run democratically. It was formed with the interests of profit in mind. It was like a war zone in Seattle for a while. There were tens of thousands of people in the streets, all kinds of colors and causes. At first, the city was really welcoming. There was food for people, there were strangers who just let us stay in their houses. I stayed at a house of two women, both doctors, who were partners, and they had two kids. They fed us and had a hot tub they let us go in when we were all dirty and smelly.

I was kind of skeptical but really excited, especially when I saw all these union guys talking to me about women's studies. I was explaining what women's studies was about, and they were explaining why they were in unions. We were really different, but we were able to unite. They were curious about us, the students, and we were curious about them. I really loved the excitement and the camaraderie of people around me who cared about the same thing. But there were also a lot of people living there who felt invaded, pissed off—the police especially. It just gradually got polarized and there would be just battles between hundreds of protesters.

Back at school that year, my friends and I all got together and organized this sit-in again to form a workers' rights consortium: a monitoring group that goes to college-apparel-producing factories around the world that have complaints lodged against them. We wanted the university to support that, and they did, after a while. Madison has had a long history of student-labor stuff, but colleges and universities, most, are the center of privilege. Most of the people don't care. They learn about the world and inequality, they learn about racism, they learn about everything, but it's not their goal to make things better. It's their goal to make their lives whatever they want. I got really involved with the Students Against Sweatshops nationally, so I met a lot of students like me around the country. I've only been out of a school for a year, and I'm transitioning to having a working lifestyle.

At first, my parents thought it was kind of crazy. Especially when I went to jail. [*Soft laugh*] I was just there a couple of hours after the sit-in. They were mad. Now they're pretty happy. I think they're proud that we're trying to change things, even though they're still right wing. My twin sister and brother are now both involved in the Worker Rights Consortium. I was the first one to get involved politically. She was more countercultural. Like an environmentally conscious hippie.

I guess my hope kind of changes. Before September eleventh, it seemed like we could concentrate more on one specific thing, just eliminating sweatshops that produce college garments. Now it's more overwhelming. There's millions of people dying in this country or that country, and our country that's doing it, that's killing civilians. I still know there's a lot of people out there that feel the same way. They need to be talked to. They need to learn like I did. I see really good hearts in a lot of people. It doesn't matter how much privilege you have, although the privilege can totally blind you to the world's problems. But I see a lot of people who are willing to sacrifice stuff in their lives to make change, to make a difference. At Madison, the whole new freshman class, we had twenty kids show up to this meeting. It wasn't like that five years ago. You really had to go out and find people. It's becoming more and more commonplace for people to feel like it's a good thing to do.

Bob Hemauer

He accompanied Mollie McGrath during her visit. He is twenty-three. He is a big kid, could be a football running back. He is enthusiastic about his doings, as though astonished at what is happening in his life.

I WAS A BIG GEEK in high school, just kind of not popular. I spent a lot of time reading books. I knew from a really early age that I didn't like the way politics worked. It's not right, for example, that factories close in this country and the people who own the factories make a ton of money while all the people who are working there get kicked out. I knew I was for change, however vague that is, and I just kind of floated around. It's difficult for people who aren't confident in themselves to insert themselves into a movement sometimes.

I'm from a small town in eastern Wisconsin, West Bend, a working-class town in a part of a state which to this day remains extremely conservative. My parents run a paint store. My dad's been working there since he was sixteen years old. He's fifty now. I've got a younger brother and kid sister. I talk with my mom and dad about my activism. It's odd, 'cause a lot of folks I know aren't really able to talk about it. My parents are comfortable where they are, but they're very open-minded. They just want me to be happy, and they know that working for social change and social justice is what makes me happy.

Mollie and I became close during the college sit-in. It was the second sit-in in two years over sweatshop issues on our campus, and we were all U-locked with each other by the neck in our chancellor's office. U-locks are those bicycle locks. Over the course of the sit-in, which was five days, I called my parents twice. Once I was in the chancellor's office at the beginning of the sit-in, when they were threatening to call in the cops and haul us up. I had this U-lock on and I picked up the phone in there and called my mom. "Hey, Mom, you're probably going to see some stuff on the news. I'm okay." She was like, "That's fine, honey, just stay safe, be careful." I didn't call her again until five days later, and all this stuff was on the news. "Oh, Mom, I'm in jail now." There were fifty-four people total that were arrested. They kept me in for the better part of a day; everyone else got out in a few hours. My mom and dad are timid about political expression, but they've been supportive of me. We've had dialogues, and they've moved their politics from center Democrat to slightly further left. In my hometown the Democrats are a fringe group, and anyone else is crazy. [*Laughs*]

Like everyone my age, I had self-esteem problems. But I got involved. I started doing some political-campaigning-type stuff for Senator Feingold. That wasn't for me. I started doing labor solidarity stuff, talking with students and organizing students because that's your constituency. I found it really rewarding to hear that the stuff we were doing was helping workers who lived in Madison. Becoming friends with actually working folks was really inspirational.

There's this factory in Madison, the Rock Town Factory. It's represented by the Paper and Allied Chemical Employees, PACE, Local Twelve-oh-two. Rock Town was threatening to close the plant. First, management wanted twelve-hour shifts, which absolutely kills families. It's an erosion of workers' rights. People fought and died for the eight-hour day, right? To take the twelve-hour day would be a major setback.

The Student Labor Action Coalition that I work with on campus met with some folks in this union and got involved with the struggle. We kind of said, "Yes, we want to support you in what you do." We, the students, would be out when the union would be doing pickets. When they threatened to close the plant six months later, we were there. Unfortunately, we lost that fight, but the experience of meeting working people who are struggling to save their lives and their jobs, and helping them, was incredible to me. At first there was a little bit of wariness from the union folks, like "What are these people all about?" But after a few years of working together, they really love having the energy of the student movement. There's a spark there. There's definitely a marked difference when you go to, say, a student conference and a labor conference. At the student conference, you'll definitely get more sense of urgency, like this is something we need to *do*. With the union folks, they recognize that the struggle isn't a sprint, it's a marathon. The two combined form a great symbiotic relationship. The students move union folks to do things they wouldn't necessarily feel comfortable doing. They're the crazy kids up front making the racket. But now, I feel, they look upon us as allies.

The union we work very closely with is the blue-collar technical employees union on campus, the American Federation of State, County, and Municipal Employees, Local One-seventy-one. They have great progressive leadership. The University of Wisconsin uses a lot of limited-term employees or temps. There's a lot of abuse. What SLAC, the Student Labor Action Coalition, is trying to do is get students educated. What the university will do is hire someone at seven-fifty an hour to be a cook, let's say. According to state statute, you can only work half a year, six months, a thousand and forty hours as a limited-term employee. But what the university will do is hire people and just slightly change their job classification and keep them on for years and years and years. We have a woman who's working really closely with us, a limited-term employee, an LTE, who had been working at the job for nine years. She went public, as a whistle-blower, and got fired. What we're trying to do is build consciousness among students about how the university squeezes its workers dry. These people work without benefits, without retirement, without anything. I've been involved with this group for almost four years, and we haven't had more people than we have now. Every week we're getting a couple of new people. I can't even tell you. It's so exciting. We had a meeting on Thursday, and three limited-term employees just walked in from seeing the posters. These three workers, whom no one knew, just walked in, heard about the meeting, are excited to do organizing with other LTE's.

I graduated, and it's kind of a weird time for me. A lot of activists, when they graduate, go through this kind of "Oh, my God, what am I going to do?" I don't want to get a corporate lame job and move out to the suburbs. What I've chosen to do is stick around in the student group to provide some continuity. Another thing about the student group, they have a lot of energy, but they don't have a lot of institutional memory.

I'd like to be able to look back on my life and say that I made a positive difference in a very specific way. I don't want a street named after me, but I want to be able to be content knowing that I helped.

You can look around today and feel absolutely crappy about the world. But to me, the hope comes in the struggle. I have firm belief that things will be better in a major way soon. I don't know how soon, especially looking at history, but I'm an incurable optimist.

Lynn Siebert

"I'm twenty-three, a year out of Knox College in Galesburg, Illinois, where I also grew up.* I am an only child. My father is a professor of political science at Knox College, and my mom is a registered nurse. I grew up in a pretty conservative community. Religious figures were constantly writing into the local newspaper condemning anyone who wasn't conservative Christian: condemning gays, condemning liberals. My dad always considered himself independent politically."

FOR YEARS I HAD NO IDEA what I wanted to be. In college I thought that journalism was the way I wanted to go. That's not what I'm doing now. I'm working as a union organizer for SEIU [Service Employees International Union] Local Eight-eighty. We're a union that organizes all the people in the service industry. Our local organizes home care workers, home day care providers, and child care providers who work in their home. Most of the time, I organize home child care providers.

It's not like there's a shop floor, it's not like somebody who's going to go organize a factory. These people all work in their individual homes spread out all over the state. We take the union to them, going door-to-door.

My day? I normally head out into the field, to our turf, in the early afternoon. It's a good time for home day care providers. I knock on doors. I have a list of names. Through the Freedom of Information Act, we are able to get a list of all the licensed child care providers. There are probably about ten thousand providers in the state of Illinois, and somewhere around half of them take care of children whose parents are low-income and qualify for state assistance. Especially here in the Chicago area, it's mostly women of color doing this kind of work. The state pays these providers well below the market rate. For somebody who pays privately for child care, the market rate here in Chicago is probably around thirty-three dollars a

*Carl Sandburg's hometown.

day. The state pays these providers here in Cook County twenty to twenty-one dollars per child per day. Say if they had three children in their day care, which is about the minimum they would have, they would make about six dollars an hour.

I have my list, I have my map. I park my car, and go and knock on the doors of the people on the list. There was a woman named Bertha Rose, a provider who lives in Austin, on the West Side of Chicago. When I went to knock, she was sitting on the porch waiting for a van to pick up some of the children she was taking care of. I introduced myself: "Hi, I'm Lynn, from the home day care providers union, I'm here because providers are organizing to fight for better rates, better benefits, more of a voice and more respect for the kind of work that you're doing." That's another thing: most of these women don't have any health insurance. They don't get any of those benefits with their job. The state considers them independent contractors.

So Bertha invited me to come sit down on her porch. I started out by asking her some questions about her work: how long she'd been doing child care, how many children she was taking care of, what the ages were of the children. They were mostly toddlers, two to four years old, some infants. She didn't expect me. Sometimes when I knock on doors people say, "A union? I didn't know we had a union." But other times, they may have gotten our newsletter in the mail, they may know other providers who are members of the unions. There's kind of a buzz through the home day care community because providers get together. They have associations, they have friends who do the same work. So they may have heard of a union already.

[*Laughs*] I've been met with kids saying, "Mom, there's a white lady at the door." I get mistaken sometimes for a licensing representative with DCFS [Department of Children and Family Services]. They're the ones that license providers, and they do unexpected visits from time to time. Sometimes they may think I'm a cop or a social worker. I explain why I'm there. Usually I'm right in the door within minutes, sitting on somebody's couch having a conversation with them about what needs to be done.

In the case of Bertha, it was a conversation about what specifically she does in a given day: changing diapers, feeding the kids meals and snacks, putting them down for a nap, taking them to the park, going to the library. Then we talk about how she feels about what the state is paying. Generally our success rate is high. Most everyone that we talk to signs an organization card for representation with the state. Most of those people are dues-paying members.

We're organizing groups of people that were once thought to be unorganizable. It's not what I originally saw myself doing, but it's definitely what I'm happy doing now. I think a lot of people my age are doing this kind of work because they're dissatisfied with how things are. We're helping to mobilize a group of people, poor women of color normally, who aren't thought of as political heavy-hitters. But by bringing these people together, they can have a voice, they can have a say politically. I wouldn't be doing this work if I didn't have hope. Maybe enough of us are not being heard from. Our agendas aren't mainstream. Especially with the political climate as it now is. People are, I think, looking for alternatives, looking for ways in which they can change the system in maybe some kind of quietly radical way.

Mine isn't a nine-to-five job. It's not something where you go in, punch your time card, go home at the end of the day, and leave it behind. It's much more consuming than that. Union organizing isn't the only such job. My roommate's a teacher, and she's the same way. She's constantly thinking about her students.

The people that I work with at Local Eight-eighty wouldn't want to be working a typical nine-to-five job. I could look at what I do in the short term and say, "This is a year where we didn't win anything." The reality is that there are people who have been with this union for twenty years, fighting for what look like very small rate increases, getting up to six, seven dollars an hour. I can't be negative about not winning a raise this year when they're still out there fighting. We did a big action in the State of Illinois building when the governor was threatening to cut home care workers' hours. Six of our members took arrest, were taken off in riot cuffs, one of them eighty-one years old. She's been a member of this union for twenty years. The union that I work for is a fighting union. We have to be committed to a bigger vision. We are growing.

Maggie Morningstone

She works in Alderwoman Helen Shiller's office. At the moment I arrive, she is simultaneously answering the phone and helping a neighborhood person fill out a form. She is twenty-six and ebullient.

SOMETIMES PEOPLE CALL ME or come into this office and say, "I'm thinking about buying a condo in the area, but I feel really nervous because I see homeless people on the street and people that are not like me, and that scares me." Oftentimes I tell them that I feel safer walking down Broadway at midnight than I ever did crossing the quad when I went to the University of Illinois. The reason is because I feel a part of this community. Even if I don't recognize the faces on the street, I know these people are looking out for each other. That's a beautiful thing, that's a hopeful thing.

If you're in the middle class, if you're not very poor or very rich, I think you have a bigger capacity for hope because you have less stress in your life. If you don't have a lot, then you're worried about getting something. If you have a lot, then you're worried about keeping it. But if you have just a little bit, then you can just live.

OK, I'll tell you a story. A couple of weeks ago there was a fire in a building on Beacon Street. I just happened to be in the neighborhood and saw the fire. It's lots of six-flats. It was about ten-thirty in the evening, and all these trucks were coming by. I called Helen* and she met me over there. We found one woman who wouldn't be able to live in her apartment again, it was too badly burned. She was visibly upset, shaking, and wasn't really making much sense. We really wanted her to go to a hospital, but she said no. Finally she agreed, if Helen and I could drive her there. She was in her mid-fifties, living by herself. We take this woman, Susan, into the hospital. We went to get a Pepsi out of the vending machine, and when we got back, Susan was having an epileptic seizure in the emergency room. There wasn't much else we could do for her that night, but we made sure

*Helen Shiller.

295

that the Red Cross would contact her. A week went by and we didn't hear from this woman. One day, she walks into the office looking much better. She had checked herself out of the hospital against medical advice. She just wanted to get her stuff settled: find a new place to live, see what was left over from the fire, get herself going again. So we took her over to the apartment building, and all of her stuff was gone. So we got Susan set up with a brand-new apartment. We got her some toiletries, we got her a little bit of food, vouchers for clothes. I happened to have an extra television. She really wanted a television, to help her relax. She was already on disability, so she was getting a steady income. We had a new apartment for her, a refrigerator, a fan, a microwave, this new TV of mine that I gave her. The very next day we found out that this woman was getting kicked out of this new apartment because she took my television and sold it for money to buy crack. Somebody caught her smoking that crack in the building and they said, "Sorry, you can't live here anymore." Sometimes you get a raw deal. But I would much rather have had that happen than automatically assume that someone is going to give you the shaft.

Oh, sure, things like that frustrate me every day. But not enough to make me want to quit. It frustrates me that there are only twenty-four hours in a day. I'm not so concerned about the world of tomorrow. I'm more concerned about participating in what we do today. And making sure it continues tomorrow.

HIGHER LEARNING

Liliana Lineares

We're in Harvard Yard. She is a custodian. She's seated with her daughter and with her interpreter, Minsu Longiaru, an Indonesian law student, who started a legal aid group here for the working people.

I WORK AT THE medical school on the Longwood campus of Harvard, which is downtown. I have a part-time job. We do mopping, dusting, keeping the windows clean. We keep everything impeccable. I have a pretty big work area that I have to finish within three and a half hours. I work from six in the morning until nine-thirty in the morning, Monday through Friday. I'm married and I have children. After nine-thirty, I go home, I do my errands, I do my cooking, my cleaning, and I wait for my daughter to get home. Sometimes, in the afternoons, to supplement my part-time job, I take care of two little girls. I've been working at Harvard for the last three years. I'm often looking for ways to get another income. In 2000, I also worked on the census, in Spanish. I had that as another part-time job. In 2001, I started taking classes from the Red Cross. After that I became more involved with some of the activities here at Harvard. Going to meetings, working with the union, things like that.

During April and May, I worked for the union as they were trying to organize new workers for the master contract. Before the contract negotiations, there was a lot of stress in the workplace. The supervisors were telling you: "Do your work, that's it, we don't want to hear any more about it." Now, after the contract negotiations, the administration has totally changed. The supervisors are much more flexible. We have sick days, we have raises, we have benefits and vacations. Before, if you were sick, you had to come in to work anyway because you couldn't really use a sick day or you were worried that if you had to miss a couple of days, you would lose all of your vacation days. Now the workers have realized that they have the power to change things and make them better.

The students helped us. What happened between the students and the workers was an emergence of a really tight relationship, a sort of common affection rose between us. Before the taking of Massachusetts Hall, I didn't have this feeling. When it happened, when the sit-in happened, at first really nobody could believe it. It was almost like a form of salvation that the students had finally become conscious of our problems. Before the student strike, I definitely saw them as privileged people who were very different than me. After the sit-in, I saw that it wasn't like that.

My feelings about hope have changed. What we realize is that we're not alone. Now we have a community of students who are out on the front lines. We have a workshop this Saturday. We're trying to build an organization, the worker center, where students and workers can be involved with one another. Before, a lot of people didn't know my name. I was a stranger to the students, and the students were strangers to me. At most, I sort of recognized faces. Now, I know a lot of students by name, and they say hello to me. I know Minsu, I know Aaron. I know Greg, Runa, Lara, and there's a little red-haired boy. It has been very good for me to be involved in this. It's like I'm just putting in my own little grain of sand. Not only for myself, but for the people who come afterwards.

I don't really see myself as somebody special serving the movement. It's not that somebody knows *my* name, my name isn't that important. Workers all across this campus have gotten their names in the *New York Times*. For us it was really about winning the best benefits that we could for our co-workers. At this moment, I feel very motivated. And it's not just because I'm going to be having a second child. I want to be able to continue, to move ahead in my work. I want to be able to improve the situation of my children, my family. Most of all, I want to contribute my own grain of sand.

At this point, I don't really feel tied down or held back by fear or any need to conform with what other people are doing. I have a lot of hopes, I have a lot of dreams. I'd like to buy a home. I would like my children to be able to have careers and work as professionals. I don't want to be the kind of person that dwells on the past. A lot of sad things have happened in the past, but the important thing is to keep on and to live. You really have to live, you really have to struggle. I do have my family in Peru, my father and my brothers and sisters, and I want to make things better for them, too. Life is very different, but at the same time, this country offers a lot of opportunity. I only hope that God will give me the ability to be able to achieve all the dreams that I have.

For me, the most important thing is that they respect us as workers. I think almost fifty percent of the workers here are women, and most of them are mothers. We will risk everything for our families because the most important thing is that we are earning our money, we are earning our salary honorably. In Lima, I worked in a business, and it was basically like Macy's. I worked there for fifteen years, from when I was eighteen until about thirty-four. Most of my salary I got from commissions. It was a middle-level salary. In our country, you don't earn that much money.

In Lima, I lived with my parents until I got married. I was the oldest of six children, three girls and three boys. I was the person who had to support my family. My father and my second sister and I were the ones that were working. I and my sister had to give up studying so that I would be able to work to support my family. My mother stayed home with my brothers and sisters. The four youngest, they're all professionals. The two oldest, we're both workers. We were a family from humble origins. We have an expression, *del pueblo*: we're from the people. Now I'd say we're more of a middle-class family.

I got married and the reason I came to the United States is really because of my husband, who was a policeman in Peru and had to come here because of the domestic terrorism. He was granted political asylum, and then he brought us over. We were separated for three years. When I came to the United States, I had a lot of different feelings, emotions, reactions, very mixed because of what you are leaving behind and what you find once you get here. It was painful because I was leaving behind all of my family in Peru, and sometimes when you get to the United States, it's almost like a big monster, everything is so big in the city.

I arrived in the United States on May twenty-ninth, 1999, and I began to work at Harvard on August twenty-third. When I first started working, I didn't know about what rights we had as workers.

I just accepted my situation, and it was just very conformist. I figured that's the way it has to be. In Peru we have a saying: you have to pay your dues at the beginning. So you begin with patience, and later things get better. As time went on, and I really began to inform myself and get more involved, I saw that things really don't have to be this way.

For me, my dream when I was a little girl was to be a professional, to have a career, to marry, to have children, to have a family that was like the one that I came from, and to have a pretty house. I don't think you could ask for anything more than that from God. I wanted to be a social worker, helping people. The way I see my life right now is that it's really going to change. I see a better future. I have many hopes for progress, that things will get better for my daughters, the one I have now and the one that is coming, also for my family in Peru. Now I'm thirty-eight, I'm not going to become a professional at this point. I hope to have more time with my family, maybe a house. I hope that perhaps one day my daughter will be able to have a career, because I was never able to have one. I also have hopes that I will be able to keep my health, and the people I know will have their health. That's all that one can ask for.

What happened here at Harvard between the workers and the students did play a very important role in my hope. I see it as a determining factor. I still feel like I have a lot to learn. It's important not to be the kind of person who just works and doesn't try to learn other things. I do want to learn and I feel that I learn more each day and become closer to achieving my hopes.

Bob Kelly

"I'm a glorified custodian, a building manager here at Harvard. The student groups come to me and I reserve the rooms for them. I've worked here fourteen years full time, and three years part time."

WHEN I FIRST CAME, I didn't like the students at all. I resented them a great deal, and I just looked at them as wealthy snobs. They don't see you. Some of them won't speak to you. If they see you in the street, they don't see you. I had resentments towards them, and it's taken a while over the years.

I began to notice how serious some of them were, how committed. This one girl student used to work in the projects. I'd see her crying some evenings about what had happened that day with her girls. She ran a little group of girls. She couldn't do enough for them.

When this living-wage campaign started, it was really run out of this building. I'd notice those students working nights and days, they'd be here running off copies and have meetings all night. They'd be in here at seven-thirty in the morning, going out postering. They were doing something that they would gain nothing from. You know what I mean? These were student volunteers, and all they were doing was getting the university to frown on them and maybe give them a hard time. And the risks that they put themselves through. I mean, like when they occupied the building there, they jeopardized their academic careers, and it wasn't like they were going to walk out of there and have a raise themselves. Those kids stuck it through. It's wonderful to see a generation of these people that went to bat like that, with nothing to gain for themselves. What does it give you? Hope is what it gives you.

Something happened here that I never saw before. I remember the sixties when they had the demonstrations here. I used to hang in a barroom over in Somerville, the next city, a blue-collar town. It was like two different worlds. Everybody was looking at the students as hippies and drug addicts, and we were all just blue-collar people. The two groups never mixed. So this never happened before. The workers who did the work around the university, I noticed, got to like the students. Instead of "We're taking care of spoiled little rich kids," it's "Can you believe they're doing this for us?" Things that never would have happened were it not for the students. Boy, people can surprise you.

Greg Halpern

He was one of the leaders of the Harvard Living Wage Campaign's sit-in strike of 2001. "I grew up in Buffalo, New York. I'm twenty-four now. My father is a professor of political science at the State University of New York, Buffalo. He specializes in civil liberties and civil rights. My mother is a corporate lawyer. They separated my freshman year of college. I didn't really see that coming. I think they were different people, and when I left the house, they sort of drifted apart."

I WAS AT HARVARD, studying American history and literature. I don't think it was the right major for me. I love photography and spend all my time in the darkroom. My senior year I started photographing workers on campus and interviewing them. I felt like there was a very powerful drive among the undergraduate community to be successes in the very traditional sense. Something like seventy-five percent of my classmates go on to be doctors, lawyers, businessmen, or consultants. I always felt there wasn't quite enough room for an alternative lifestyle. So I moved off campus—I'd never felt very welcomed—and my childhood friend from Buffalo, Aaron Bartley, moved in with me. He was a labor activist.

The Living Wage Campaign at Harvard on behalf of all the custodians who work there got started the fall of '98. Aaron really dragged me to the first meeting. There were four of us: one other student, and a union representative. The custodial union in Boston had been one of the most corrupt unions around. The old president is now in jail. That was SEIU [Service Employees International Union], Local Two-fifty-four. It was a disaster. The janitors thought all the union did was take their dues. People's rights were abused constantly, especially immigrants. The local custodial wages were around eight dollars and fifty cents, and some food service workers went lower than that. In real wages, their wages have dropped over the previous ten years. Even after the raise we got them with the sit-in, their wages are still lower than they were ten years ago. And

Harvard has an endowment of twenty billion dollars, the largest of any university in the world.

For me it was an enlightening, almost humiliating experience to have my eyes opened and see around me workers I hadn't seen before, and whom I was sure I had looked right through in the past.

I was embarrassed by that. I was on the lunch line at one point, and a friend of mine made a joke about how terrible the food was. I laughed, looked up, and caught the eyes of a young black woman behind the counter, glaring at me. I was deeply embarrassed. At the same time I was reading your book, *Working*. I started to see people around me. I think other students had that experience, too. A lot of us came from families that didn't teach students about the person who is cleaning that bathroom, or serving you food, or who's cleaning off the chalkboard when you leave. My dad was enlightened. He grew up very, very poor, and still somehow I didn't get that consciousness. When my dad went to college, he slept in the same tiny room with his brother and grandmother. Yet somehow I didn't connect his experiences with the people around me, because I was born into this privileged life.

It was only a matter of weeks before we had forty people at our weekly meetings. We sent letters to the president of Harvard. We had rallies once a month. Hundreds of people, professors, politicians, shouting, chanting, dancing in public, but nothing happened. Ninety-five percent of the students walked by. I had the distinct feeling that most of them sort of snickered. There was a real stigma we had to overcome.

People looked at us and thought we were nostalgic for the sixties or we wanted to be hippies, foolish notions that ignored why we were truly there. We got fed up. Three years of rallies. To organize a rally like that would take days and days of forty people working. I was a senior when it began.

My senior spring, I did an independent study with Robert Coles. I started interviewing workers. I got totally hooked on it. I put the interviews up on campus—I blew them up into ten-foot-size pages with workers' words on them and stuck them in the science center, which is the public space for students. I got a surprisingly strong reaction. People would read them and say, "My God, I never thought about that person I saw sweeping down there." Or they thought, *My God, I never knew that they felt that about us, the students.*

It's going to sound corny, but it felt like I had all of a sudden seen the world around me differently. I had never been involved in activism. I never did anything. And it felt really good. It felt great. I remember the first time I chanted at a rally—"What do we want? Living wage. When do we want it? Now!"—I was embarrassed. I thought, *What am I doing?* I was on my own campus, screaming that outside the president's office. At first I was very self-conscious, and then it just felt very good to be out there.

We always knew that a sit-in would probably have to be our final step. We kept delaying it because we thought we didn't have the student support. As students kept graduating, our best members kept leaving. We were so fed up. Finally there was a meeting and people felt we should do the sit-in. "We're sick of rallies, chanting...we gotta do it." I had drifted from the campaign because I thought, *Nothing's going to become of this. It's become an after-school club, nothing's getting done.* I got fed up. But when I heard that there might be a sit-in, I came back. When the word got out, thirty new people showed up. We had fifty or sixty people at the meeting about whether or not to have the sit-in. This was spring 2001. We were in a common room for students. We're all sitting in this circle debating. Everyone had a turn to say yes or no.

The general sentiment in the room was no, forget it. I was so fed up. I'm two years out of school, I'm already feeling like a hanger-on. My turn came—I felt, *Here is the moment.* I thought of this custodian, Bill Brooks, who cleaned the room that we were sitting in. He was sixty-five years old, works two full-time jobs, sleeps four hours a night, and he told me in his interview that at this point in his life, work had become a self-inflicted wound. It was the most amazing thing anyone had ever said to me about work and about what it did to him. I think work actually took his life from him to a large degree.

The workers were very surprised to see students get out there and do this. A lot of them were afraid to show their faces and get involved because they know you don't want to mess with Harvard. If professors can get denied tenure for doing this kind of thing, imagine what could happen to an illegal immigrant custodian who barely understands English if he shows up at a rally with his uniform on. I don't blame them. They didn't show up to rallies until the union started to get involved and gave them a little more courage to come out. One guy told me his supervisor said he would get docked a half hour's pay if he showed up at a living-wage rally. He said his union rep—this is how corrupt the union local was—told him the same thing.

We contacted the media before we did anything. We had a press list, contacts. This is common, but for us it was new. We didn't know about this stuff. We sat in twenty-one days. I brought a can of tuna fish and two bananas, 'cause I thought, *Oh, we'll be in there overnight, they're gonna freak out and give us a living wage.* I thought the administration would literally lose it when they saw that fifty students took over the president's office. [*Laughs*] That's how foolish and hopeful I was.

I couldn't sleep for a night because I was so nervous. I'd never done anything like this. I packed a big backpack, put clothes in it, a little bit of food, a sleeping bag, and the worker testimonies that I had collected. Other kids all brought backpacks. And we all brought cell phones. As soon as we got into the building we wanted to make calls. Everyone wrote down a hundred names, and the first day we started calling everyone we knew, every contact we had in the press, every professor, every student, every relative, anyone we knew who might do anything to support us. It was ridiculous, a bunch of kids who looked like this consulting advertising team. It was weird. We were activists, but it was a very Harvard scene: kids with laptops and cell phones networking!

We ran in the door, and halfway through, the secretary tried to jump in front of us, but we just plowed our way in. Massachusetts Hall is where the president's office is, and there's this thing where the doors automatically shut. The receptionist pressed a panic button and all the doors automatically shut. We ran quick enough so that before the door could shut, we got into the office of another top administrator. We took over the lobby where the receptionist is, one meeting room, the hallway, the bathroom, and one office. We couldn't get the president's office. We sat down and linked arms. There were fifty of us. We started chanting: "What do we want?

Living wage!" The cops immediately came, and everyone starts chanting, "We will not be divided."

I'm getting chills now, talking about it, and I got chills then. This is in the first five minutes. The cops say, "You're all trespassing, you all have to leave." There was a guy with a video camera, and they tried to pull him out. They grabbed his camera, and he said, "I'm not leaving." That's when we all started chanting, "We will not be divided." The cops realized they would have to pick us up and carry us out of that building. There was this moment where all the cops and the police chief thought, *We're in a pickle now. What do we do?* In 1969, they arrested the kids who took over University Hall at Harvard over the Vietnam protests. They called in the police and the kids got beat up, and the next day this bloody Harvard kid's face was on the front page of the news. I know the cops were thinking: *We're not going to do that again, that's a PR nightmare.* So they treated us with kid gloves.

At first the cops said, "Nothing comes in the door." But they realized, *If we don't let anything in, these kids are going to go hungry, and it's going to be a hunger strike.* Imagine what the press would say. Fifty Harvard kids go on a hunger strike for the workers. So they started handing us food. You could show up with a bag marked *Greg* and the cops would hand it to me. Friends were bringing bags of brownies, personal food packages. With time, the cops grew to be sympathetic because they knew we were in there for Harvard workers. I think the cops honestly were a little bit impressed, but at first they were pissed off. I didn't sleep the first night. I lay down in the hallway between the bathroom and the reception room, and there were cops walking up and down the hallway the whole night. I would open my eyes and see this big black leather boot walk right by my head. I was so panicked. At first, we thought they were going to try to wake us up in the middle of the night and drag us out. We kept one person up every night for twenty-one days.

We had a whole team of students on the outside—fifty on the inside and at least fifty on the outside. With time, it would be hundreds on the outside. This team went to the dining halls, door-to-door. They were spreading the news word of mouth. It was a secret that we were going to have this sit-in, right? We couldn't tell anyone. But as soon as we went into the building, students started telling other students, knocking on doors. It was a tough job because most students really didn't care. They thought we were out there to get attention for ourselves or were nostalgic for the sixties. The conservative student paper ran a story making fun of us. There's a lot of that nowadays, where people make fun of activists because they don't trust their motives. It's not like Vietnam, it doesn't have the same intensity.

After about three days, a guy from NPR [National Public Radio] called and came to the rally. That was our first national news piece. Then the *New York Times*, the *Washington Post*, the *L.A. Times* picked up on it. All sympathetically. Bob Herbert, from the the *New York Times*, wrote two pieces for the editorial page. He called us Harvard's heroes, which was pushing it. We were not heroes. There was nothing truly heroic about doing the sit-in. It wasn't until Harvard students saw the op-ed page of the *New York Times* that they thought, *Well, maybe these kids are not just in it to get attention.* And then three hundred professors came out. There were a few very devoted faculty who supported us. They sent e-mails like wildfire to all the other faculty, and quickly got about three or four hundred signatures, and took a full-page ad out in the *Boston Globe*. Finally the president, Neil Rudenstine, came in and he said he wouldn't negotiate. He'd be happy to talk to us about a living wage as soon as we left their building. He said it was an inappropriate forum, it was coercive. We said, "Hell, no, we've been asking you to talk to us about this living wage for three years, and you've done nothing." The administration had formed a committee to look into it, and the committee said, "It's an interesting idea, but no, no living wage." That was what we got after three years. So we said no. "The only thing that we've got going for us is this building. All of our power lies in the fact that we're sitting our butts down right now in this building, and we're not giving it up." So secretly, to save face, Harvard started negotiating. "We'll negotiate, but we'll do it secretly."

I think students began to see custodians differently. When you look through someone, when you pass someone in the hallway and don't make eye contact and you don't say hi, and in four years you don't go up and talk to the same person who cleans the dining hall or your room, you're clearly not respecting them, you're not thinking of them as a person. After the campaign, there were plenty of students who finally began to think of workers as people they could know. And so there were friendships formed. We have barbecues at my house now where workers come, and we go out together to bars or just hang out. That certainly never happened before. Maybe we earned their respect. Before, I think there was a lot of bitterness, and rightfully so, for these students who made them feel invisible, spoiled brats running around with their cell phones and BMWs.

The sit-in was the most hopeful thing I've ever been a part of. It was very emotional for me. Most of us on the inside just broke down during the sit-in, just lost it. It felt like an insanely uphill battle, because the first few days, no one was out there in support of us. The press didn't cover us for the first two days. We hadn't slept, and we thought we were going to get our butts kicked. Honestly, we thought we might get arrested. So there were ups and downs of extreme, intense depression, and extreme, intense joy and hope. We'd get a newspaper brought in, or sometimes we'd get Internet access, and when a good news piece came out, we'd all gather around and read it, and there'd be extreme happiness and joy. Slowly the crowds gathered every night on the outside. The final rally there were probably three thousand people outside.

At night people would come out and sing, they would hold candles. As the workers got courage, they would come out, too. The dining hall workers and food workers delivered pizzas. They knew why we were there. We were sitting in for them. Sometimes they would cry and thank us for being on the inside. They could only get so close—the police put up a ten-foot barrier. Once a worker came up and shook my hand, crying, to say thank you. The cop yelled at him, "What did I tell you? Get back! You're not allowed to get by that window." I screamed at the cop afterwards, because I thought he shouldn't have screamed at the custodian—all he wanted to do was thank me. But there were lots of moments like that.

I'd much rather be a naive fool than be cynical. I don't mind being called a fool if I'm foolishly believing in a better world. It sounds cheesy, but why else be alive? Honestly. What else is there? It's worth living to be happy, to have a nice house, to have a good marriage, and to raise kids, and I want to do those things. But the bigger questions . . . What's the point of being alive if you're not hopeful that you can do a little something to make the world a little better?

The world is sometimes a really miserable place. My mom thinks I'm depressed too often. She tells me to be a little happier than I am. The only thing you can do to make yourself feel a little better about the world is to *try* to make it a little better. And some people say, "Oh, that's selfish, you're trying to help other people to make yourself feel good." But if you can make yourself feel better *and* help people at the same time, there's nothing wrong with that. It's a hell of a lot better than simply devoting your life to making yourself and yourself alone feel better, which is what a lot of people do with their time, with work, try to make money and make themselves as happy as possible.

This sit-in, people thought we were such idiots. They told us that to our faces. We invited a lawyer to come to our meeting the night before the sit-in to tell us legally what could happen to us. He told us he thought we shouldn't do it, it wouldn't be effective. He was just one of hundreds of people who told us we shouldn't do it.

We sat in that building for three weeks, without a shower, fifty people. That place stank. Because we made a sacrifice—small compared to what a custodian goes through every day—three weeks sitting in that smelly building, people thought, *Wow, this must be really something.*

Edward Childs

He is fifty-one. "We're in Harvard Yard, at the Phillips Brooks House, three buildings away from Mass Hall, where the sit-in occurred."

I'VE BEEN A COOK at Harvard for twenty-seven years. Chief steward of the union here. We have five hundred and fifty workers in the cafeterias, in the food department.

As a student at UMass, I'd been working part-time in hotels.* I grew up at the end of the civil rights and antiwar movements and was part of it. A friend called up and told me they were trying to organize a union at the university here. There was a campaign to up the wage fifty cents, which, at that time, was a big raise. I says, "OK, I'll take a semester off and come here to help organize." And I've been here ever since. I had been studying math at college, but I got the union bug, and the union bug is much stronger than anything else.

I grew up in the public housing projects. At that time in Boston, the way the city segregated the communities was they would have all-white projects or all-black projects. Ours was all-white. My father was in and out of jobs, primarily as a cook or a truck driver. He was a baseball player at one time, an outfielder, Warren Childs. He was the number-one pick of the Boston Red Sox as a rookie. But just before he was about to start, he had to go to World War Two. He went to the Battle of the Bulge and got shot up. When he came home, a wounded veteran, he had no job. No baseball. My mother worked off and on, and then she became disabled.

Growing up in the public housing projects, what I saw was the civil rights movement, but because of the high segregation in Boston, there was no inlet for white working-class youth to get into the civil rights movement and join with Martin Luther King. The segregation was also mental. The white working class, who were very poor in Boston, could never learn how to organize their own communities,

*UMass is the University of Massachusetts.

311

to better themselves. So I was looking for an inlet. I found it through the antiwar movement.

My grandfather, my mother's father, was from Ireland. He was extremely progressive. He had fought in the movement over there for civil rights. He was very antiracist. I stayed with my grandparents a lot. During the summer, my parents would send me over to get me away from the projects. So it was from my grandparents I got that feeling. These past twenty-seven years at Harvard have been interesting. As we would organize campaigns, we'd always solicit support, both from other unions and the community. During the years of the South African movement here—the divestiture movement— we would get shop stewards committees to be part of that. The students, who were active, didn't understand that the workers should be part of it, but the South Africans did. When they came to visit the campus, they met with us as much as they did with the students. The unions here have probably between thirty-six hundred and four thousand workers. For years, there was an organizing drive. Harvard kept trying to stop the union. A big part of early life for me here was helping the clerical workers get a union. We were the biggest union on campus—the hotel and restaurant workers union, HERE [Hotel Employees and Restaurant Employees International Union], Local Twenty-six. We helped bring in a more progressive slate.

The conditions at that time were segregation. Women were very mistreated. The conditions for nonwhite workers were pretty intolerable. We did a big campaign against that. We set up a respect campaign. We actually put a "respect" clause in our contract, saying that there can be no discrimination, no insults, nothing the manager can do to insult or disrespect our workers. When I came here we had the big campaign on the pay, and over the years we had three walkouts and a strike. Through that campaign, we probably got the best wages for dining hall workers. Even though we were probably at the top of our industry, we still weren't paid that well. Then Harvard came up with a scheme of contracting to outside contractors who paid a lot less, a lot less. We struggled over that through the years.

During the living-wage struggle, the custodians had a corrupt union, so much so that the international put them into receivership, so they were in transition. It wasn't so much corrupt as totally incompetent. They were caving in to everything. So we made sure that our workers reached the custodians, because a lot of them eat at our cafeteria. We talked union to them. We also identified some of their leaders, so we could tell our union organizers, "Hey, this is a good leader, you should go after this person." Then suddenly, we have a relationship with the students. We had them come in and help picket with us. I remember one time at the faculty club, they brought in new rough, tough management, who were abusing our people. So, we set up a campaign at the faculty club and picketed them. We had the students actually go in and disrupt. The kids also brought their own tactics in. One thing they did was get that yellow police caution tape and surround the whole building with it, the students did.

Some of us had looked upon them as, "Well, they're nice, but they're not going to help us." But others of us said, "We need them, we need them." We did have an attitude, generally, amongst the workers that these are privileged students, and they only look for us when they need something. We pretty much don't exist, our families don't exist. We can't plead our issue because they don't understand us. Why should they? They have what they want. A lot of our workers understood some students through our relationship with the black students, 'cause over the years, we've had rallies with the black students around discrimination. We joined with the black students in trying to demand black professors here.

The majority of our people are immigrants. Either from the Caribbean Islands, Asia, Latin America. We have a lot of Portuguese, Cape Verdeans, and black Americans. A lot of people have an understanding from their homes. We just did a campaign on Iraq, on what sanctions by the U.S. are doing. We did a survey, and most of our people actually come from countries that were sanctioned by the U.S. They got a feeling that sanctions are bad because that's what drove them here in the first place. Those who aren't from there are black Americans, or women. Women were being told by Harvard, "Oh, you can't become a cook because women can't cook." What do you do? You send us home to cook, right? So we had to have a campaign. That forced Harvard to allow women to cook on campus.

We had been working with the students ahead of time. The day we heard of the sit-in, within five minutes we called up all the shop stewards in the different dining halls to orientate the workers. By the end of lunch, most of our workers were wearing buttons on the job: *We Support the Living Wage Campaign.* That was the button the students were putting out. We had the students go to each dining hall and give them to the workers, and the workers all put them on.

The workers were ecstatic. You couldn't talk to workers without seeing smiles on their faces from one side to the other. They were seeing students who understood. We called for a rally that evening, because the university wouldn't allow anything in—they wouldn't allow food. We called for our contract committee to meet that evening. We were preparing for negotiations. Our committee met in a building in Harvard Yard. Everybody was very, very happy. We decided we have to intervene, that this is a struggle for *us*. So what we did is we bought pizzas, and we marched to the site of the sit-in, where the president's office was.

We marched in chanting that we want a living wage. We had a whole bunch of pizzas, so we had a whole bunch of workers carrying pizzas. Our workers were real angry at this time, because when we were met with the police, they said nothing comes into this building, and we said, "Listen, these are our students. Our job is to feed them. We're either going to feed them through the front door, or through the windows, or whatever, but we're going to feed them." Some of our workers were really ornery now, and they were just going right into the police line. So the police called up their superiors, and within fifteen seconds, they said, "OK, you can go in and feed them." The police were just following orders. They were probably told by their superiors, "Don't worry, it's not going to go anywhere. They'll be gone in the morning."

One of our workers was a cop's cousin. She was saying, "You're not going to stop me, 'cause you'll never come to my house again!" [*Laughs*] We were determined to get the pizza in. We also outnumbered them. So we went right through the front door. After that, they allowed us to feed the students whenever we wanted. We went into our halls and we got the main meals. Then management, seeing that they couldn't really stop us, joined with us. We said to management, "Our students are in the halls. We have to feed them. And this is the food. If they can't come to us, we should go to them." They agreed. Each dining hall took turns and brought meals to the students. Actually, they probably ate better than the regular meals because the workers went nuts in feeding them. They all went in delegations. Any special foods we had, they got.

Those twenty-one days, we had meetings in all the halls to organize support for the students. We were supposed to negotiate in June. We said, "We want negotiations now. If not, then we're striking *now*." We held a rally at the church across the street from Mass Hall, where the sit-in was. We marched to the place. Three hundred workers with their families came. And when we marched, the community came. So we had hundreds and hundreds of workers. They filled the whole street out there.

Our workers went from, before the sit-in, like, "This is going to be a hard contract." The unions weren't winning very much and we felt the economy was starting to tilt backwards, especially in our industry. The hope was not great. When this sit-in happened, that whole attitude changed. Now we have a momentum, and I think hope for us was momentum. We had the students, we had the publicity, and not only that, when we looked at each other, we had each other. Even our weak workers were enthusiastic.

The custodians, with each contract, were getting less and less money. We negotiated while the sit-in was going on. We won a good contract for our industry, for the food workers. The maintenance workers, they won a good contract. This was a huge victory. When a struggle like this happens, not only do you feel that the immediate union situation is better, but also the international situation. A lot of people talk about their homes now, whether they're from Portugal, Venezuela, Colombia. A lot of our union discussion now is to help out in the situations there. Harvard workers now have a lot more hope than the workers in the other places that didn't have this struggle. This hope does carry a long way. We're having a discussion right now of helping out the black reparations movement.

We met two weeks ago with the Middle Eastern workers. We have some Palestinian workers, and some Moroccan workers. When 9/11 happened, we met with all the workers. The president of our union put out a statement saying that if anybody from our union is harassed, that we'll intervene, whether it's at Harvard, or in the hotels, or out in the community, by the police or by anybody. The whole union got together on that. This is great hope. Whether we're winning something concretely or not, we have a lot of hope, and I think hope means a lot more than concrete winning every time. Because we have a future.

EPILOGUE:

THE PILGRIM

Kathy Kelly

She has visited more countries, cities, and small towns not listed in Baedeker's guidebooks than anyone I have ever known. Her hosts have been the men, women, and children whose homes have been under constant fire. Her pilgrimages have one purpose: to reveal the lives of war's innocent victims. Baghdad is where she is at the moment of this writing, on the eve of her country's preemptive strike on Iraq.

She has been arrested by our government countless times. For all I know, she may hold the track record. She has founded a peace group, Voices in the Wilderness. A good number of its members have followed her course. She weighs less than a hundred pounds, and is now in a hospital, still bearing witness.

I GREW UP out on the Southwest Side—this was the working-class Southwest Side—of Chicago in an area of bungalows and scrawny little parks. We thought my mother was a mutant at first. There were just three of us, and we couldn't understand why all the other families would be so large. So we'd be on our knees with novenas to St. Gerard, the patron saint of pregnant mothers, and then my mother had three in one year. The twins were just eleven months apart from my brother Jerry. I was the middle child. We grew up, the Kelly kids, thinking that Mom and Dad, Officer Friendly, the parish priest, and the nuns all wanted to keep us happy, and we were. We were real secure. I hardly knew problems existed. That neighborhood was very, very close to Gage Park, where the Reverend Dr. Martin Luther King was hit by a stone. It was actually a neighborhood that had lots of problems. I was really lucky. The high school teachers I had held up values for us that I might not have otherwise seen. My parents were very kindly and certainly against war. They had been in London during World War Two.

My mother grew up in a very poor part of Ireland. When her mother died in childbirth, the father really wasn't able to care for the children. So she was sent off as an indentured servant, to work in monasteries. That's how she ended up in England. My father had studied with the Christian Brothers, but he left the order and joined the U.S. Army. He was a young GI in London, fell in love with my mother, and they married. After the war, my father was a Catholic high school teacher; he taught math.

I attended an experimental high school: half a day Catholic school, half a day public school. We'd have math in the morning and riot in the afternoon because the neighborhood still was very, very racist. But it was a wonderful experiment. I don't think my parents were racists. There was a sense that there wasn't much that could be done about problems. It was something I needed to overcome. But we never heard hateful words about other people in our household. My mother understood the underdog quite well.

There was a sense that you should always try to share what you have with other people. But most of the visions would have come from reading the lives of the saints. That's all that was in the library. And there were all these stories of nuns who went off to China and did good things. But really, what I think most affected me was—do you know the film *Night and Fog*?* It's a very hard film to watch. They had classical music in the background, very haunting, and just panned in on the camps. You could see that there were rows and rows of bungalows across the way, and what did folks do? Why didn't they smell the burning flesh? That had a big impact on me. I thought, *I never, ever want to be sitting on the sidelines or sitting on my hands in the bleachers and just watch some unspeakable evil happen.*

I sure thought that my life was good, though. I was a pretty happy kid. When I learned about Reverend Dr. Martin Luther King, I felt great hope. I also was among those who felt a lot of hope associated with Bobby Kennedy. His assassination did bring down that hope. I

*It was a French movie about the Holocaust, directed by Alain Resnais. His more celebrated film was *Hiroshima, Mon Amour.*

don't think I picked up again that things could change until I fell in with these people who would just say, "Look, I'm responsible. It's not what are the leaders going to do, it's what am *I* going to do? Am I going to take the weapons out of my own personal budget? Am I going to personally take responsibility to put a plate of food in front of somebody who's hungry? Am I going to have a crash room in my home and take a homeless person into my home?" So we wouldn't always be asking the government to solve problems; we'd change these patterns of lifestyle ourselves. And then find out it's not hard. It's interesting and easy and attractive.

I was a late bloomer. I went through the Vietnam War like Brigadoon in the mist. I never got involved in anti–Vietnam War activism. I feel very sad about that now, but I understand when people sit one out, because that was me. I still had this kind of fatalism that said you can't really do anything about these big problems. I would cry over the *New York Times*, and that was about it.

I was living in Hyde Park, working on a master's degree in theology at the Chicago Theological Seminary. When I was studying for that degree, I realized that I never, myself, saw any poor people, and so much of the scripture has to do with hearing the cry of the poor. So finally I found my way over to a soup kitchen. Just to find someplace where I could put into practice some of what was being preached.

Finally, I came up to this neighborhood, to Uptown. I call it the do-gooder's ghetto. I met Karl Meyer, one of Dorothy Day's protégés. He was a very good writer who had converted to Catholicism and had all the enthusiasm of a convert. He had sat with Dorothy Day and others to protest the civil defense air-raid drills, when they refused to go underground during the Red scare of the 1950s. They'd sit on park benches and be arrested. He went to Rikers Island at a very young age—for refusing to take shelter during the air-raid drills. What they were saying is there was no shelter from nuclear bombs, that the best way to find security was to stop paying for these weapons. He became a war tax refuser and kept a house of hospitality going here in Chicago for at least thirteen years. Then he went to prison during the Vietnam War. His father was a congressman from Vermont, one of the only Democrats opposed to the war.

I was the wealthiest person on my block in Uptown. I was earning seven thousand dollars a month as a Catholic high school teacher. Other people's homes were abandoned buildings. Everybody I knew on the block was eating at the soup kitchen. That's when I began to think, *This won't do. I can't take a third of an income and turn it over to the federal government to buy weapons when I'm going into my classrooms trying passionately to teach children not to rely on weapons.*

I had been teaching high school way down on the South Side. I'd take the train every day all the way down to Ninety-fifth and Throop Street to an African American all-girls Catholic high school. I was teaching religion, but I was also starting to experiment with teaching nonviolence and peace. Then I switched to St. Ignatius College Prep. After my first year there, I said to the Jesuits, "Look, if it's OK with you, I'd like to lower my salary beneath the taxable income. I can't pay for these weapons any longer. I've got to take it out of my personal budget." This was, of course, the influence that Karl had. I saw that he was able to do it. The schools were great. They said, "OK, but you tell us where you want the money that you're not taking to go." I was Lady Bountiful. Every paycheck, I'd say, "Well, I want this amount to go to the soup kitchen, and this amount to go for a Catholic Worker house of hospitality, and this amount to help resist U.S. intervention in Central America." And those checks would just go flying out. I haven't paid any taxes to the federal government since 1980.

They wrote me off as uncollectable one year. They said that they were going to give up, but I think they might be trying again. After we started the Voices in the Wilderness Campaign, there was a new effort to collect. The IRS became my spiritual director. [*Laughs*] Because if you're not going to give any money to the government for weapons, and you don't want them to come and take something from you, you can't really own anything. So I don't know how to drive a car and I don't want to learn. I don't own anything, really, and I'm quite happy to live the way I do.

I rent an apartment that we use as the base for Voices in the Wilderness—it's a campaign to end the economic sanctions against Iraq. We work out of my home. A number of us had been in Iraq during the [first] Gulf War. We camped as a peace team on the border between Saudi Arabia and Iraq. It was hard to say we were nonpartisan, because actually we were dependent on the Iraqi people.

We tried to set up camp in Kuwait and Saudi Arabia as well. I stayed over there for about six months. When I came back I was ready to say that the war was over and turn the chapter. But by 1995, we started to realize that the war hadn't ended, it had just changed into economic warfare that discriminated directly against the most vulnerable people.

That's where I go back to *Night and Fog*. Can you know something is going on, be powerfully aware of it, and say, "Well, there's not anything really we can do about it"? The answer for me is no, we have to try to do what we can. The thing that had a big impact on me was going to a U.S. prison for a year for planting corn on a nuclear missile silo site.

There were one thousand of those silos in the Midwest, and one hundred fifty around Kansas City. You wouldn't even know that they're there. You almost have to train your eye to look for the white sticks that protrude from the ground. Eventually you get the hang of it. It looks like a backyard garage in terms of size. These are like razors in a loaf of bread, sewn all through the breadbasket of the United States—the place that's meant to grow corn and wheat, and we were harvesting weapons of mass destruction.

I was arrested for criminal trespass. I waited there until the authorities came. I informed them we were there. The Gumps put up a sign: *We Shall Study War No More.** Others of us fanned out. We went to fourteen different sites. There were fourteen of us.

I went onto a site by myself. I remember climbing the fence and sitting on top of this missile silo lid, and then seeing an armored

---

*Jean and Joe Gump were devoutly Catholic parents and grandparents, who lived in a middle-class suburb, west of Chicago. They were highly respected in the community. Jean was president of the high school PTA, the League of Women Voters, and executive secretary of the town's Human Relations Council.

On Good Friday, 1986, she and four young Catholics, young enough to be her children, committed an unlawful act. "We commemorated the crucifixion of Christ by entering a missile site near Holden, Missouri. We hung a banner outside the chain-link fence that read: SWORDS INTO PLOWSHARES, AN ACT OF HEALING. Isaiah 2, from *Scriptures*. It was a Minuteman II silo, vehicle coming toward us with a machine gun mounted on top. Sol-diers got out in full camouflage with helmets and rifles. "All person-nel please clear the site, hands in the air, step to the left, step to the right." I cooperated. They told me to kneel down, and they hand-cuffed me, and they left one soldier with me. The other three went off, maybe to get the manual and find out what to do next. So I was kneeling handcuffed and I started to talk to the soldier they'd left. He was behind me and had a gun to my head. I told him I was teaching kids who were part of two different gangs in my neighbor-hood. At the end of every year there would be three of them dead. I talked about how we didn't want to see money going to buy weap-ons of mass destruction, instead of taking care of these kids. I asked him, "Do you think the corn will grow?" He said [*Southern accent*], "I don't know, ma'am, but I sure hope so." Then I said, "Do you want to say a prayer?" He said, "Yes, ma'am." I think we said the St. Francis peace prayer: "Lord, make me a channel of your peace. Where there is darkness, let me sew light, where there is sadness, joy, where there is despair, hope . . ." We said amen together, and then he said to me, "Ma'am, would you like a drink of water?" I said, "Oh, yes." I was very, very thirsty. For him to unscrew the canteen and pour water down my throat—it was like a mother robin drop-ping worms down a throat—I think he had to put his gun down. I was handcuffed. He said, "Ma'am, would you tip your head back." And I did, and he poured the water down my throat.

I do think that he taught me so much that day. Here's this young soldier who took a risk in order to do an act of kindness for a perfect

---

a first-strike weapon. There are 150 such missiles. Each of these could decimate an area of seventy-two miles. And all the children and others. We wanted to make this weapon inoperable. And we succeeded."

Her account of the arrest and and what followed reflects her natural sense of the absurd. She was sentenced to eight years at the Alderson Women's Federal Prison in West Virginia. It was reduced to six.

Since then, she and her husband, Joe, who had himself committed an act of civil disobedience and was sent to the Sandstone Federal Penitentiary in Minnesota, were freed. Neither has recanted nor paid any fine. They are still at it. (*The Great Divide*, Pantheon, 1988.)

stranger. Maybe the manual said, *Keep your prisoner fed and watered,* but I'll bet it didn't say to put your gun down to do it. This was at the height of the cold war. What it says to me is that you can't have a cartoonized view where there are the "good guys" and the "bad guys." Life doesn't work that way. I don't think it's ever a good idea to point at an individual or a group and say, "Those people can't possibly change or accomplish any good." That's where our hope is, in a profound belief that people can change.

I saw that young soldier in court and I winked at him. I think if there's such a thing as mental telepathy, he was trying to say to me, *Please don't tell that story!* I hope he'll forgive me today.

I didn't have a jury trial. I fasted for twelve days asking for a jury trial, but we didn't get one. We had a magistrate. I was convicted and sentenced to one year in prison. I said that we have a right to try to claim our right not to kill, and that we're not shouting fire in a crowded theater, we're giving a very rational call, because these weapons were aimed at children and families in the Soviet Union, and their weapons were aimed back at us. The magistrate liked all of us quite well, I think. Personally he seemed to almost show a little bit of affection. He was going to let us have our day in court, but there was no way he wouldn't find us guilty.

He sent me to maximum security, Lexington, Kentucky. I learned that prison is a very, very, abysmally stupid, meaningless place. I did nine months there. I call it a world of imprisoned beauty. I never met the bad sisters. I was in maximum security, too. I met women who could have been my co-workers, my next-door neighbors, relatives. They were lovely women, by and large. I would say a good ninety percent of the women were there for nonviolent reasons, mainly related to drugs. It's understandable when women are in situations that are bleak and they don't have the money to meet their kids' needs. There's this shortcut. It's like my Irish ancestors bootlegging in this country. They see a possibility to get some money quickly. It's very tempting to get involved in the drugs, but prison isn't a way to solve the problem.

They were mostly African American and Hispanic. I met some incredibly interesting and funny and genuinely authentic characters. There were fifty-eight of us in the entering class. Of that fifty-eight, twelve passed a sixth-grade literacy test. I was the one who knew how to type, so I'd write letters for them. That's how I got to know some of their stories.

I told them why I was there. Otherwise they would have thought I was a snitch because I had such a short sentence. They called me "Missiles." They'd say, "Missiles, you ain't nothin' but a minute," because my sentence was so little.

This was '88, '89. At that point, the war on drugs was beginning to heat up and the prison industry was starting to grow. So that was an opportune time to learn a lot about the prison industry in the United States. I came out of prison in '89 and joined Roy Bourgeois outside Fort Benning and the School of the Americas. That's the place where we've trained people to use terror tactics in their countries. Some of the graduates were instrumental in killing the Jesuits in Central America, the four women nuns that were raped and killed and Archbishop Romero [of El Salvador]. We did a long fast. Roy went for thirty-six days, I stopped at twenty-eight.

My last fast was forty days, August 2001, in front of the United Nations and across from the U.S. mission to the UN, protesting the economic sanctions against Iraq. These sanctions have cost the lives of over a half a million children. They've directly targeted civilians. We're now looking at close to eleven years of a policy that has completely failed. I've gone to Iraq fifteen times now, in direct, open, and public violation of the economic sanctions. We bring medicine and relief. We've visited homes and hospitals. We've gotten to know some families. I lived there for seven weeks during the summer of 2000, in the poorest part of Basra and southern Iraq.

Each time we go we're threatened with twelve years in prison, a one-million-dollar fine, and a two-hundred-and-fifty-thousand-dollar administrative penalty. We've got a one-hundred-sixty-thousand-dollar prepenalty notice in December of 1998. My passport was confiscated in February of 1998. Some of the team members had their belongings taken. But by and large we've been treated with kid gloves. I don't know if they ever will impose these penalties. They told me to go down and get a new passport.

You know what we're going to do now? Twelve of us at least are going to walk from Washington, D.C., to New York City under the banner *Our grief is not a cry for war*. Did you hear the statements that some people made after the September eleventh attacks saying, "Please don't retaliate, please don't kill civilians in the name of my loved one who died"? They were very eloquent: "Our son would never have wanted violent retaliation." So we're going to carry those words. We want to pay reverence to those words. Walking to end war, hunger, and revenge. Then we'll have smaller walks that'll be joined by big numbers of people in each of the named cities along that route. And from there I'll take off to Baghdad.

I feel hope in the young people. I see them every day. They are showing me their readiness: "We're going to change our lifestyles." Jeff, one of the young people you know, he won't be driving across country anymore because he got rid of his car. That's where we see a lot of hope.

My dad came to live with me for the last seven years of his life. During that time I saw a lot more of my siblings. They came to visit Dad, and they got to know my community, and that was a very good coming together. It wouldn't have happened otherwise. I think they're sympathetic. I think that they're very representative of mainstream American life, which quite often has an emphasis on taking care of the children within your own family. The best way to take care of the children here is not to ignore the cries of children elsewhere.

It's so ironic, because some of the people who could best understand what people experienced in Manhattan on 9/11 are people who are targeted civilians elsewhere. One thing that many Americans can't understand is that on September twelfth there was so much of an effort to help rebuild, to help people overcome this terrible tragedy. Condolences came in from all over the world. In Iraq, five thousand of their children die every month. There hasn't been condolence, just more and more punishment heaped on these people. And yet, when I go over there, and I don't even have to say why I'm there, people just spontaneously say in their language, "You are welcome. Sit down and have tea." We are always treated with dignity and hospitality and forgiveness. That's been my constant experience.

I just feel lucky. If my life had gone in another direction, maybe I would have been happy, I don't know, but the grass doesn't look greener to me right now. I've seen the kids in Iraq pull their parents beyond despair. I've watched them do that on the streets in Basra.

These people in Basra have every reason to be severely depressed, but they've got these gleaming kids who are racing down the street with two plastics as their kites or their toys. I see them do that and I realize that kind of hope can't be abandoned, and I'm not going to give in to despair.